"Davis's masterful treatment of the historical ɪ provides a foundational understanding for tl contemporary, French self-understanding as a builds a framework for understanding the ne with its contingent practical challenges currem̰y ᴄ...ᴇ.ʙ...ʙ ----- ʊ ⁊ and immigrant populations in France."

—**Daniel Sheard**, Assistant Professor, John W. Rawlings School of Divinity, Liberty University

"In his book, *Rise of French Laïcité*, Stephen Davis has done what few Anglophones have dared to attempt, address and translate a unique French concept—*laïcité*—for the non-French. In so doing, Davis provides painstaking details as to how and why an understanding of history must inform contemporary social, cultural, and missional engagement."

—**Richard Kronk**, Assistant Professor of Global Ministries, Toccoa Falls College; former church planter in France (1995–2013)

"Who can understand *La Laïcité à la Française*? Often mistranslated, almost always misunderstood, Davis's historical, sociological, and missiological work meticulously clarifies this complex and fundamental trait of French society. A must-read for all gospel workers who venture onto French soil!"

—**Raphael Anzenberger**, Director, RZIM France

"This is an excellent and insightful summary of the history of *laïcité* in France since the Reformation. I strongly recommend it for missionaries in their second to fourth year in France. . . . This book will help them understand the French values and how to better share the gospel in light of these values."

—**David R. Dunaetz**, Book Review Editor, *Evangelical Missions Quarterly*

"Stephen Davis has written an important historical study on the rise of secularism (*laïcité*) in France. From the domination of the Roman Catholic Church at the Reformation to its separation from the state in 1905, the road was long and rocky. Constitutionally strengthened in 1946 and 1958, *laïcité* is being challenged today by the rapid growth of Islam, France's second largest religion, and its pursuit of recognition in the public space. A truly engaging story."

—**Jeff Straub**, author of *The Making of a Battle Royal: The Rise of Religious Liberalism in Northern Baptist Life, 1870–1920*

Rise of French Laïcité

Evangelical Missiological Society Monograph Series

Anthony Casey, Allen Yeh, Mark Kreitzer, and Edward L. Smither
SERIES EDITORS

A Project of the Evangelical Missiological Society
www.emsweb.org

Rise of French Laïcité

French Secularism from the Reformation
to the Twenty-First Century

Stephen M. Davis

PICKWICK *Publications* · Eugene, Oregon

RISE OF FRENCH LAÏCITÉ
French Secularism from the Reformation to the Twenty-First Century

Evangelical Missiological Society Monograph Series 7

Pickwick Publications
An Imprint of Wipf and Stock Publishers
199 W. 8th Ave., Suite 3
Eugene, OR 97401

www.wipfandstock.com

PAPERBACK ISBN: 978-1-7252-6409-0
HARDCOVER ISBN: 978-1-7252-6410-6
EBOOK ISBN: 978-1-7252-6411-3

Cataloguing-in-Publication data:

Names: Davis, Stephen M., author.

Title: Rise of French Laïcité : French Secularism from the Reformation to the Twenty-First Century / by Stephen M. Davis.

Description: Eugene, OR: Pickwick Publications, 2020 | Evangelical Missiological Society Monograph Series 7 | Includes bibliographical references and index.

Identifiers: ISBN 978-1-7252-6409-0 (paperback) | ISBN 978-1-7252-6410-6 (hardcover) | ISBN 978-1-7252-6411-3 (ebook)

Subjects: LCSH: Laicism—France—History. | Secularism—France—History.

Classification: LCC BX1528 D38 2020 (print) | LCC BX1528 (ebook)

Manufactured in the U.S.A.   08/06/20

This book is dedicated to my wife, Kathy, who has faithfully served the Lord with me around the world for over forty years. My life and ministry have been immensely enriched by her love, encouragement, and faithfulness. Without her, this book would have never been written. She truly is God's gift to me.

Contents

Abbreviations

APPEL	Association pour la promotion et l'expansion de la laïcité
CFCM	Conseil français du culte musulman
CLR	Comité Laïcité et République
CMB	Christian of Maghrebi Background
CNEF	Conseil national des Évangéliques de France
EU	European Union
FEPC	French Evangelical Protestant Church
FLTE	Faculté libre de théologie évangélique de Vaux-sur-Seine
FNLP	Fédération national de la libre pensée
FPF	Fédération protestante de France
IBN	Institut Biblique de Nogent-sur-Marne
NC	Nouveaux convertis or nouveaux catholiques
RPR	Religion prétendue réformée
UEEL	Union des Églises évangéliques libres de France
UEPAL	Union des Églises protestantes d'Alsace et de Lorraine

Preface

CHARLES TAYLOR HAS ARGUED that secularity must be understood in terms
of public spaces "allegedly emptied of God or of any reference to ultimate
reality."[1] He then asks the pressing question which his monumental work
seeks to answer: "Why was it virtually impossible not to believe in God in,
say, 1500 in our Western society, while in 2000 many of us find this not only
easy, but even inescapable?"[2] In France, the answer might be largely understood from its religious history beginning with incipient laïcité during the
Protestant Reformation in the 1500s, the introduction of religious pluralism, the rejection of the transcendent as source of authority, the evolution
of laïcité to a prominent and constitutional value of French society, and the
marginalization of religion evacuated from the public square.

This book traces the history of the rise and development of laïcité in
France from the sixteenth-century Protestant Reformation to the Law of
Separation of Churches and the State in 1905, followed by changes in French
society in the twentieth and twenty-first centuries. French laïcité presents
a specificity in origin, definition and evolution which arises from a unique
societal context which led to the official separation of Church and State in
1905. Laïcité has been described as the complete secularization of institutions as a necessity to prevent a return to the Ancien Régime characterized
by the union of Church and State. To understand the concept of laïcité, one
must begin in the sixteenth century with the Protestant Reformation, Wars
of Religion, and religious tolerance granted by the Edict of Nantes in 1598
under Henry IV. This has been called the period of embryonic laïcité with
the tolerance of Protestantism and incipient pluralism. The Revocation of
the Edict of Nantes under Louis XIV in 1685 reestablished the union of the
throne and altar which resulted in persecution of the Huguenots who fought
for the principle of the freedom of conscience and religious liberty.

---

1. Taylor, *Secular Age*, 2.
2. Taylor, *Secular Age*, 25.

The Law of Separation of Churches and State (*Loi concernant la Séparation des Églises et de l'État*) was enacted in 1905 in fulfillment of the French Revolution's attempt to remove the Roman Catholic Church as the State religion. The law abrogated the 1801 Napoleonic Concordat with the Vatican, disestablished the Roman Catholic Church, ended centuries of religious turmoil, declared state neutrality in religious matters, and continues as a subject of debate and dissension one hundred years later with the emergence of Islam as the second largest religion in France. The question at the turn of the twentieth century concerned the Roman Catholic Church's compatibility with democracy. That same question is being asked of Islam in the twenty-first century.

Introduction

IN HIS BOOK LE *Château de Ma Mère* (*My Mother's Castle*),[1] Marcel Pagnol
recounts the childhood story of young Marcel (b. 1896) who debated within
himself the existence of God. This took place upon his uncle's return from
midnight mass one Christmas Eve. During the service the uncle prayed
that God would send the family faith. "Of course," Marcel told himself, "I
knew that God did not exist, but I was not completely sure. There are lots of
people who attend mass, and even people who are serious. My uncle himself
speaks to him often yet he's not crazy." Upon further reflection, he arrives
at a conclusion which he admits is not really rational: "That God, who does
not exist for us, certainly exists for others: like the king of England, who
exists only for the English."[2]

This quaint story about a young French boy illustrates what many
French people in fact believed at that time and sheds light on the contemporary conflict in French society concerning the place of religion and belief in
God. During this period, France enacted the Law of Separation on December 9, 1905, which formalized the rupture of Church and State. The law of
1905 guaranteed liberty of conscience to believe or not believe, and the free
exercise of religion for those so inclined. The State would no longer provide
subsidies for the four recognized religions—Catholic, Lutheran, Reformed,
Jewish—and would practice neutrality in order that no religion be favored
above another. The Vatican vigorously protested this law while Catholics
in France, both clergy and laity, were themselves divided in their acceptance of the law's provisions. Decades later the French Constitutions of 1946
and 1958 reinforced the substance of the law of 1905 in their first article:
"France is an indivisible, laïque, democratic and social Republic. It ensures
the equality of all citizens before the law without distinction of origin, race
or religion. It respects all beliefs. Its organization is decentralized."

---

1. All translations are my own.
2. Pagnol, *Le château*, 127.

One must look to the law of 1905 as a pivotal historical point, setting in motion a particular French conception of separation of Church and State (or in this case separation of the Church *from* the State). The Law of Separation was enacted in the context of centuries of Roman Catholic domination, the sixteenth-century Reformation and Wars of Religion, the French Revolution of 1789, the rise to power of Napoleon and the 1801 Concordat with the Vatican, the restoration of the monarchy (1814–1830), and the intense struggle between clerical and anticlerical forces in the early years of the Third Republic (1870–1940) highlighted in the Dreyfus Affair at the end of the nineteenth century. This book is focused on understanding the French concept of laïcité and its historical development and how laïcité shaped French society in the twentieth century. We will also examine the resurgent debate over the disputed meanings and applications of laïcité in the twenty-first century in light of challenges from Islam and the emergence of Islamic fundamentalism (*intégrisme islamiste*).[3]

Professor of anthropology John Bowen presents an interview with a high-ranking French official in the Central Bureau of Religion (*Bureau central des cultes*). The official commented on the differences between religion in France and the United States. He recounted complaints received along the spectrum from Scientologists to evangelical ministers who felt that the system of laïcité should be changed. His response was simply, "They do not understand French history. Even the French Scientologists with whom I meet, even if they understand it some, they say that they cannot explain it to their American colleagues. So are we supposed to change our laws because you have trouble explaining France?"[4]

In the century following the law of 1905 there have been endless debates, essays, and books discussing, debating, and dissecting the law of 1905 and its implications for modern society. There are those who return to the law of 1905 as a touchstone or a lens through which they view and interpret current events and challenges to laïcité. There are others who assert that the law is often misapplied when it results in the suppression of the place of religion in French history, considers religion as a subject taboo in public schools, and leads to laws deemed discriminatory toward certain religions. The growth and influence of Islam in France has been the single major factor in a renewed debate on laïcité and on the question of the compatibility of Islam in a laïque Republic.

Despite the wealth of research on French religious history and on the concept of laïcité and modern challenges it presents in a pluralistic society,

3. Maslowski, "Les chrétiens avec ou sans Dieu," 214.
4. Bowen, *Headscarves*, 17.

relatively little has been written on laïcité in English. At the outset, it should be noted that there is disagreement about whether the term *laïcité* should be used or its English equivalents *secularism* or *secularization*. Olivier Roy distinguishes between secularization as a phenomenon of society that does not require any political implementation and laïcité as a political choice which defines in an authoritative and legal manner the place of religion in society.[5] He argues that laïcité is specific to France and incomprehensible in Great Britain where customs agents can wear the veil, as well in the United States, "where no president can be elected without speaking of God."[6] The word laïcité itself was not used in the law of 1905 but is found in the French Constitutions of 1946 and 1958. Patrick Cabanel suggests that, although some claim *laïcité* is untranslatable in other languages, the word *national* might be an acceptable synonym in certain contexts.[7] His book is an excellent source for the meaning of words related to laïcité.

From a historical perspective, Jacques Barzun's monumental work *From Dawn to Decadence* begins with the year 1500 AD and sets broad historical parameters for this volume. He affirms that "textbooks from time immemorial have called it [1500] the beginning of the Modern Era."[8] Barzun considers that the years 1500–1660 were "dominated by the issue of what to believe about religion," the years 1661–1789 "by what to do about the status of the individual and the mode of government," and the years 1790–1920 "by what means to achieve social and economic equality."[9] Following Barzun's taxonomy, the first modern period opened in Europe with the Reformation in Germany under Martin Luther in 1517 and provides a convenient reference point to understand the foment of history in forming the French consciousness and setting the scene for future, interminable clashes between Church, State, and citizens.

Luther's Reformation in Germany crossed into France where the seeds of Reformation were alternately sown and uprooted. Donald Kelley, in his book *The Beginning of Ideology* and Holt in *Renaissance and Reformation in France*, examine the influences of the Reformation and the religious conflicts which arose.[10] Kelley has a chapter in which he demonstrates the important role of printing in disseminating both Reformation and counter-Reformation ideology, where the "war of words" preceded the Wars of Religion. Philip Benedict

5. Roy, *Laïcité face à l'islam*, 19–20.
6. Roy, *Laïcité face à l'islam*, 29.
7. Cabanel, *Les mots de la laïcité*, 64.
8. Barzun, *From Dawn to Decadence*, xvii.
9. Barzun, *From Dawn to Decadence*, xvii.
10. Kelley, *Beginning of Ideology*; Holt, "Kingdom of France."

and Virginia Reinburg likewise present the importance of the printing press in the dissemination of the evangelical faith in France through the writings of Luther and Calvin.[11] Holt explains how the Wars of Religion "proved to be the single most dangerous threat to the French state and monarchy before the Revolution of 1789."[12] These books provide essential historical elements on the early clashes between Protestantism and Catholicism which become crucial in understanding the growing desire for the promised Republican liberty in the 1789 French Revolution.

French religious historian Alain Boyer makes a significant contribution in a chapter on Protestants and their relation to the law of 1905. He states that during the French Revolution, generally speaking, Protestants regarded with envy the Declaration of the Bill of Rights [1791] in the United States.[13] He also notes that Protestants accepted the 1801 Concordat between Napoleon and the Vatican because of the favorable treatment accorded Reformed and Lutheran believers. However, they found fault in that the Concordat gave a place of eminence to the Catholic Church and assumed that the head of State would be Catholic.[14] He further asserts that the great majority of Protestants, especially Reformed believers, and even more so members of free churches [Églises libres], were favorable toward the separation.[15]

One particularly noteworthy historical event preceding the law of 1905 was the Dreyfus Affair. L'Affaire, as it has become known, demonstrates the competing forces at work to either reestablish the monarchy and Church in power or to solidify and advance the unfulfilled ideals of the 1789 Revolution. Among the books which connect l'Affaire with the religio-political struggles are the works of Cahm and Begley. Cahm observes, "French Catholicism at the end of the nineteenth century still bore the mark of the Church's traditional theological anti-Judaism, based on the twin ideas of the Jewish people as deicides and as the embodiment of Evil."[16] A more recent work by Louis Begley notes "the struggle over the role of the Catholic church in education and the state, which the church lost when a law voted in on December 9, 1905, terminated the concordat between France and the Vatican and provided for a strict separation between church and state."[17]

11. Benedict and Reinburg, "Religion and the Sacred."
12. Holt, "Kingdom of France," 23.
13. Boyer, *La loi de 1905*, 71.
14. Boyer, *La loi de 1905*, 69–70.
15. Boyer, *La loi de 1905*, 72.
16. Cahm, *Dreyfus Affair*, 90.
17. Begley, *Dreyfus Affair*, 56.

L'Affaire provides a window to see more clearly the impulses at that time for Church and State separation.

One of the observations made in this book is that the marginalization of religion has taken place in its removal from public space. Guy Haarscher affirms the classic understanding that laïcité is a political concept where the State does not privilege any religious confession and ensures the free expression of conscience to everyone. He does, however, recognize that laïcité might push religion strictly into the private sphere. In light of the multiculturalist experiences of many nations, Haarscher attempts to reconcile the law of 1905 with its contemporary ideal in France.[18] Olivier Roy, cited earlier, is one of many French intellectuals questioning the role of laïcité in French society. His writings are indispensable for anyone wanting an insider perspective. He has written extensively on laïcité in confrontation with Islam. He recognizes that Islam's presence in France has raised questions about whether Islam is compatible with *laïcité française* and whether Islam is a threat comparable to or greater than the threat of Catholicism at the beginning of the twentieth century. He warns against making laïcité a civil religion requiring adhesion to a body of common values and concludes that the problem is not Islam, but contemporary forms of the return of religion.[19] Jean Baubérot is one of the most prolific writers on the topic of laïcité.[20] He advances the idea of a plurality of laïcités from sociological, historical, and political perspectives. Baubérot also writes on religious themes—the foundations and evolution of religions and the intersection of faith and laïcité.[21]

The French concept of laïcité casts a long shadow over France in contemporary times and provides a lens for understanding current attitudes and events. As stated earlier, the law of 1905 reflects a culmination of events in France's history and a precursor of events which would frame the French Constitutions in 1946 and 1958. Henri Pena-Ruiz asserts that the experience of the wars of religion and the persecutions tied to creedal obligation contributed greatly to the emergence of a laïque conscience.[22] Those interested in understanding the French laïque conscience, or religious worldview, cannot afford to neglect the historical events preceding and surrounding the law of 1905, the far-reaching consequences of the law in the development of a culture imbibed with laïcité, and the present-day challenges in understanding

18. Haarscher, *La Laïcité*.

19. Roy, *Laïcité face à l'islam*, 172.

20. Baubérot, *La laïcité*; *Histoire de la laïcité*.

21. Baubérot, *Petite histoire du christianisme*; Baubérot and Carbonnier-Burkard, *Histoire des protestants*.

22. Pena-Ruiz, *Qu'est-ce que la laïcité?*, 265.

a laïque nation with varying degrees of hostility or indifference to religion. France mesmerizes and mystifies Americans. We are often baffled by their general indifference to religion and their laws forbidding religious symbols in public schools, full-face veils in public places, and even the interdiction of burkinis on French beaches. Understand laïcité and one will gain insight in beginning to understand France and its people.

1

Laïcité and the Religious Question

ANY ATTEMPT TO UNDERSTAND the history of French laïcité is confronted with the challenge of where to begin, what to include, and what to omit. For present purposes, it must suffice to survey major events, personages, and themes which marked French history and contributed to the emergence of juridical laïcité in the early twentieth century. We seek to understand the historical context out of which the French concept of laïcité arose, the implications of the 1905 legal separation of Church and State, the demise of religion in France, and the current revival of interest in the subject of laïcité with the emergence of Islam and its claims. According to French philosopher and historian Marcel Gauchet, the history of laïcité in France is closely linked to the history of the State as one of the major actors in the process of the removal of religion from the public sphere. Although this has happened elsewhere, in France there has been a greater marginalization of religion.[1]

French history might be likened to peeling back layers of an onion, where one not only weeps, but one also finds the need to go deeper to the core. This book does not attempt to provide a comprehensive treatment of French history on which almost countless volumes have already been written. The history of the great nation of France is long and vast with innumerable events of importance and influence. Few nations have had a greater influence on world events than France. As historian William Stearns Davis observes:

> France has been a participant in, or interested spectator of, nearly every great war or diplomatic contest for over a thousand years; and a very great proportion of all the religious, intellectual, social, and economic movements which have affected the world either began in France or were speedily caught up and

1. Gauchet, *La religion dans la démocratie*, 41.

1

acted upon by Frenchmen soon after they had commenced their working elsewhere.[2]

One of the most well-known events in modern history is the French Revolution. Gildea asks whether the French Revolution was good, bad, or both at the same time or at different times. How did the ideals of 1789 lead to the Terror of 1793? How did the guillotiners become the guillotined? The answers often depend on whom you read and on the precommitments and perspectives of the writers. The interpretation of events may differ according to the underlying agenda or political loyalties of the reader. To this day there are divergent opinions from different quarters of French society, from those on the political Left to those on the Right. On the political Right, there are those who contend that the French Revolution was a disaster in its attack against the Church and monarchy and that it ruined the advanced economic status of France when compared to other European nations. The Terror of 1793 was the natural consequence of anarchy, and revisionists cannot paint over the destruction of a society that the monarchy might have been able to reform if given time. On the political Left, defenders of the Revolution claim that the Revolution continues and the terror was justified to safeguard the Republic and procure freedom. Robespierre was a hero and admirable in his defense of the nation against monarchists and religionists. In fact, the guillotine was seen as more humane than former methods of torture and persecution, and both revolutionaries and counterrevolutionaries committed atrocities.[3]

These observations do not devalue historical recording and recollection. They act as safeguards in recognition of one's own prejudices and those of others. They provide evidence that consensus is lacking on the interpretation of historical events, that there is no single collective memory among French people, and that outsiders should tread carefully and avoid stereotypical misrepresentations of the history of others. However, given the above-mentioned cautionary remarks, there are broad brushes which appear incontestable. Few nations have experienced the centuries of upheaval suffered by the French people in the name of religion. This history contributed to the separation of the established Church from the public sphere, juridically in 1905 and constitutionally in 1946 and 1958. Over the last century there has followed a rapid demise of the dominant religion with the inauguration of a laïque Republic. Cesari observes:

2. Davis, *History of France*, 2.
3. Gildea, *French History*, 15–17.

> For reasons particular to France's historical situation, most nota-
> bly the resistance of the Catholic church to the law of separation,
> this rejection of religion eventually took on a radical character.
> The conception of secularism [laïcité] in France is thus an ex-
> tremely rigid one, in which any and all signs of religion must be
> eradicated from public space.[4]

On one hand, this book examines the failures of the established
Church in France to be truly Christian in many respects, particularly in
its monopolistic form and in wielding political power prior to its forced
disestablishment in 1905. The failures of the Church in France are well
documented, and many failures have been recognized by the modern Roman Catholic Church. Without question the Church battled forces opposed
to her authority and resisted until all resistance became futile. At times, the
Church contested attempts to remove her from political power. At other
times, she made compromises with secular authorities. At most times, she
sided with monarchism in both its absolute and constitutional forms. For
example, as will be seen later, the Church gave her allegiance to Napoleon
III (1808–1873) during the establishment of the Second Empire (1852–
1870). This would contribute to the Church's undoing in the Third Republic
(1870–1940) when anticlerical Republicans came to power in 1879 determined to regulate the Church-State problem once and for all.

On the other hand, in all fairness to the spirit of that age, even if the
Church had been faithful to her calling, the conflict between the Church
and State was perhaps inevitable. The arrival of the Reformation with its
emphasis on the authority of Scripture, the priesthood of the believer and
the freedom of conscience, the invention of the printing press, and later
Renaissance humanism in France with its emphasis on individual autonomy, conspired to undermine the Church's authority. Man was placed at
the center of the universe and became master of his own destiny on earth.
The great eighteenth-century philosophical movements inspired by critical
thinking, the progress of knowledge, and the ideals of tolerance and liberty
sharpened the conflict against prevailing religious thought. Barzun affirms
that "the zeal for explanation by measuring the regularities of nature kept
strengthening Deism and atheism and weakening the credibility of a Providence concerned with individuals. Western culture was inching toward
its present *secularism*."[5] In the nineteenth century, the conflict intensified
with scientific progress, the elevation of reason, and the influence of Cartesian thought. Man became master of nature. Religious dogmas, ancient

4. Cesari, *Islam and Democracy*, 76.
5. Barzun, *Dawn to Decadence*, 378.

texts, and devotion to tradition previously passed on from generation to generation were viewed as backwards and prescientific. With the entrance of democracy and universal suffrage, the only source of legitimate power was found in the people which replaced the divine unction consecrating the monarchy. All this conspired to put an end to the mingling of political and religious authority and the union of the throne and altar.[6]

From the time of the conversion of Roman emperors to Christianity to the official separation of Church and State in the early twentieth century, the Church held or sought political power and declared itself as the only true religion as found in Holy Scriptures.[7] Now, after centuries of Christian influence, the rapid dechristianization of France and most of Western Europe has taken place in a relatively short period of time. Today the great cathedrals of France are mostly known as tourist attractions. Church attendance on any given Sunday has steadily declined. This decline has been well documented and statistically France has had sharper declines than her European neighbors.[8] Dechristianization has been described as the disappearance in the West of a politico-religious system which entailed an obligatory faith and practice for everyone. This phenomenon is generally understood by historians to have begun with the French Revolution in 1789, not merely as a single event, but as a decade of Revolution which forever altered the course of French history.[9]

French History and Laïcité

The relation of French history to the concept of laïcité is complex. The contributing events span centuries of interminable crises between the dominant Church and its rivals for power or with those seeking reform. In modern times, this panorama of events extends from the Protestant Reformation and Wars of Religion in the sixteenth century to the ideological battles in present-day France. At stake today is the meaning and relevance of laïcité in a pluralistic, democratic society. According to Bowen, "In the dominant narratives of laïcité, history has moved toward the removal of religion from the public sphere. . . . The law of 1905, celebrated as having proclaimed the separation of church and state, was but the outcome of a long period of struggle, with its Revolutionary thesis and Restoration antithesis."[10] In present discussions and

6. Gaillard, "L'invention de la laïcité," 9.

7. Delumeau, *Le christianisme*, 21–22.

8. Greely, *Religion in Europe*, 208–11.

9. Delumeau, *Le christianisme*, 190.

10. Bowen, *Headscarves*, 21.

debates on the place of laïcité, the invocation of the law of December 1905 on the separation of Churches and State figures prominently. One hundred years after the law was enacted, proponents and opponents of laïcité have recourse to varied interpretations and applications of the law of 1905. One incident in 2014 involved the mayor of La Garenne-Colombes who was criticized for allowing a Christmas manger scene on public property purportedly in violation of the law of 1905. His response was to remind his attackers that France has an ancient Christian culture. He criticized the ignorance of those who ignore that fact or who misunderstand the law of 1905, who wave the laïque flag but do a disservice to laïcité.[11]

From a historical perspective, one of the distinguishing factors of French laïcité is that it resulted from a break with the past and with religious power structures. Jean-Claude Monod explains that laïcité was introduced by the Reformation, prepared intellectually by the Renaissance, initiated by the French Revolution, and was founded largely on autonomous reason devoid of religious assumptions.[12] Patrick Cabanel advances what he considers a global hypothesis in his understanding of French history. He asserts that every century over the last five hundred years France has changed the solution for dealing with the religious question which was opened by the definitive implantation of the Protestant Reformation with the Edict of Nantes in 1598 as the starting point. According to him, the Reformation forever changed the religious equation in France. He estimates that by 1560 one out of ten French people was won over by the Reformation and converted to Protestantism. That number fell to one out of fifty by the end of the eighteenth century. These figures are considered by Cabanel as measures of a double failure—the failure of Protestantism to take root in France and the failure of the monarchy to effectively treat the Protestant question. He does not consider the Edict of Nantes tolerant, pluralistic, or laïque. He argues that Protestantism was temporarily authorized and protected, yet still trapped as a minority until France once again found its unity in the Catholic religion in what he calls a coexistence in intolerance.[13] The Revocation of the Edict of Nantes in 1685 was followed by a new edict of toleration in 1787 when it became evident that Protestantism was not going to disappear. To this edict was added state recognition of three other religious confessions alongside the Catholic Church with the Concordat of 1801. A hundred years of relative peace followed until the events of the nineteenth century

---

11. Juvin, "Crèche de Noël."

12. Monod, *Sécularisation et laïcité*, 47.

13. Cabanel, "La question religieuse," 167–69.

which would lead to the unraveling of the Concordat and the enactment of the Law of Separation in 1905.[14]

Cabanel looks at two major thresholds of laicization. He sees the first threshold with several characteristics established during the revolutionary and Napoleonic periods. The first characteristic was institutional fragmentation. Although religion was no longer coextensive with French society, religion remained an institution structured by the State under the Concordat. The second characteristic was State recognition of the religious needs of its citizens and the provision of salaries for ministers of different religious expressions. Religion was maintained as the moral foundation of society and the practice of catechism was continued in public schools. The third characteristic was an incomplete religious pluralism in State recognition of four religious confessions—Catholic, Reformed, Lutheran, Judaism. Established laïcité was the second threshold which covered most of the twentieth century and appears to most people today as the definitive framework in defining relations between the State (public domain) and churches (confined to private spaces). In this threshold, religion was no longer considered an integral part of societal structure and was banished to the private sphere where it experienced a loss of legitimacy and where religious needs were no longer socially recognized. The State withdrew recognition of the religious confessions included in the Concordat, the Catholic Church lost its privileged place, minority religions became juridical equals, and the State, at least in principle, observed a benevolent neutrality.[15]

The importance of these two thresholds will be seen later in the challenges to laïcité in the early period of the twenty-first century to determine whether a third threshold has now appeared. The arrival of this third threshold might have been signaled by the writings of Nicholas Sarkozy (b. 1955), president of France from 2007 to 2012. As Minister of the Interior from 2002 to 2004, he also had conferred on him the position of Minister of Religions. During this earlier period, he wrote a book entitled *La République, les religions, l'espérance*. In the form of an interview, he presented laïcité in service to liberty and religion in service to society. A major chapter was given to Islam and the Republic in which he describes two variations of Islam: one official and reassuring represented by the Grand Mosque in Paris; one unofficial and worrisome in which a militant extremism was developing.[16] It is significant that he wrote this book during the time when two French citizens were held hostage by Islamic militants. In his preface he declared that the

14. Cabanel, "La question religieuse," 171.

15. Cabanel, "La question religieuse," 174–75.

16. Sarkozy, *La République*, 59.

kidnappers were fanatics who claimed the Islamic faith which professes the opposite of what they became and had nothing to do with God.[17] Further, he distanced himself from his predecessors and their apparent indifference toward religions and considered that in past years sociological questions had been overestimated and religious reality largely underestimated.[18] He spoke with an uncommon frankness in stating that religion occupied a central place in France at the beginning of the third millennium. He further clarified that the place of religion is not "at the exterior of the Republic; it is not a place in competition with the Republic. It is a place in [dans] the Republic."[19] The landscape of France has changed several times in the past and is once again undergoing change and challenges in the present.

Christian France

As we now turn to examining the place of Christianity in French history and the emergence of laïcité, important questions and distinctions must first be raised concerning the nature of French Christianity and Christendom. In posing questions on the re-evangelization of Europe, Wessels asked, "How Christian was Europe really? To what extent has it been de-Christianized today?" He initially responded that Europe was largely Christianized by AD 750 if one uses the marks of baptism and other religious rituals. However, he questions "how deeply this Christianization had really penetrated in the so-called Christianized areas" and agrees with Dutch historian Jan Romein that "mediaeval Christianity was only a thin veneer."[20] French philosopher Luc Ferry adds that many associated with the Christian faith were attached to the religious form as such, but the content, the message of love, was hardly evident in the reality of human relations.[21]

French historian Jean Delumeau goes further in declaring that one cannot even speak in terms of medieval Christianity and that the Christianization of Europe in that period was unsuccessful. He questions what was really accomplished in seven or eight centuries of evangelization and notes that both Protestant Reformers and their Catholic adversaries viewed the peasantry, which constituted the vast majority of Europeans, as ignorant of

---

17. Sarkozy, *La République*, 9.
18. Sarkozy, *La République*, 13.
19. Sarkozy, *La République*, 15.
20. Wessels, *Europe*, 3–4.
21. Ferry, *L'homme-Dieu*, 245.

Christianity, given to pagan superstitions and to vices.[22] With this assessment Newbigin concurs:

> When we speak of a time when public truth as it was understood and accepted in Europe was shaped by Christianity, we do not—of course—mean that every person's behavior was in accordance with Christ's teaching. In that sense there has never been and there can never be a Christian society. But Europe was a Christian society in the sense that its public truth was shaped by the biblical story with its center in the incarnation of the Word in Jesus.[23]

Delumeau further asserts that one can speak of medieval Christianity only by an abuse of language or by holding to the myth of a golden age, and that those living during that period often lived as if they had no moral code.[24] This specialist in Catholic Church history claims that Christianity, in its dealings with non-Christians, often practiced the law of the strongest. Christianity was proclaimed, theorized, and institutionalized but never really evident in the way people lived. It was a project or a dream that was wrongly taken for a reality.[25] In pre-revolutionary structures, with the marriage of Church and State, it was necessary that everyone belong, willingly or not, to the cultural and moral framework established by the Church. For many it was simply "conformism, resignation, and forced hypocrisy."[26] When the Church lost its force, people regained their liberty outside the Church. McManners observes that "'Christian Europe' was a social-intellectual-cultural complex and not a concentration of converted believers" and supports that assertion with a quote attributed to Anatole France (1844–1964) who observed years later that "Catholicism is still the most acceptable form of religious indifference."[27]

We are far from the days when the subjects of European kings were required to hold the faith of their sovereign and their ancestors. It may be extremely difficult for moderns to even imagine life under an imposed religion in light of the freedom of choice—religion or no religion—which most Westerners enjoy today. Yet we must understand that for centuries of European history, secular authority was at the service of ecclesiastical authority with the accompanying constraints and restraints on personal liberty.

22. Delumeau, *Le christianisme*, 90.
23. Newbigin, *Gospel in a Pluralistic Society*, 222.
24. Delumeau, *Le christianisme*, 29.
25. Delumeau, *Le christianisme*, 41.
26. Delumeau, *Le christianisme*, 73.
27. McManners, *Church and State*, 10.

Christianity existed as a politico-religious system present in the daily life of subjects. The configuration of Church and State structures ensured that the form of Christianity which was held by those in power was rarely transformed into anything resembling biblical Christianity. It was coupled with the dominant physical presence of churches and monuments serving as a constant reminder that people lived in a Christian nation.[28]

This somber interpretation of church history may appear one-sided in ignoring the contributions of the Catholic Church throughout history. It is undeniable that the Church has had great influence over the centuries, has done good works, has provided relief to the suffering, and has contributed to advances in knowledge and civilization. However, no good works done can ever justify the fact that the Christian Church as it was known in France often failed to live Christianly and that opposition to the Church in many quarters arose against the evil done in the name of God. It was not for the good the Church had done that led to the separation of Church and State. It was the Church's intolerance, oppression, and complicity with political power and its refusal to allow dissent or competing belief systems that contributed to her undoing.

It may also be helpful to distinguish between Christendom (*chrétienté*) and Christianity (*christianisme*). The former refers to people and places where Christianity dominates; the latter refers to the religion founded on the teaching, the person, and the life of Jesus Christ.[29] Douglas Hall affirms that although "the Christian faith entered the world as a movement containing provocative and anti-institutional elements, it eventually expressed itself in well-defined institutional forms."[30] On one hand, Christendom dominated for centuries in European history and its institutions developed and expanded in their exercise of political control. On the other hand, Christianity was never meant to be an earthly political power. Many of the objections to the Christian faith should be seen more as reactions to Christendom rather than reactions to Christianity.

The beginning of official Christianity in Europe is dated to the conversion of Constantine (272–337) in the fourth century AD. The distinction between Church and State was erased with privileges accorded to the Church and the intervention of the emperor in the affairs of the Church. Early on, other religions were tolerated. Later under other emperors, such as Theodosius (347–395) who created a state religion, other religions were persecuted. In AD 498, following victory in the battle of Tolbiac, Frankish

28. Delumeau, *Le christianisme*, 22–23.

29. Robert et al., *Nouveau Petit Robert*, 428.

30. Hall, *End of Christendom*, 6.

King Clovis (466–511) received Christian baptism on Christmas Day from the bishop of Reims along with three thousand followers.[31] According to De Monclos, the exact date of Clovis's baptism remains controversial.[32] In any case, this event is regarded as the beginning of Christian France, or Christendom, a fusion of the political and religious spheres, and "the first of the Germanic nations to espouse the orthodox Christianity of the empire."[33] McCrea notes,

> The first time medieval chroniclers described an event as "European" was the victory of Christian Frankish forces over a Muslim army at Poitiers in 732 . . . [then] with the crusades of the eleventh century, Western Christianity became synonymous with a European identity which defined itself against the Islamic and Byzantine Orthodox Christian civilizations to its south and east.[34]

After the fall of Rome in AD 476, "the absence of Roman hegemony increased the power of the church in medieval Europe. With the church's ascendancy, 'Christendom' appeared—a single society with two expressions of power. The coronation of Charlemagne by Pope Leo III in 800 made the question of who governed Christendom less clear."[35] The rule of the Carolingians, in particular the reign of Charlemagne (742–814), inaugurated a royal theocracy under the Holy Roman Empire, in "an attempt to refound the old Roman Empire of the West, but on a strictly Christian basis."[36] In other words, the monarchy by divine right (*droit divin*) was installed in power through the coronation and by the consecration of the Church. The king supported the Church in establishing pontifical states with financial and military participation.

At the death of Charlemagne in AD 814 the feudal period began during which time the Church represented the only organized power. This was the beginning of a pontifical theocracy where the spiritual power of the Church displaced political power as primary in governing the affairs of the people. A movement known as Gallicanism emerged in France to encourage the autonomy of the French Church from papal power. As a result of schism, a French pope was installed in Avignon in 1309 by Philippe Le Bel (1268–1314). Historically, there were two forms of Gallicanism. The ecclesiastic form affirmed the autonomy of the French Church from Rome. The

31. Chaunu and Mension-Rigau, *Baptême de Clovis*, 10.

32. Montclos, *Histoire religieuse*, 19.

33. Walker et al., *History of the Christian Church*, 150.

34. McCrea, *Religion and the Public Order*, 18.

35. Lillback, "Church and State," 678.

36. Davis, *History of France*, 34.

political form emphasized the authority of the French king over the temporal organization of the French Church. This latter form will be prominent in the 1801 Concordat promulgated by Napoleon Bonaparte (1769–1821) of which more will be said later.[37]

During these early periods of Christian France there was no religious pluralism. "In the medieval West one had no choice but to be born into the (essentially unique and indivisible) Church. . . . In the Middle Ages the Church's affairs were matters of State, but only for the elite who made the decisions."[38] In the seventeenth century, Louis XIV (1638–1715) would combat Protestantism according to the principle "one law, one faith, one king."[39] The absence of the modern concept of religious pluralism was true in most of recorded history. According to Newbigin, "Although the world has been a religiously plural place for as long as we know anything of the history of religions, most people for most of history have lived in societies where one religion was dominant and others were marginal."[40] France was unexceptional in her imposition of a State religion. Her exceptionalism lies more in the degree she has been emancipated from religion and in the history behind her present religious condition.

There were attempts throughout French history to provide religious rights for Protestants and other faiths and relief from the control of the dominant Church. Much of the success was short-lived and the freedoms obtained were lost at the whims of monarchs, revolutionaries, or Republicans. For example, in 1598 the Edict of Nantes was enacted under King Henry IV (1553–1610) who had converted from Protestantism to Catholicism. Under the terms of the Edict, Protestants were granted substantial religious rights and a measure of religious liberty. From a religious point of view, the edict granted considerable concessions to the Protestants, notably in the institution of the principle of liberty of conscience in all the kingdom and the complete liberty of worship in all the regions where Protestantism was established before 1597. From a political point of view, full amnesty was granted for all acts of war. Civil equality with Catholics was guaranteed and there was a provision for the right of access to public employment. Protestants retained territorial possession of places of safety in more than one hundred cities in France, including La Rochelle, Saumur, Montpellier and Montauban.[41] The Edict was revoked by Louis XIV in

37. CNEF, *Laïcité française*, 12–13.
38. Cameron, *European Reformation*, 198.
39. Baubérot, *Petite histoire du christianisme*, 59.
40. Newbigin, *Gospel in a Pluralistic Society*, 25.
41. Carenco, *L'Édit de Nantes*, 3.

1685 and followed one hundred years later by the Edict of Tolerance promulgated in 1787 in favor of the Protestants. They would again be granted limited rights but not allowed to meet publicly for worship.[42] We learn through these events that at these times in French history, the State held the authority to grant religious freedom without grounding these rights in anything but the power of the State. There was little recognition of any divine right to freely worship the God of one's understanding or recognition of the freedom of conscience to not worship any God.

42. CNEF, *Laïcité française*, 13.

2

Reformation and Incipient Laïcité

THE PROTESTANT REFORMATION, BEGUN under Martin Luther (1483–1546) in Germany in 1517 and continued shortly after in France under John Calvin (1509–1564), provides a convenient and significant reference in our understanding of historical influences in French society and religious experience. As Reformation church history professor Euan Cameron asserts,

> The personal motives for the reformers' conversions are ultimately inexplicable. However, this overlooks the fundamental point: they were personal motives. One did not become a first-generation reformer by habit, compulsion, or default. Where any evidence exists, it suggests that the reformers reached their position only after serious and earnest heart-searching. They were some of the most conscientious revolutionaries ever to rebel against authority.[1]

Five hundred years later, the Reformation's historical and religious importance cannot be exaggerated. "No other movement of religious protest or reform since antiquity has been so widespread or lasting in its effects, so deep and searching in its criticism of received wisdom, so destructive in what it abolished or so fertile in what it created."[2] The late Catholic historian John Bossy questioned the use of Reformation in the singular while recognizing he had no better alternative. He wrote, "Yet it seems worth trying to use [Reformation] as sparingly as possible, not simply because it goes along too easily with the notion that a bad form of Christianity was being replaced by a good one, but because it sits awkwardly across the subject without directing anyone's attention anywhere in particular."[3] Cameron asserts that although there were reformations throughout Europe in Catholic nations, Reformation

1. Cameron, *European Reformation*, 131.

2. Cameron, *European Reformation*, 1.

3. Bossy, *Christianity in the West*, 91.

in the singular is reserved "for a particular process of change, integrating cultural, political, and theological factors in a way never seen before and rarely since."[4] Walker recognizes that the "defensive action to the Protestant threat is appropriately called the Counter-Reformation" and also that "one may properly speak of an indigenous Catholic Reformation of the sixteenth century."[5] Yet the localized attempts at "spiritual renewal would not have won the support of popes and prelates—would not have been 'institutionalized,' so to speak,—were it not for the profound shock administered to the church at large by the Protestant Reformation."[6]

The Protestant Reformers clearly believed that the Roman Catholic Church had departed from the truth of Scripture. Protestants generally consider the term Counter-Reformation a better descriptor of the Council of Trent (1545–1563) whose decrees "were clear and definite in their rejection of Protestant beliefs."[7] The Catholic Church may have experienced reforms, renewals or reformations in areas of practice, piety, and missionary zeal, but did not experience Reformation in the weighty sense of the word which describes the reestablishment of apostolic doctrine. Alister McGrath explains Luther's theological priority:

> For Luther, the reformation of morals and the renewal of spirituality, although of importance in themselves, were of secondary significance in relation to the *reformation of Christian doctrine*. Well aware of the frailty of human nature, Luther criticized both Wycliffe and Hus for confining their attacks on the papacy to its moral shortcomings, where they should have attacked the theology on which the papacy was ultimately based. For Luther, a reformation of morals was secondary to a reformation of doctrine.[8]

Luther became a priest in the Catholic Church in 1507 and received his doctorate in theology from the University of Wittenberg in 1512.[9] Early on Luther accepted the Church's teaching that God gives grace to those who do their best. According to Gerald Bray,

> It took a spiritual crisis in his own life to shake Luther out of this way of thinking. He did his best but discovered that it was not

4. Cameron, *European Reformation*, 1.

5. Walker et al., *History of the Christian Church*, 502.

6. Walker et al., *History of the Christian Church*, 502.

7. Walker et al., *History of the Christian Church*, 510.

8. McGrath, *Luther's Theology*, 19–20.

9. Bloch, *Réforme Protestante*, 13.

good enough. . . . After much searching, he found the answer in the words of the prophet Habakkuk, quoted by the apostle Paul in his letter to the Romans: "The just shall live by faith" (Rom 1:17; cf. Hab 2:4). The scales dropped from his eyes as he realized that it is by grace that we are saved through faith and not by our works, however meritorious they are in themselves. The foundations of the old system were shaken to the root, and the result was the Protestant Reformation.[10]

On October 31, 1517, Luther nailed his famous ninety-five theses on the door of the Castle Church in Wittenberg and was ordered by the Church to recant his error. Benedict describes Luther's resistance:

> He dug in and soon was calling for a reduction in the sacraments from seven to three (later two) and the abolition of the monastic orders, while denouncing the Church of Rome as hopelessly corrupt. Although excommunicated by the pope and condemned by the Imperial diet of Worms, he was protected by the Elector of Saxony. Thanks to the printing press, Luther's example and ideas galvanized widespread agitation for change in the structure of the Church across the German-speaking world. Parisian booksellers also began to sell his writings to eager customers as early as 1519. The Sorbonne condemned Luther's teaching in 1521, and secular laws soon made possession of his writings a crime.[11]

Luther translated the Greek New Testament into German in 1522 and the Hebrew Old Testament into German in 1534, the latter considered a foundational work for modern German. He is credited with establishing five fundamental principles or *solae*: *sola scriptura*, *sola fide*, *sola gratia*, *solus Christus*, and *soli Deo Gloria*. These scriptural truths set his teaching apart from the teaching of the Church and announced an inevitable rupture.[12] Luther's influence in France would soon be eclipsed by that of Calvin, yet "between 1528 and the 1540s, Luther was by far the most widely translated foreign theologian in this period."[13] Questions have been raised about the Reformation's necessity or inevitability. "Such questions cannot be answered with any degree of confidence. The fact remains, however, that Luther himself regarded the Reformation as having begun over,

---

10. Bray, "Late-Medieval Theology," 93.

11. Benedict and Reinburg, "Religion and the Sacred," 135–36.

12. Bloch, *Réforme Protestante*, 17–18.

13. Benedict and Reinburg, "Religion and the Sacred," 137.

and to have chiefly concerned, the correct understanding of the Christian doctrine of justification."[14]

Calvin was born in Noyon, France in the region of Picardy. He received a classical education through which he acquired an encyclopedic knowledge of authors from antiquity and from the patristic period. He later studied law until the death of his father in 1531.[15] In 1533 he converted to Protestantism and in 1536 wrote the first edition of his Institutes of the Christian Religion, "which evolved through subsequent revisions into the most forceful and successful exposition of Reformed Protestantism of the sixteenth century."[16] He established himself in Geneva in 1541 and began calling upon believers living in places with no Protestant church to separate from the Catholic Church and if necessary relocate to a place where they could worship freely:

> As growing numbers of French evangelicals heard this call and fled to Geneva, the number of Genevan presses multiplied, and clandestine networks were established for distributing their products throughout France. . . . No less than 178 French-language editions of one or another of Calvin's treatises, sermons, and commentaries appeared during his lifetime. His sharp critique of Catholic theology and worship and uncompromising call for separation from it increasingly dominated evangelical propaganda.[17]

The Reformers proclaimed the divine authority of the Scriptures and encouraged personal Bible reading. Consequently, there was no longer one authoritative voice and interpreter of the Holy Scriptures. As people began reading the Christian Scriptures for themselves the divide between ecclesiastical authority and the faithful grew. Andrew Fix writes,

> For centuries the Catholic church had maintained that the only criterion of truth for a religious proposition was the authority of church tradition, pope, and councils. Luther proposed a radical new standard for religious truth at the Diet of Worms in 1521 when he maintained that whatever his conscience was compelled to believe when he read Scripture was religious truth.[18]

Baubérot asserts that in France in the early 1500s the piety, theology, and practices of the Church were not in crisis. He describes

---

14. McGrath, *Luther's Theology*, 21–22.

15. Bloch, *Réforme Protestante*, 14.

16. Benedict and Reinburg, "Religion and the Sacred," 138.

17. Benedict and Reinburg, "Religion and the Sacred," 138.

18. Fix, *Prophecy and Reason*, 9–10.

pre-Reformation times as a vast market of salvation and quest for personal salvation, which led a host of men and women to choose the religious life, the way of Christian perfection governed by perpetual vows of poverty, chastity, and obedience.[19] At least initially, the new ideas which came from Germany found favorable soil in diverse intellectual and religious milieu.[20] As Trueman and Kim observe, "France, with a strong monarchy, a vibrant intellectual culture at the University of Paris, and indeed, an interest in exerting independence from the Roman church, looked in the early sixteenth century like fruitful soil for Protestant reform."[21] There were also attempts at reform from within the Church which targeted the clergy and religious life. Those who called for reform denounced the abuses of the clergy at all levels of the hierarchical ladder, from the absentee bishops accumulating undeserved privileges, to the ignorant and concubinary village priests, and to the lazy and drunken monks.[22] Jonathan Bloch considers it an error to imagine that Christianity in France was united and strong at the dawn of the Reformation and maintains that pagan elements were present in the various expressions of Catholicism. He explains that this situation permitted Protestantism to progressively gain a foothold without meeting the resistance that a united Catholicism would have provided.[23]

Prior to the Reformation, the monarchy and the Church were wedded without religious competition. Kelley states that "within a generation the ostensibly religious upheaval precipitated by Luther involved not only the formal break-up of Christendom but a whole range of secular disturbances." He further affirms that the Reformation must be understood "not merely as a changing design upon a historical fabric but as a violent, multi-dimensional, and perhaps multi-directional process which needs examining from several angles."[24] Scholars uniformly look to the Reformation as the beginning of religious, social, and political turmoil in France which would destabilize both the monarchy and the Church. Eugène Réveillard, deputy of Charente-Inférieure, wrote in 1907 that the Reformation, in the measure it brought back religion and Christian churches to the purity of their origins according to the intention of the Reformers, marked the beginning of the restoration

---

19. Baubérot and Carbonnier-Burkard, *Histoire des Protestants*, 14–16.

20. Baubérot and Carbonnier-Burkard, *Histoire des Protestants*, 13.

21. Trueman and Kim, "Reformers and Their Reformation," 136.

22. Baubérot and Carbonnier-Burkard, *Histoire des Protestants*, 16.

23. Bloch, *Réforme Protestante*, 7.

24. Kelley, *Beginning of Ideology*, 7.

of the principles of liberty of conscience and of worship, and at the same time, the separation of powers—civil and ecclesiastical.[25]

Xavier de Montclos considers it a mistake to only see reciprocal rejection and condemnation in the Reformation or Counter-Reformation. He believes that these two great branches of Christianity in modern times both responded to calls for a deeper and more evangelical religious life.[26] Monod regards the sixteenth century as marked by several significant changes. First, it was the beginning of the individualization of faith which made adherence to faith traditions possible but not obligatory. Second, it was the time of the pluralization of the faith which in time would find protection by law. Monod considers that the religious revolution and schism of the sixteenth century, characterized by pluralism and individualism, led to relativism and the possibility of the "subjectivation of religious teaching."[27]

In a few decades, the Reformation's influence in France "not only shattered the unity of religion, but it led to the contesting of the monarchy itself."[28] This new religion became known as Calvinism and its followers were called Huguenots.[29] According to Kelley, "The origin of the term 'Huguenot' has been long debated. The present consensus is that it derives from the word for the resisting Swiss confederations (*Eidgenossem*), but it seems to have emerged during the conspiracy of Amboise, and opponents of the 'foreign house' of Guise construed it as designating their allegiance to the descendants of the royal dynasty of 'Hughes' Capet."[30] However, Carter Lindberg states that "the French Calvinists preferred the term *Réformés*, the Reformed. Catholic satires of the time called them *la Religion Déformée*."[31] The first Reformed churches appeared in France beginning in 1555. In 1559 a national synod gathered in Paris and adopted a confession of faith which was ratified in 1571 at La Rochelle and called *La Confession de la Rochelle*.[32] By 1561–1562 Calvinism became a considerable power in the kingdom, about two million people. Among them were academics and former religious workers, bourgeoisie from legal and commercial professions, representatives of high and low nobility, whose conversion led

25. Réveillard, *La séparation*, 23.

26. Montclos, *Histoire religieuse*, 57.

27. Monod, *Sécularisation et laïcité*, 48.

28. Holt, "Kingdom of France," 23.

29. Carbonnier-Burkard, *La révolte des Camisards*, 13.

30. Kelley, *Beginning of Ideology*, 257.

31. Lindberg, *European Reformation*, 282.

32. Carbonnier-Burkard, *La révolte des Camisards*, 10.

to the conversion of entire cities and villages.[33] This Protestant religious expression "threatened the perception of nation forged by both king and subjects, because the king's own coronation oath required him to protect and defend his realm and his subjects from heresy."[34] Montclos asserts that beginning in 1540 persecution became practically systematic with many Protestants dying at the stake. Their strength and determination frightened the Catholic hierarchy and constrained the authorities to seek a solution.[35] The growth of this new faith raised fears and concerns that needed to be addressed by the royal family since the converts to Protestantism "were simply too numerous to suppress."[36]

Wars of Religion

The concept of the inseparability of King and Church would initially lead to compromises under Catherine de Medici (1519–1589). The Edict of January accorded the Huguenots partial rights to privately practice their religion in government approved places in January 1562. Religious gatherings were forbidden in population centers where the Huguenots were concentrated. According to Lindberg, "Huguenot public worship was allowed in private homes in towns and outside the towns' walls. This was the watershed for French Protestantism."[37] The edict was rejected by most French Catholics who raised the question, "How could the regent, wife, and mother of a king of France advocate the Huguenots' legal right to exist within the kingdom, when the king's own coronation required their suppression?"[38] It was a fundamental principle that the "coronation oath required him to protect and defend his realm and his subjects from heresy" and that "much of the symbolism and ritual of the coronation itself served to imbricate the monarchy and the Catholic Church together, making Protestantism or any other form of heresy a threat to royal authority."[39] The authorities of the Church considered Catherine's edict in contradiction with the Council of Trent (1545–1563) which had anathematized the heresy of Luther and Calvin. She soon became aware of the dangerous situation in which the edict placed her and sought to side with and placate the Catholic faction. War seemed

33. Montclos, *Histoire religieuse*, 60.
34. Holt, "Kingdom of France," 23.
35. Montclos, *Histoire religieuse*, 60.
36. Holt, "Kingdom of France," 25.
37. Lindberg, *European Reformation*, 289.
38. Holt, "Kingdom of France," 25.
39. Holt, "Kingdom of France," 23–24.

inevitable. "The Huguenot political and military resources were not sufficient to bring France into Protestantism, but they were strong enough to
ensure their existence as a rebellious minority."[40]

The massacre of Protestants in Vassy in March 1562 by the Duke of
Guise foreshadowed the bloodshed which would follow in the Wars of
Religion for almost forty years. At stake was the status of the Reformed
religion in the kingdom.[41] At Vassy, the Duke, with 200 armed men, came
across a large congregation of Huguenots gathered in a barn for worship and set upon them. Some 70 Huguenots were killed and many more
wounded. The incident sparked more massacres, and the religious wars
were on.[42] The result was tragic and "only after four decades of civil war
would the nation re-emerge with any semblance of community, imagined
or otherwise."[43] Around this time, Sébastian Castellion (1515–1564), who
ministered alongside Calvin for a time in Geneva, wrote in the preface of
his *Traité des hérétiques* (1554), "Who would want to become a Christian
when they see that those who confess the name of Christ are bruised at the
hands of Christians, by fire, by water, by sword, and treated more cruelly
than robbers and murderers?"[44]

The landscape of post-Reformation France was permanently altered.
There would follow in the next centuries an innumerable succession of
contestations, religious suppression, upheavals, bloodshed, governmental
turbulence, and riots in the streets. It seemed that under then-present
structures of government there could be no peaceful coexistence between
two competing religions especially now that "when the Huguenots took
up arms they lost the image of a persecuted church. And when in 1562
they looked to English Protestants for assistance . . . they lost their patriotic credibility."[45] However, Catherine de Medici's Edict of January 1562
had broken with the past and "made France the first Western European
kingdom to grant legal recognition to two forms of Christianity at once."[46]
According to historian Philip Benedict,

> Within three months, violent Catholic rejection of the legitimacy
> of toleration combined with Protestant hopes for the imminent
> triumph of their faith to plunge the country into the first of a

40. Lindberg, *European Reformation*, 290.
41. Carbonnier-Burkard, *La révolte des Camisards*, 14–15.
42. Carbonnier-Burkard, *La révolte des Camisards*, 15.
43. Holt, "Kingdom of France," 25.
44. Delumeau, *Le christianisme*, 81.
45. Lindberg, *European Reformation*, 290.
46. Benedict, "Wars of Religion," 147.

deadly cycle of wars that would recur eight times over the next three decades. So frequent and gruesome were the massacres accompanying these conflicts, so searing the sieges, and so numerous the assassinations of leading political actors, that the events of the "time of religious troubles" burned themselves into French and European historical memory for centuries to come.[47]

In short order, the inability for two incompatible faiths to live peacefully side-by-side led to the massacre on St. Bartholomew's Day on August 24, 1572, which then spread from Paris to other cities.[48] What began as a "controlled operation against the leading Protestant noblemen grew into a vast bloodletting by ardently anti-Protestant members of the civic militia, who had allowed themselves to believe that the king had finally sanctioned the long-hoped-for eradication of all Huguenots."[49] Benedict claims that "if the exact division of responsibility for the massacre may never be apportioned with certainty, its broader ramifications are clear."[50] The massacre "precipitated a massive wave of defections from the Protestant cause. In the wake of the killing, Charles IX forbade the Reformed believers from gathering for worship—to protect them against violence, his edict proclaimed, but also because he undoubtedly realized that the massacre might end the Protestant problem once and for all."[51]

As the massacres continued in the provinces for several months, fearful Protestants defected and reembraced the Catholic religion. Others fled to find refuge abroad or in Protestant-controlled regions in France. It has been estimated that "Kingdom-wide, for every person killed in the St. Bartholomew's massacres, dozens returned to the Catholic fold or fled abroad."[52] One Catholic historian reports that Pope Gregory XIII (1502–1585), upon receiving the news of the massacre, decreed a jubilee of thanksgiving, struck a commemorative medal, and commissioned Italian artist Vasari to immortalize the event by a fresco on the walls in the Vatican *Sala Regia*.[53] Protestants and Catholics were both prisoners of a system of thought that considered heresy the greatest enemy and mutual extermination an act of justice in the name of God.[54] One major consequence of the massacre was

47. Benedict, "Wars of Religion," 147.
48. Benedict, "Wars of Religion," 155.
49. Benedict, "Wars of Religion," 156.
50. Benedict, "Wars of Religion," 157.
51. Benedict, "Wars of Religion," 157.
52. Benedict, "Wars of Religion," 158.
53. Delumeau, *Le christianisme*, 32.
54. Delumeau, *Le christianisme*, 35.

"a flurry of publications about the limits of obedience to royal authority that made the years after 1572 one of the most fertile periods of political reflection in all of French history."[55] Another consequence was the change in relations between Catholics and Protestants shocked by the brutality of the massacre on a previously unknown scale:

> Episodes that had become common during the previous twelve years—Protestant attacks on holy images or religious processions; Catholic attacks on Protestants returning from worship or seeking to bury their dead; the cold-blooded slaughter of neighbours of the opposite faith—all but disappeared from most corners of the kingdom after 1572, in part in revulsion from the sheer scale and horror of the events of that year.[56]

According to G. R. Evans, "The massacre had its effect, because it removed many of the leading figures of the Protestant movement and sent many Huguenots into exile in more sympathetic lands, and it may have contributed in that way to the eventual triumph of Roman Catholic dominance in France."[57] The following years cycled through brokered peace and revocations, times of limited freedom of worship for Protestants, and times of outcry and Catholic outrage whose "manifestos spoke of a 'holy and Christian union' to defend the Roman Church against 'Satan's ministers' and of restoring provincial liberties 'as they were in the time of king Clovis.'"[58] The 1572 Saint Bartholomew's massacre had not produced its desired effect to rid the kingdom of schismatic Protestants and in the course of time led to "a growing, if still begrudging, acceptance of the argument that religious toleration was less an evil than endless warfare."[59] As a result,

> Many of both faiths [Catholics and Protestants] drew the lesson that where two religions were so deeply rooted in a single country that even violence could not exterminate them, a measure of toleration was preferable to the costs entailed in trying to restore religious uniformity, although no French author was as yet willing to defend freedom of worship as a positive good under all circumstances.[60]

---

55. Benedict, "Wars of Religion," 159.
56. Benedict, "Wars of Religion," 161.
57. Evans, *Roots of the Reformation*, 352.
58. Benedict, "Wars of Religion," 162.
59. Benedict, "Wars of Religion," 163.
60. Benedict, "Wars of Religion," 174.

In light of these events, Gaillard dates the concept of laïcité in France to the Edict of Nantes in 1598 conceived by Henry IV to end the civil and religious torment which plunged France into chaos. He calls it "embryonic laïcité."[61] The State became the guarantor of civil peace and liberty of conscience for the two religions. The edict's import lay in considering individuals in two ways. First, as political subject, the individual was expected to obey the king, regardless of confession. Second, as a believer, the subject was free to choose his religion which was now considered a private matter. It is said that in the life of Henry IV, also known as Henry of Navarre, former Protestant and Huguenot leader, there "had never been a consistent practice of Huguenot morality."[62] However, his conversion to Catholicism and the Edict of Nantes brought the Wars of Religion to an end. His edict opened access for Protestants to universities and public offices. Protestants were allowed garrisons in several towns, most notably the port city of La Rochelle. Many in the Catholic Church disapproved, "railed violently against it, and cast innuendoes at the sincerity of the 'conversion' of the King, but Henry forced its general acceptance as a part of the law of the land."[63]

It is noteworthy that in seventeenth- and eighteenth-century France four cardinals (Richelieu, Mazarin, Dubois, and Fleury) and one archbishop (Loménie de Brienne) held the position of prime minister.[64] Of these perhaps Richelieu (1585–1642), who served during the reign of Louis XIII (1601–1643), was the most able and has become the best known. It was said that "Louis XIII reigned, but that Richelieu governed."[65] Richelieu battled the Huguenots more out of political than religious motives. He was responsible for the siege and the fall of the Huguenot stronghold, La Rochelle. With the surrender of La Rochelle, the Huguenots lost political influence but retained their religious rights for another fifty years. This was one period of French history when "French Protestant lived with Catholic in a peace and harmony seldom seen elsewhere in any part of Europe save in Holland."[66]

The Edict of Nantes of 1598 survived almost a century before its revocation, during which time French Catholics and Protestants cohabitated in relative calm (1598–1685).[67] However, as early as 1629 with the Edict of Nîmes under Louis XIII, the Huguenots experienced the loss of some

61. Gaillard, "L'invention de la laïcité," 20–21.

62. Davis, *History of France*, 125.

63. Davis, *History of France*, 127.

64. Delumeau, *Le christianisme*, 97.

65. Davis, *History of France*, 134.

66. Davis, *History of France*, 135.

67. Dusseau, "L'histoire de la Séparation," 13.

gains and their pastors had the right to preach, celebrate the Lord's Supper, baptize, and officiate at marriages only in villages and cities authorized by the Edict of Nantes.[68] His successor, Louis XIV, grandson of Henry IV, governed as an absolute monarch and claimed the divine right as God's representative on earth. The French clergy pressured the king and obtained the Revocation of the Edict of Nantes on October 17, 1685, also known as the Edict of Fontainebleau. The king's subjects were compelled to adopt the religion of the one who ruled by divine right. Protestant worship was forbidden in France and the edict led once again to the departure of thousands of French Protestants.[69] Protestants lost the right to have separate cemeteries and were compelled to receive the sacraments of the Church. Many Protestants buried their dead in their cellars or gardens. To this day in the Cévennes, private cemeteries are common and allowed by exemption.[70] The banned religion became officially designated RPR, *religion prétendue réformée* (so-called reformed religion).[71]

A cursory look at the articles of the Edict of Revocation reveals the drastic measures undertaken to extirpate the Protestant religion in France. Article one ordered the demolition of Protestant temples. Articles two and three forbade all religious assemblies with the threat of prison. Articles four, five, and six ordered the expulsion within fifteen days of all Protestant pastors who refused to convert to Catholicism. Article seven outlawed Protestant schools. Article eight obliged all infants to be baptized into the Catholic Church and receive religious instruction from village priests. Articles nine and ten forbade Protestant emigration under the threat of galleys for the men and imprisonment for the women. Article eleven stipulated punishment for those who relapsed into heresy in refusing the sacraments of the Church. Article twelve granted the right to remain in the kingdom to the not-yet-enlightened RPR conditioned by the interdiction of assemblies for worship or prayer. Many methods were utilized to pressure Protestants to convert. The Church opened centers of conversion (*maisons de conversion*) and placed mounted troops (*dragons*) in Huguenot homes (*dragonnades*) to ensure their attendance at mass. In effect, the Edict of Revocation forced hundreds of thousands of dissidents to convert to the prince's religion without allowing them liberty to leave the territory.[72] The fear of the *dragons* led to waves of conversions among entire villages and accelerated the

68. Montclos, *Histoire religieuse*, 67.

69. Montclos, *Histoire religieuse*, 69.

70. Cabanel, *Les mots de la laïcité*, 16.

71. Carbonnier-Burkard, *La révolte des Camisards*, 9.

72. Carbonnier-Burkard, *La révolte des Camisards*, 17–19.

disappearance of the RPR. In only a few months hundreds of thousands of Protestants converted to Catholicism. Those who converted were called NC (*nouveaux convertis or nouveaux catholiques*) and placed under strict surveillance. In their deaths the refusal of extreme unction could lead to their bodies being dragged in the streets and the confiscation of all their possessions which could not be passed on as inheritance. Those captured while seeking to flee the kingdom were sentenced to life on the king's galleys or imprisoned for life. It has been estimated that from 1685 to 1715 over 200,000 Protestants escaped and emigrated to places of refuge including Geneva, England, Germany, and Holland.[73]

In Gaillard's opinion the specificity of French laïcité cannot be understood apart from the memory of the Edict of Nantes and its later Revocation. The Catholic Church welcomed the Revocation, aligned itself with the Royal State, and instituted the Counter-Reformation with the rejection of religious liberty and freedom of thought.[74] Religious unity was reestablished, and the Revocation engendered a return to oppression. André Chamson's *Suite Camisarde* presents the Revocation as a foundational event which sheds light on the religious, regional, and historic collective memory of the Cévenol region of France and the war of the Camisards. The Camisards were Calvinist Cévenol insurgents during the persecutions which followed the Revocation of the Edict of Nantes. They owe their name to the white shirt they wore over their clothing in order to be recognized among themselves.[75] The Camisards fought to defend and to reclaim their religious rights obtained under the Edict of Nantes in 1598. They fought above all for the liberty of conscience to freely worship the God of their religion. The war was triggered by the desire of Louis XIV to impose one law and one faith which tore apart the Cévennes from 1702 to 1705. Thousands of men were imprisoned, deported, sent to the galleys, tortured, and more than five hundred villages suffered the great burning [*le grand brûlement*].[76] The power of the Church and the exclusion and exile of hundreds of thousands of Protestants would harden antagonisms for the next century. Yet, according to Montclos, the idea of tolerance was born.[77]

One of the ironies of the Revocation of the Edict of Nantes by Louis XIV is found in the defeat of the French almost two centuries later in the Franco-Prussian War in 1870 which will be discussed later. Thousands of Protestant

73. Carbonnier-Burkard, *La révolte des Camisards,* 21–23.

74. Gaillard, "L'invention de la laïcité," 21–22.

75. Robert et al., *Nouveau Petit Robert,* 335.

76. Chamson, *Suite Camisarde,* iii.

77. Montclos, *Histoire religieuse,* 69.

Huguenots, who refused to convert to the king's religion, fled the waves of persecution for places where they could practice their religion unmolested. In 1870, the descendants of persecuted Huguenots from the previous century were counted among Prussia's military forces. France was soundly defeated at one of the most devastating battles in French military history at Sedan, a center of French Protestantism until the persecution following the Revocation. The humiliating defeat resulted in the capture of Emperor Napoleon III and his army and ended the Second Empire.[78]

War of Ideas

Changes in the world of ideas preceded radical change in Europe. According to Fix, "Few transformations of worldview have been as decisive and influential as that which changed the religious worldview of traditional Europe into the rational and secular worldview of modern Europe."[79] The sixteenth century experienced what Jean-Michel Ducomte calls a *"laïcisation de la pensée"* with the influences of diverse Renaissance thinkers like Erasmus (1466–1536), Francois Rabelais, and Giovanni Pico della Mirandola.[80] Erasmus and Luther were contemporaries with some shared criticism of the Church and criticisms of each other. As Stumpf explains it,

> Erasmus criticized scholastic jargon not only because of its lack of elegance but even more because it obscured the true teachings of the Gospels. . . . He sensed a deep incongruity between the simple teachings of Christ and the opulence and arrogance of the Papal Court. . . . But he was neither a religious skeptic nor did he become a Lutheran. His was a lover's quarrel with the church. He wished to harmonize the church's teaching with the new humanistic learning.[81]

Erasmus and Luther have been compared in this way: "If Erasmus looked back to antiquity for the treasure of the classics, the Reformers, particularly Luther, looked back to the primitive community of Christians for the original spirit of Christianity. In this way the Renaissance and the Reformation both epitomized a revival of the past."[82] Walker asserts, "The Renaissance was far from being a revival of paganism" and the humanists

---

78. Smiles, *Huguenots in France*, v–vi.

79. Fix, *Prophecy and Reason*, 5.

80. Ducomte, *La Laïcité*, 5.

81. Stumpf, *Socrates to Sartre*, 208.

82. Stumpf, *Socrates to Sartre*, 209.

"perceived no fundamental contradiction between classical and Christian ethics. . . . Renaissance culture, in short, though primarily 'secular' and 'laic,' was not intrinsically 'irreligious' or 'anticlerical.'"[83] However, faith and reason became recognized as two distinct modes of knowledge. Free will won the day against blind religious devotion and the political arena ceased to be considered as the fulfillment of a divine project. Scientific and technical progress in both the fifteenth and sixteenth centuries associated with Ambroise Paré, Copernicus, Kepler or Galileo, contributed to demonstrate that human reason was equipped with the capacity of investigation. There were no longer absolute truths. There were only convictions or hypotheses, all necessarily relative. With Descartes (1596–1650) arrived methodological doubt leading to a new orientation with man thrown into history and seeking to change its course.[84]

The seventeenth century likewise left its mark on the world of ideas. Fix writes,

> It has long been accepted that the great discoveries of the Scientific Revolution of the seventeenth century played a major role in the gradual displacement of the traditional European religious worldview by an outlook based on reason and secularism. . . . The demonstrated power of human reason to discover the fundamental natural laws governing the operation of the physical universe awakened in people a great confidence in the ability of reason to provide humankind with knowledge of other vital aspects of human experience as well.[85]

The eighteenth century was marked by the Enlightenment (*le siècle des Lumières*), known also as the Age of Reason. This period extends from the death of Louis XIV in 1714 to the French Revolution in 1789. The laicization of the State in France finds its origins in the philosophy of Enlightenment thinkers in opposition to religion and the power of the Catholic Church.[86] Enlightenment philosophy created the conditions for the recognition of laïcité as a principle of a society open to freedoms and philosophical thinking, some agnostic, some atheistic, yet detached from religion.[87] Many of these great thinkers were deists and not opposed to religion as such. They were

83. Walker et al., *History of the Christian Church*, 394.

84. Ducomte, *La Laïcité*, 4–5.

85. Fix, *Prophecy and Reason*, 7.

86. Jeantet, "L'école et la laïcité," 29.

87. Coq, *Laïcité et République*, 36–37.

hostile toward an intolerant religion which became humanly and politically unacceptable.[88] Kärkkäinen provides the following caution:

> With regard to a more tolerant attitude toward other religions, we should not ignore the radical transformation of intellectual climate brought about by the Enlightenment. Before the Enlightenment and the rise of classical liberalism that followed, most people took it for granted that an exclusive claim to the superiority of Christianity needed no extensive justification. The Enlightenment eradicated major pillars of orthodoxy, however, and left theology and the church to rethink major doctrines and convictions.[89]

In Davis's view, "The spirit of the age may be summed up in four words—Montesquieu, Voltaire, Rousseau, and Encylclopædists. In them, were to lie almost all the Revolutionary law and the prophets."[90] Whether theists like Voltaire or Rousseau, or atheists like Diderot, the philosophers shared the idea of the necessity of separation between the Church and State. Montesquieu advanced a theory on the separation of powers; Voltaire advocated for an enlightened monarchy; Rousseau chose the Republic, but they all condemned the obscurantism of the Church, symbolized by the affairs of Calas, Sirven, and Chevalier de la Barre.[91]

The Enlightenment cried out for the autonomy of the individual, equality, and tolerance. Luc Ferry remarks concerning the Enlightenment thinkers, that with their critique of superstition, many have considered the birth of a democratic universe as the effect of a rupture with religion.[92] The publication of l'Encyclopédie (1751–1780) with 150 scholars, philosophers and specialists from a multitude of disciplines pushed the quest for knowledge and was condemned by the Church. Gaillard describes the times as a "blast of knowledge in constant movement shaking things up, like a steady tide against the cliffs of dogma. And when the insatiable thirst of change met the aspirations of the enlightened nobility, of the dynamic bourgeoisie, and of the miserable commoners, the result was the Revolution."[93]

Each of the above-mentioned philosophers and others merit more attention than can be given here. Stumpf sees them as "dissident voices who challenged the traditional modes of thought concerning religion,

88. Mamet-Soppelsa, "Les femmes et la laïcité," 40.

89. Kärkkäinen, Theology of Religions, 19.

90. Davis, History of France, 223.

91. Dusseau, "L'histoire de la Séparation," 13.

92. Ferry, L'homme-Dieu, 37.

93. Gaillard, "L'invention de la laïcité," 22.

government, and morality. Believing that human reason provides the most reliable guide to man's destiny, they held that 'Reason is to the *philosophe* what grace is to the Christian.'"[94] Among these men, Barzun considers Voltaire "the Enlightenment personified and the supreme master in all genres."[95] Voltaire, born François-Marie Arouet (1694–1778), did not live to see the French Revolution. Yet he is representative of Enlightenment personages who were influential in their advocacy of freedom of and freedom from religion. French was considered the diplomatic language of the eighteenth century and Voltaire's writings were read throughout Europe. He was no friend to religion, at least as he knew it in France. As a Deist, he mercilessly attacked the established Church in France. For him the Church represented "all the traditionalism, mediævalism, intolerance, and political absolutism as it then existed in France."[96] He became the idol of free thinkers and the reference for an enlightened bourgeoisie. He considered Catholicism harmful to the nations and Christianity as the principal cause of injustice in the world.[97] History records the example of Voltaire's defense of the chevalier, Jean-François de la Barre, who was condemned to death in 1766 for refusing to remove his hat at the passing of a religious procession. The defense was in vain and the nineteen-year-old chevalier was executed, decapitated, his body burned, and for good measure a banned copy of Voltaire's *Philosophical Dictionary* was added to the flames.[98]

Walker captures well Voltaire and his genius, a man who has achieved almost mythic status:

> In Voltaire, eighteenth-century France had its keenest wit. No philosopher, vain, self-seeking, but with genuine hatred of tyranny, especially of religious persecution, no one ever attacked organized religion with a more unsparing ridicule. . . . Voltaire was a true Deist in his belief in the existence of God and of a primitive natural religion consisting of a simple morality and in his rejection of all that rested on the authority of the Bible or church.[99]

In his *Philosophical Letters* Voltaire contrasts religion in France with the religious tolerance he found in England during a period of exile there. He states, "If one religion only were allowed in England, the government

94. Stumpf, *Socrates to Sartre*, 290.
95. Barzun, *Dawn to Decadence*, 378.
96. Davis, *History of France*, 226.
97. Montclos, *Histoire religieuse*, 81.
98. Monod, *Sécularisation et laïcité*, 52.
99. Walker et al., *History of the Christian Church*, 584.

would very possibly become arbitrary; if there were but two, the people
would cut one another's throats; but, as there is such a multitude, they all
live happy, and in peace."[100] What Voltaire described in England, at least in
the first two statements, somewhat accurately depicts the history of religion
in France as he had known it. The multitude of religions and any ensuing
peace and happiness were a long way off in France. The relation of Voltaire
to laïcité is debated and the term did not yet exist at the time he wrote.
We have seen, however, that Gaillard speaks of embryonic laïcité originating in the sixteenth century.[101] André Magnan, professor emeritus at the
University of Paris and president of honor of the Société Voltaire, considers Voltaire the precursor of notions of laïcité in his thought and writings
in opposition to religious fanaticism.[102] Philosophy professor Christophe
Paillard disagrees with the claim that Voltaire represents a step which led
to the elaboration of the concept of laïcité. He argues that Voltaire never affirmed the necessity of the religious neutrality of the State. To the contrary,
he affirms that Voltaire believed the State needed to exercise control over
religions to prevent them from imposing themselves on peoples' consciences.[103] In any case, Paillard admits that Voltaire is situated between tolerance
and laïcité, the latter word invented one hundred twenty-five years after his
death.[104] He concedes that Voltaire created the intellectual climate of that
which Jean Baubérot conceptualizes as the "first threshold of laicization,"
which one might interpret as interconfessional tolerance.[105]

Tolerance and incipient laïcité are related ideas in Voltaire's search
for freedom from religion. It is important, however, to understand the
origin and nuances of the French word *tolérance*. The word comes from
the Latin *tolerare* which initially had the sense "to bear," "to endure," or "to
put up with" in a pejorative sense that which one could not prevent. The
edicts of tolerance in the sixteenth and seventeenth centuries, sometimes
called edicts of pacification, were concessions to which the monarchy
resigned itself in order to stop the bloodshed. It was not until the time
of Voltaire that tolerance became a virtue, not simply resignation. Paillard develops the Voltairean concept of tolerance as a principle of media-
tion between the ancient notion of State religion, *Cujus regio, ejus religio*
[whose realm, whose religion], and the present conception of the laïque

100. Voltaire, "Presbyterians," 219.
101. Gaillard, "L'invention de la laïcité," 20–21.
102. Magnan, "Lire Voltaire pour être libre."
103. Paillard, "Voltaire," 35.
104. Paillard, "Voltaire," 44.
105. Paillard, "Voltaire," 50.

State. He contends that Voltaire, more than anyone else, made tolerance a positive and universal value to the point of imposing it on public opinion as the cardinal virtue of an enlightened spirit.[106] Denis Lacorne describes the tolerance advanced by Voltaire and others in the context of terrorist attacks which have afflicted Europe for several years:

> The great emancipating project for the freedom of conscience and the freedom of expression, inaugurated in the sixteenth century and generalized in the century of the Enlightenment, continues to be fought throughout the world. . . . The very conceptions of tolerance have evolved from one century to another up until now, but their final object remains the same: tolerance is that which leads to religious pluralism, whatever may be the nature of relations between Churches and the State.[107]

The tolerance found in the edicts of tolerance of the sixteenth and seventeenth centuries, however, was viewed negatively by "princes and peoples who were unable to conceptualize tolerance as an 'amicable coexistence' of religious communities separated by strong doctrinal differences."[108] Lacorne explains how tolerance in a pejorative sense was transformed from a pragmatic inconvenience to what he calls the *tolérance de Modernes*. This modern tolerance produced rights and new freedoms—freedom of conscience, the free exercise of religion, the freedom of expression and by extension the freedom to blaspheme.[109] The struggle for these freedoms would eventually lead to the Law of Separation in 1905. Today, in the context of religion, and particularly in the context of radical Islam, "this tolerance has its limits and the ultimate limit is fanaticism."[110]

The influence of Enlightenment thinking contributed at least indirectly to the development of laïcité and the eventual separation of Church and State. Dusseau argues that its firstfruits are found in philosophers' ideas as well as in political practices of the French monarchy.[111] When Enlightenment philosophy imprinted its mark on the movement of ideas, there was an intense clash with the all-powerful Church in its total alliance with the absolute monarchy.[112] The ideals of tolerance, equality, and autonomy could not exist alongside religious constraints imposed by a State

106. Paillard, "Voltaire," 36–37.

107. Lacorne, *Les frontières*, 9.

108. Lacorne, *Les frontières*, 11.

109. Lacorne, *Les frontières*, 11–12.

110. Lacorne, *Les frontières*, 13.

111. Dusseau, "L'histoire de la Séparation," 13.

112. Gaillard, "L'invention de la laïcité," 22.

Church. These ideals would ferment and lead to the French Revolution at the end of the eighteenth century.

Revolution

Ducomte considers that the French Revolution marks the starting point of the laicization of French society and her institutions. The term laïcité was not yet in use at the time. Its substantive form appeared as a neologism in the nineteenth century in the context and struggle of removing the Church's influence over public education. Laïcité however gave a name to a reality which already long existed beginning with the French Revolution and the attempts to free the State from all confessional control.[113]

The French Revolution has been described as "the most far-reaching political and social explosion in all European history."[114] It was more than an event. It was a series of events which played out for a tumultuous decade. The period extends from 1789 to 1799 with the introduction of a constitutional monarchy and the inception of the disestablishment of the official and dominant Church. "The Revolution, for those who made it, was the construction of a new political order symbolised by the terms liberty, equality, and (later) fraternity."[115] The arrival of the Revolution must be viewed as a break with the past model of governance (*Ancien Régime*) with its societal divisions and the mingling of Church and State in the affairs of the citizenry. Michel Vovelle has characterized the Ancien Régime by three interlocking themes. Economically, in its mode of production, the nation was dominated by the feudal system; its class structure revolved around a three-tiered hierarchy; its political system was one of absolutism, the divine right of kings consecrated by the Church.[116] "Absolute monarchy legitimated by divine right was replaced by the sovereignty of the people with power vested in their elected representatives."[117]

The Revolution would be interrupted with the coup d'état and rise to power of Napoleon Bonaparte in 1799 followed by his ascension as hereditary emperor in 1804. He became the founder of the First Empire which lasted until his defeat at the Battle of Waterloo in 1815, then exiled on the island of Saint Helena until his death in 1821. However, the ideals of the Revolution would return in force and compete with counter-revolutionary

---

113. Ducomte, *La Laïcité*, 3.

114. Davis, *History of France*, 244.

115. Gildea, *French History*, 20.

116. Vovelle, *Révolution française*, 6.

117. Gildea, *French History*, 20.

forces for the next century. Davis quotes approvingly French historian Ernest Lavisse to describe this period:

> No country has ever influenced Europe as France did between 1789 and 1815. Impelled by two dreams—the dream of a war against kings on behalf of the people, and the dream of the foundation of an empire of the Cæsarian or Carolingian type—the French armies overran the continent, and trampled underfoot as they went, much rank vegetation which has never arisen again.[118]

He further states, "There is not a single civilized man on the earth today whose life, thought, and destinies have not been profoundly influenced by what happened in or near France during those five and twenty years of action, wrath, and fire."[119] Davis's remarks may sound like hyperbole to those in the twenty-first century as he writes from his early twentieth-century perspective. However, the influence of the French Revolution on future generations cannot be denied. The Revolution's significance undoubtedly goes far beyond the nation of France and has been studied and considered an essential foundational moment, not only for French national history, but in the history of humanity.[120]

There is some debate as to whether France was more miserable than other European nations at the time of the Revolution. In Davis's opinion "the French were probably, all things considered, the most progressive, enlightened, and in general fortunate people of continental Europe."[121] While that may be true in relative terms, we may question whether this description applied to the common people. The pre-revolutionary feudal system functioned in a world dominated by a rural economy. The majority of the French population, estimated at 85 percent, was concentrated in rural areas. The French peasantry lived under the seigneurial system where the seigneur levied heavy taxes and meted out justice. Roger Magraw discusses the social-political consequences of the Revolution and the mobilization of the peasantry. In his opinion, "it was the anti-seigneurial peasant revolution of 1789–1793 which swept away the ancien régime."[122]

It should then come as no surprise that the populace in principle welcomed the French Revolution. The atrocities of the Revolution and the Reign of Terror which followed are well known and in hindsight rightly

118. Davis, *History of France*, 268.
119. Davis, *History of France*, 268.
120. Vovelle, *Révolution française*, 4.
121. Davis, *History of France*, 243.
122. Magraw, *France 1800–1914*, 3.

criticized. Less well known is the oppression endured by the people under
the nobility and the clergy which wielded secular power. An assessment of
life in France at the time of the Revolution provides a sobering picture of
the wealth of the Church and its princes. In 1789, France had a population
of 26 million and 130,000 clergy. The clergy, representing a tiny fraction of
the population, possessed large swaths of territory in the kingdom.[123] The
pre-revolutionary social hierarchy in France was composed of three orders
or estates (*les trois états*): clergy, nobility, and peasantry (*le tiers-état*). The
first two groups were largely exonerated from the crushing taxes imposed
on the peasantry. Added to the contempt felt by the peasants was their exclusion from the ranks of military officers. Magraw states, "Until 1789, the
'Second Estate,' some 1 percent of the population, owned 25 percent of the
land and monopolised posts in Army, Administration, and Church, giving aristocratic bishops and monastic heads access to income from church
lands and tithes."[124] The monarchy was the third rail in the structure of
the Ancien Régime, having reached its zenith under Louis XIV and then
greatly weakened under the mediocre Louis XVI (1754–1793) beginning
in 1774. The king remained the living symbol of a system in which the
Church was the state religion and which hardly flinched during the last
years of the Ancien Régime by the promulgation of the Edict of Tolerance
in 1787 for the benefit of Protestants.[125]

    Montclos sketches three grand moments which constitute the revolu-
tionary process regarding religion. These are the Civil Constitution of the
Clergy in 1790, the antireligious terror from October 1793 to April 1794,
and the separation of the Church from the State in the 1795 Constitution.
He remarks that during the Terror there was a brutal fight against persons
and possessions led by proconsuls who not only preyed on Catholicism
but also on Protestantism and Judaism.[126] These moments coincided with
the foundational texts of the Revolution—the Declaration of the Rights of
Man and the Citizen in 1789, the Civil Constitution of the Clergy in 1790,
and the Constitutions of 1791 and 1795. The Declaration was adopted on
August 26, 1789, and would soon be considered foundational for modern
politics in France. These revolutionary actions ended the Concordat of
Bologna from 1516 between King Francis I (1494–1547) and Pope Leo
X (1475–1521), known especially for the sale of indulgences to embellish
Saint Peter's Basilica in Rome. The adoption of this early Concordat had

123. Delumeau, *Le christianisme*, 46–47.
124. Magraw, *France 1800–1914*, 15.
125. Vovelle, Révolution française, 9.
126. Montclos, *Histoire religieuse*, 87.

introduced a division between high clergy composed of courtesans and a lower clergy which was often poor and lacking in both status and possessions. This Concordat had recognized papal power over national councils where the king was accorded authority to name those to ecclesiastical positions—abbots, bishops, and archbishops.[127]

The Revolution introduced sweeping changes in France. Religious liberty was proclaimed and activities transferred from the Church to the State (i.e., civil status, marriage). The State introduced legal divorce, abolished religious crimes of blasphemy, heresy, and sorcery, and adopted a revolutionary calendar.[128] Despite open revolt against the Church, the French people were not yet ready to exclude God from the life of the nation. Religious references remained in French official documents until the 1946 Constitution of the Fourth Republic (*des droits inaliénables et sacrés*) and were later excluded from the 1958 Constitution of the Fifth Republic still in effect to our day. Article 10, one of the most oft-cited statements of the 1789 Declaration, recognized the liberty of opinion and declared that no one should be disturbed for their opinions, not even religious ones, as long as their expression did not trouble the public order (*Nul ne doit être inquiété pour ses opinions, même religieuses, pourvu que leur manifestation ne trouble pas l'ordre public établi par la Loi*).

The Civil Constitution of the Clergy in July 1790 was preceded by other actions against the Church to weaken her position in France. A year earlier, in August 1789, the clergy lost its position as the first of the three orders in France. In November 1789, all the possessions, property, and holdings of the Church became property of the nation. The National Assembly elaborated what would become part of the future Constitution concerning the organization of the Church of France. Priests were required to take an oath of allegiance to the nation, to the king, and to the Constitution. Many clergy refused to obey this law. Their refusal was at the origin of political conflict which led revolutionary France toward a civil war.[129] The Constitution of 1791 was short-lived and would be followed by several others as issues arose and were addressed in 1793, 1795, 1799, 1802, and 1804. The Constitution of 1795 founded the First Republic. The Constitution of 1802 established Napoleon Bonaparte as First Consul for Life (*Premier Consul à vie*). The Constitution of 1804 named Napoleon emperor. That these were tumultuous times is an understatement.

127. Bloch, *Réforme Protestante*, 11.

128. CNEF, *Laïcité française*, 13.

129. Bruley, *La séparation*, 40–41.

Many have tried to capture the essence and the seismic importance of the French Revolution. Evangelical missiologist Paul Hiebert writes,

> The Holy Roman Empire had been in decline since the late Middle Ages, but it was the French Revolution that shattered the sacred foundations of history. The secular state emerged based on rationalism and the will of the citizens. Public life was now the realm of reason alone and had no place for a seemingly unknowable God. Religion was relegated to the private sphere of life and seen as imagination, and God ceased to be relevant to public life. A rigidly materialistic, atheistic philosophy emerged that reduced the spirit to matter and morals to social constructs defined in terms of material progress.[130]

According to Stumpf, "Some saw in the Revolution a contest of power whose effect was to destroy the legitimate power and authority both of the government and of the church, an effect that could only result in the further destruction of the institutions of the family and private property."[131] Former pope Benedict XVI (b. 1927) likewise understands the importance of the French Revolution in the disintegration of the spiritual influences without which Europe would not have come into existence. He asserts that religion became a private matter related to feelings, irrelevant in the public square, and reason became the supreme arbitrator to determine what is best for civil society. The pope argues,

> The sacred foundation for history and for the existence of the State was rejected; history was no longer gauged on the basis of an idea of a preexistent God who shaped it; the State was henceforth considered in purely secular terms, founded on reason and on the will of the citizens. For the very first time in history, a purely secular State arose, which abandoned and set aside the divine guarantee and the divine ordering of the political sector, considering them a mythological world view.[132]

However, the Revolution was well received in many Protestant quarters, at least in its ideals if not in its reality. Protestants welcomed with favor the Revolution which brought about their emancipation from the intolerance and persecution at the hands of the Church.[133] They had received limited civil status rights in 1787. Then in 1789 they were granted equal

---

130. Hiebert, *Transforming Worldviews*, 142.

131. Stumpf, *Socrates to Sartre*, 355.

132. Ratzinger, *Europe Today and Tomorrow*, 20–21.

133. Vovelle, *Révolution française*, 22.

rights and the liberty of worship. The Assembly tacitly authorized them to organize at their discretion, which they did notably in opening places of worship in cities where that had been previously forbidden.[134]

The removal of the Catholic Church from public influence and the overthrow of the monarchy were among the objectives achieved by the Revolution. The tithe, the Church's principal source of revenue, was eliminated in August 1789 in the name of fiscal justice. The Civil Clergy Constitution of 1790, which nationalized French Catholicism, was approved by Louis XVI. Tolerance was granted to non-Catholics and ecclesiastical properties were nationalized. The number of bishops was reduced. Priests and bishops were elected by districts and departments respectively and both became civil servants remunerated by the State. Pope Pius VI (1717–1799) condemned this action and priests were divided between those who swore loyalty to the Republic and those who looked to Rome for guidance. Persecution and division followed.[135] Walker explains,

> When the tremendous storm of the French Revolution broke, it swept away many of the privileges of the church, the nobility, the throne, and kindred ancient institutions. The revolutionary leaders were filled with rationalistic zeal. They viewed the [Catholic] churches as religious clubs. In 1789, church lands were declared national property. . . . The constitution of 1791 pledged religious liberty. Then in 1793 came a royalist and Catholic uprising in the Vendée, and in retaliation the Jacobin leaders sought to wipe out Christianity. Hundreds of ecclesiastics were beheaded.[136]

The Revolution would not remain unopposed by the Catholic Church. The Church had its defenders even if they are not as well remembered by posterity. The Counter-Revolution continued the battle for ideas and divided France into two camps reminiscent of the Wars of Religion. The battles were not only ideological but bloody and divided France into two parts.[137] The counter-revolutionaries, many of whom had lost privileges, whose lands were confiscated and titles revoked, sought the restoration of the monarchy. In Magraw's opinion, "Religion was the most divisive issue in French society. The counter-revolution's fervour stemmed less from loyalty to King or seigneurs than from villagers' determination to defend local religious cultures against a dechristianising Revolution."[138]

134. Montclos, *Histoire religieuse*, 106.

135. Gaillard, "L'invention de la laïcité," 23–24.

136. Walker et al., *History of the Christian Church*, 668.

137. Tulard, "Contre-Révolution," para. 1.

138. Magraw, *France 1800–1914*, 159.

Louis XVI himself was executed after being found guilty of treason by the Convention on January 21, 1793. Two groups, *la Gironde* and *la Montagne*, disputed his fate. The former group, a political entity formed in 1791 by several deputies from the region by the same name, argued for clemency.[139] The latter group, among whom was Robespierre, referred to elevated places at the Convention where the political left sat led by Robespierre and Danton.[140] They demanded the king's death for public salvation and the necessities of the Revolution.[141] According to Robespierre, the Revolution required virtue and terror, "virtue, without which terror is harmful; and terror, without which virtue is powerless. Terror is nothing other than prompt, severe, inflexible justice. It is an emanation of virtue."[142] The death of the king prepared the way for further changes in the Church-State relationship. In 1795, the separation of Church and State was introduced for the first time constitutionally in France in terms close to the future law of 1905. The arrival of Napoleon would throw these separatist initiatives into confusion when he seized the initiative to bring religion into his service. Yet the future would reveal that many people freed from obligatory religious duties and rituals would soon fall away from an organized religion which no longer wielded political power. Over the next one hundred years the work of the Revolution was constantly threatened with the successive rise and fall of republics and empires. The battle for Republican values intensified while the Church fought vigorously to reverse the losses suffered under the Revolution.

Napoleon and Concordat of 1801

A religious crisis occupied France for ten years before Napoleon came to power to reverse many of the gains of the Revolution. By all accounts, Napoleon was a man without strong religious leanings. However, he recognized that the majority of French people were Roman Catholic and sought to bring the Church under his control for political purposes. An alliance with the Church became a political necessity since many French were still attached to the Church. The State needed the Church to assume tasks, such as education, that the State did not wish to administer. Pope Pius VII (1742–1823) was elected in 1800 and desired to restore the unity of the Church in a nation that was the most powerful Catholic nation at the time. As seen earlier, in 1789 the Church had been forced to relinquish its possessions and land holdings and in 1790 the Civil Constitution of the Clergy

---

139. Robert et al., *Nouveau Petit Robert*, 1154.

140. Robert et al., *Nouveau Petit Robert*, 1630.

141. Vovelle, *Révolution française*, 29.

142. Robespierre, *Œuvres*, 357.

had provoked a schism. The Church had been nationalized and its ministers were elected by church members without any consultation with or approval of the Church. In 1794, all exterior manifestations of worship were forbidden and the Church was confined to the private sphere.[143]

The Concordat was signed in 1801 between Napoleon and Pope Pius VII and "was to rule the relations between France and the papacy for more than a century."[144] The Concordat recognized that Catholicism was not the religion of the State but the majority religion of French citizens (*la grande majorité des citoyens français*).[145] Three other confessions—Lutheran, Reformed, and later Jewish—were recognized and also brought into the service of the State.[146] Although the Concordat offered a level of religious pluralism, Napoleon's objective was the control of religion for societal submission. Religions were considered a public service and on equal footing. The head of State appointed bishops while those bishops previously loyal to Rome (*réfractaires*) were forced to resign. The State retained possession of Catholic property seized after the Revolution and assured the upkeep of certain properties. In December 1804, Napoleon Bonaparte was crowned as emperor in Notre-Dame Cathedral in the presence of Pope Pius VII.[147]

After one hundred years of struggle and persecution, it was not surprising that many Protestants welcomed the Concordat imposed by Napoleon. According to French historians, Protestantism had lost half its population and it appeared that its spiritual forces were spent. Believers seemed to have conserved little of the Reformers' teaching and were marked by the rationalism of the eighteenth century. The Concordat gave Protestants access to most public positions. Pastors became paid employees of the State with an oath of loyalty to the State. Churches were reorganized into consistories which called pastors requiring government confirmation.[148]

A revival (*Réveil*), originating in Geneva, took place at the beginning of the nineteenth century with an emphasis on the evangelization of Catholics and in favor of the separation of church and State. Concordataire Protestants were divided in their views of the Concordat with the more conservative leaders coming to believe that it was no longer possible to defend it.[149] There were also efforts to unite the two concordataire Protestant churches, Lutheran and Reformed.[150] The revival was not welcomed by all

143. Gastaldi, "Le Concordat de 1801."

144. Walker et al., *History of the Christian Church*, 669.

145. Cabanel, *Les mots de la laïcité*, 21.

146. Machelon, *La laïcité demain*, 17.

147. McManners, *Church and State*, 4.

148. Baty, "Églises évangéliques," 1–2.

149. Pédérzet, *Cinquante ans*, 140.

150. Pédérzet, *Cinquante ans*, 146–49.

Reformed churches. From 1820 to 1848, independent churches of professing believers were founded and existed alongside Lutheran and Reformed
churches who themselves were divided into orthodox and liberal. The most
contentious issue concerned the necessity of a confession of faith which liberals rejected. The orthodox wanted a confession of faith but did not want to
divide the Reformed church. Several leaders, among them Pastor Fréderic
Monod and Agénor de Gasparin, maintained the necessity of a confession
of faith. After failing in their attempts to persuade others of their conviction,
they resigned from their positions, and called on others to follow them in
organizing an evangelical Reformed church.[151] Few followed Monod and de
Gasparin in their resolve which led to their association with independent
evangelical churches and the founding in 1849 of the Union of Evangelical
Churches of France (l'Union des Églises évangéliques de France) for which a
confession of faith was adopted in 1849. The two articles were clear in their
affirmation that their churches would be composed of members who made
an explicit and personal profession of faith.[152]

Conservative monarchists and Catholics desired that France return
to her status as elder daughter of the Catholic Church. The Republicans
wanted to make France the daughter of the Revolution of 1789. The
resolution to this struggle began in 1879 when Republicans gained a
parliamentary majority and worked to remove the influence of religion
and the Church from the Republic and from public school teaching. The
Republicans abrogated the 1850 Law Falloux which was a major setback
for the Church in its influence on education. This conflict between the two
Frances of the monarchists and Republican anticlericalists would reach its
summit with the arrival to power of Émile Combes in 1902 and continue
until the Law of Separation in December 1905.

Despite these tensions, the Concordat survived for over one hundred
years. "The Church believed in an alliance with the State on principle, and
the anticlerical and many other Frenchmen were glad to see the ecclesiastics
bridled by specific agreements."[153] Owing to historical factors which will be
discussed later, the Concordat survives today in the region of Alsace-Moselle. These departments were annexed by Germany in 1871 after France's
defeat in the Franco-Prussian War and were returned to France following
World War I and Germany's defeat in 1918. A condition of their reintegra-
tion into France was the continuance of the Concordat.[154]

151. Baty, "Églises évangéliques," 53–67; Pédérzet, Cinquante ans, 143.

152. Baty, "Églises évangéliques," 294.

153. McManners, Church and State, 4.

154. CNEF, Laïcité française, 14.

3

Nineteenth-Century Revival of Republicanism

UNDER NAPOLEON BONAPARTE AND the 1801 Concordat, Church and State had once again entered into an alliance. Catholicism was considered the religion of the majority of the French. The restoration of the Bourbon dynasty followed the fall of Napoleon in 1814. It was accompanied by a spirit of religious retaliation and the return of exiled supporters of the monarchy. Louis XVIII (1755–1824) made it known that he did not want to be king of two peoples. The Charter of 1814 reestablished Catholicism as the State religion. The legitimacy of royal power was once again founded on the divine right. The Concordat remained in force, but the throne and altar were once again united.[1] In 1821, bishops of the Catholic Church were given authority in religious education in secondary schools and primary school teachers required a teaching certificate from a bishop.[2] Later, under the reign of Louis-Philippe (1830–1848), the kingdom again experienced counter-revolutionary pressures yet the Church and the diffusion of her truths were seen as useful instruments favoring the docility of the people.[3] Pédérzet considers 1830 the moment of the century when the French had it best, or at least with good reason had seemingly been the happiest time. Thoughts of justice and progress prevailed with dreams of peace. The sovereigns remained, but they inspired neither fear nor ambitions. One would no longer see a Robespierre or a Napoleon.[4] Those days would not last.

A Parisian revolution overthrew the Bourbon monarchy in 1848 which set the stage for the short-lived Second Republic (1848–1851) and the election of its only president, Louis-Napoleon Bonaparte, later known as Emperor Napoleon III. Pédérzet remarked that if the Revolution of 1848

---

1. Ducomte, *La Laïcité*, 12.
2. Rognon and Weber, *La laïcité*, 25.
3. Ducomte, *La Laïcité*, 12.
4. Pédérzet, *Cinquante ans*, 1.

was a surprise for France, it was also a surprise for the churches. From the first days, they experienced great hopes and great fears at the same time.[5] During the Second Empire (1852–1870) under Emperor Napoleon III, relations with the Catholic Church became more cordial with a corresponding loss of religious liberty and repression of non-concordataire churches. As for Louis-Napoleon, "he confirmed himself in the good graces of the Clericals by sending an army to Rome to overthrow the revolutionaries there, and to renew the temporal power of Pope Pius IX."[6] Although he was "capable of anti-clericalism in some regions—his ministers viewed alliance with Catholicism as a strategic necessity."[7]

In 1850, under the Second Republic, the Law Falloux gave the Church influence in primary schools and assured that the Church had control over French youth and official participation in public teaching. In reaction, the Republicans hardened their anticlerical positions.[8] Historians agree that education was the issue which crystalized the combat between the clerical and anticlerical parties in the nineteenth century.[9] The law reversed the monopoly in education accorded to the State established by Napoleon I, granted the Church complete liberty to open religious schools, and submitted public establishments to religious control.[10] However, the law provoked the fury of many and revived anticlericalism and hatred for ecclesiastical institutions. The battle for educational control contributed to a laïque and anticlerical current—in a sense somewhat different than the word laïque previously had in the nineteenth century.[11] The battle would continue until anticlerical educational laws were enacted between 1881 and 1882 under Jules Ferry during the Third Republic. These laws attempted to reverse the gains and resurgence of the Church made earlier in the century. Public education became free, compulsory, and laïque. Religious instruction was eliminated from the curricula. Bowen notes, "From the mid–1880s to the mid–1920s, the Third Republic succeeded, through a series of decrees, laws, and negotiations, in removing the Church from the public schools and depriving the Church of its public status, a dual victory that later was to be summed up with the single word *laïcité*."[12]

5. Pédérzet, *Cinquante ans*, 132.

6. Davis, *History of France*, 463.

7. Magraw, *France 1800–1914*, 163.

8. CNEF, *Laïcité française*, 15.

9. Jeantet, "L'école et la laïcité," 30.

10. Dansette, *Histoire religieuse*, 17.

11. Rognon and Weber, *La laïcité*, 24.

12. Bowen, *Headscarves*, 12.

The year 1870 has been called "a year of decisive and paradoxical events."[13] On July 18, bishops of the Church from around the world gathered at Saint Peter's Basilica in Rome to vote their approval of the dogma of the infallibility of the Pope. Under Napoleon I and the terms of the Concordat, the French Gallican Church had looked to the State to defend her from the Holy See. This wing of the Church had increased in influence. After 1815, with Napoleon no longer in power, Ultramontanism, which looked to the Holy See rather than the State as its authority,[14] began a slow, implacable progression which led to its triumph in the 1870 papal proclamation.[15] In speaking *ex cathedra,* the Pope would be preserved from error in faith and practice. The Church now looked to Rome for her defense. With this proclamation, the Church effectively put an end to papal opposition from the Gallican wing of the Church. The Council also "gave the final authoritative and irrevocable endorsement of the Augustinian axiom by affirming that no one can be saved outside the church."[16]

The Church's support for Emperor Louis-Napoleon was to haunt the Church for years to come. Napoleon III, the nephew of Emperor Napoleon I, elected president of France in 1850, had declared himself emperor in 1852 with the support of both the papacy and the majority of French Catholics. McManners cites Montalembert that the Church operated on this principle: "When I am the weakest I ask you for liberty because it is your principle: when I am the strongest I take it away from you because it is my principle."[17] As emperor, Louis-Napoleon stood against the Prussian war machine which had already decisively defeated the armies of Denmark and Austria in 1864 and 1866 respectively. On July 19, 1870, one day after the papal proclamation of infallibility, France declared war on Prussia and suffered a humiliating defeat in a mere six weeks. Following the resounding rout of the French army at the Battle of Sedan on September 1, 1870, the emperor abdicated his throne after an uprising in Paris which ended the Second Empire. He was made prisoner by the Prussians and released into exile to England where he died in 1873. Thus, in September 1870, the Second Empire under Louis-Napoleon collapsed following two decades of rule. Many historians concur that this war dramatically influenced the course of European history. Gildea claims that "the defeat of 1870 had been catastrophic and it was a long time

13. McManners, *Church and State,* 2.
14. Robert et al., *Nouveau Petit Robert,* 2652.
15. Dansette, *Histoire religieuse,* 15–16.
16. Kärkkäinen, *Theology of Religions,* 71.
17. McManners, *Church and State,* 19.

before the Third Republic was able to register any military successes."[18] The new republic itself was "followed almost immediately by the excesses of the Paris Commune [which was] grist to the mill of critics of the revolution."[19] From a religious viewpoint, according to Dansette, the defeat in 1870 and the constitutional uncertainty provoked by the fall of the Second Empire resulted in a crisis of conscience. Many were nostalgic for the Ancien Régime which was idealized with the image of a legendary Middle Ages. They looked for a form of government more favorable to the Church which gave birth to a spirit of mysticism.[20]

From a philosophical viewpoint, Ernest Renan (1823–1892), following the Austrian defeat at the hands of the Prussian army in 1866 at the Battle of Sadowa, had already pointed to German science as contributing to its military success. Little did he know that what he wrote foreshadowed the defeat of his own nation. In 1868, two years before France's own humiliating defeat he wrote that German science, German virtue, Protestantism, philosophy, Luther, Kant, Fichte, and Hegel conquered at Sadowa.[21] Gildea notes, "The return of the Republic and Revolution in 1870–71 served to stimulate the collective memory of the Vendée. The attack on Church schools by the Third Republic was discredited by parallels drawn with the persecution of the Church and clergy during the Revolution."[22] The upheavals which followed in education, in which the Catholic Church was still involved, and in Church-State relations, would change the course of France and exacerbate the tensions between the clericals and anticlericals.

The Third Republic also witnessed, for the first time in French history, a Protestant influence which had been minimal until this time. In Dansette's view, if Reformed churches had disappeared at the end of the eighteenth century, the great events of the epoch would not have changed their course.[23] As a small minority, Protestants had been excluded from national life. They held grudges against both the Church and the monarchy. They were sometimes persecuted, sometimes tolerated, mostly voiceless until the Revolution which brought Protestantism into the national community. Dansette states that Protestants obtained tolerance at the end of the Ancien Régime, liberty at the beginning of the Revolution, and the same status for the Reformed Church as the Roman Church under the Concordat. But there was never

18. Gildea, *French History*, 101.

19. Gildea, *French History*, 24.

20. Dansette, *Histoire religieuse*, 37.

21. Renan, *Questions contemporaines*, vii.

22. Gildea, *French History*, 28–29.

23. Dansette, *Histoire religieuse*, 51.

genuine equality.[24] Divergences existed among the Protestants themselves. There were those who had fallen into skepticism and unbelief. In 1872, liberal Protestants refused a confession of faith which contained the fundamental doctrine of the deity of Jesus Christ. There were others who retained only dry cultural dogmatism. Yet there were some who experienced true renewal under Wesleyan and Genevan influences. Since religious instruction in the schools was Catholic, Protestants favorably viewed laws of laïcité regarding education. They advocated educational reform, the separation of Church and State, and social action.[25]

The strengthened influence of the Church during the Bourbon Restoration (1814–1830) and the Second Empire (1852–1870), the enactment of laws authorizing Catholic instruction in public schools in 1850 under the Second Republic, the humiliation of the nation at the hands of the Prussians at the end of the Second Empire in 1870, the rise of Ultramontanism strengthened by the claim of papal infallibility in 1870, and the new influence of Protestantism favored the rise of Republicanism and anticlerical forces to which we will now turn. Once firmly in power, the Republicans would seek the laicization of education to finally free the Republic from religious influence. They knew that those who controlled the minds of youth influenced the destiny of the nation.

Struggle for the Republic

Throughout the nineteenth century, a battle waged between anticlericalism, favorable to the ideals of the Revolution, and clericalism which kept alive the dream of a return of the Church in union with the State. Historians speak of two Frances which waged this combat. One France claimed the heritage of the Revolution with an anticlerical spirit in various degrees. "*Le cléricalisme? Voilà l'ennemi!*" was the watchword of combat launched by Léon Gambetta (1838–1882) in 1877 to unite the Left in a government program for four decades. The laïque Republic and the Catholic Church entered into conflict with alternating periods of extreme tension and others of rapprochement.[26] The other France was attached to the Ancien Régime and the marriage of throne and altar. René Rémond describes the anticlericals as so-called free thinkers and rationalists, attached to the independence of civil society, advocates of the separation of Church and State, hostile to the interference of the clergy in private life or

24. Dansette, *Histoire religieuse*, 53.
25. Dansette, *Histoire religieuse*, 56.
26. Grévy, *Le Cléricalisme*, 9.

in community activities, and who would never call themselves anticlerical. Their clerical adversaries considered anticlerical all those who did not
share their beliefs, their conception of relations between the Church and
State, or the relation between religion and common life.[27]

There was a revival of the idea of laïcité in the Third Republic in the
early 1880s, an idea which had been more or less abandoned for almost
a century as other philosophical and political ideas competed. In 1882,
although the word laïcité was not used, a law was adopted to introduce
laïcité into primary education. To assure confessional neutrality in the
elementary schools, the law removed all references to God and inserted
moral and civic instruction separated from religious reference.[28] Dansette
paints a portrait of the Republicans at this time in their opposition to the
Church and religion. He calls them laïque Republicans with two great enemies—the Church and the monarchy. They inherited a consistently irreligious, secular tradition especially during the last ten years of the Second
Empire. They were influenced by the criticism of Kant, by the evolutionary
theories of Spencer and Darwin, and by the positivism of Auguste Comte.
They firmly believed that the Revolution had snatched the French people
from the slavery in which they were held by the priests and had elevated
the people to the dignity of free men and citizens, and that the French were
freed from the shackles of the monarchy and religion, endowed with reason which alone was capable to discover truth. They claimed that Catholicism prevented the faithful from attaining earthly happiness and sincerely
believed that Catholicism was a religion for imbeciles. Dansette adds that
both Republicans and religionists tended to focus on the worst aspects
of their adversaries. Their mutual hatred prevented them from working
together in areas for the common good.[29]

As we have seen, during the Second Empire (1852–1870) under
Louis-Napoleon Bonaparte, the Church held a privileged position which
depended on the goodwill of the man who became emperor following his
coup d'état. The Third Republic followed the collapse of the Second Empire
and the struggle intensified with alternating victories and defeats for all parties. Magraw states,

> After an upsurge of popular anti-clericalism in 1870–71, the
> years of "Moral Order" (1872–77) were dominated by a Catholic
> triumphalism, memories of which fuelled subsequent Republi-
> can anti-clerical mythology. A Royalist-dominated parliament

27. Rémond, L'anticléricalisme, 8.
28. Machelon, La laïcité demain, 17.
29. Dansette, Histoire religieuse, 58–64.

urged prefects to clamp down on anti-clerical municipalities, civil funerals, and lay teachers. Funds were collected to construct the Sacré Coeur, designed to dominate the skyline of the "Paris-Babylon" in expiation of the "sins" of the Commune. Thousands of pilgrims travelled to Marian visitation sites such as Paray-le Monial to demand a Christian monarchy.[30]

Ten years into the Third Republic, the Republicans achieved a majority to undertake their agenda. Elated at their newfound power, the Republicans began to retaliate against the Church. Anticlericalism would link itself with the ideals of the Revolution to revive the struggle against the Church.[31] According to Gildea,

> They had founded a liberal Republic, in which power was concentrated in the hands of the elected representatives of the people. And they had resurrected the counter-revolutionary myth in order to legitimate their monopoly of power. The symbolism of the Revolution was duly annexed to the Republic.[32]

The notion of laïcité was in opposition to clericalism and there was also an important dimension to laïcité in denying the Church political influence.[33] According to secularist Richard Rorty, "Anticlericalism is a political view, not an epistemological or metaphysical one. It is the view that ecclesiastical institutions, despite all the good they do—despite all the comfort they provide to those in need or in despair—are dangerous to the health of democratic societies."[34] Laïcité became essentially a political concept. No religious confession or conception of a way of life was privileged in the eyes of the State. Each person's freedom of expression was guaranteed within certain limits so long as the public order was not disrupted.[35]

Anticlericalism was considered a natural response to the Church's resistance to the idea of a new world order detached from religious certitudes. Under the pontificates of Gregory XVI (1831–1846) and Pius IX (1846–1878), the Church, according to its critics, revealed its incapacity to accept the modern world and the prevailing emphasis on the autonomy of the individual. It must be noted, however, that there were different forms of anticlericalism. Largely promoted by deists and philosophers in the early

---

30. Magraw, *France 1800–1914*, 163.

31. Dansette, *Histoire religieuse*, 49.

32. Gildea, *French History*, 38.

33. Monod, *Sécularisation et laïcité*, 76.

34. Rorty, "Anticlericalism and Atheism," 33.

35. Haarscher, *La laïcité*, 4.

eighteenth century, anticlericals became progressively more radical with clearly atheistic overtones. There were some who were anticonfessional in that they opposed any interference of the Church in matters of State and sought confessional neutrality. There were others who were antireligious and sought complete religious neutrality to exclude any religious influences or even the presence of religious establishments. La Libre-Pensée (FNLP), the first militant, laïque organization was organized toward the middle of the eighteenth century and would construct a radical discourse which grew constantly more rigid.[36] Cabanel remarks that laïcité and anticlericalism are often confused in their common combat. On one hand, he views anti-clericalism as having an agenda to enact laws to separate the Church from the State. This goal was achieved in 1905. On the other hand, he sees laïcité as a long-term process which became a constitutional dimension of the French political experience.[37]

The complex events of this chaotic era would decisively contribute to the adoption of the law of 1905 which sought to settle the question of Church-State relations and regulate a new relationship. Since the sign-ing of the Concordat in 1801 there had been periods where the Church seemed to prevail and retrieve its place in French society. "The decades after 1810 witnessed a religious revival, marked by the post-Concordat reconstruction of the Church, a rise in vocations, expansion of Catholic education, 'ultramontane' piety and the emergence of a more 'personal' re-ligion involving frequent communion."[38] At times optimism reigned with the semblance of the Church prevailing over its anticlerical, Republican adversaries. McManners maintains, "The Vatican and French Catholics had been deluding themselves with the fading dream of a Christian nation, with a treaty of alliance between Church and State from which the spirit of honest collaboration was departing."[39] The Church retained a loyal core of believers but "was not fitted to face the challenges of unbelief and anticleri-calism, to reach out to win the world or to change society, nor was it fitted to fight the political battles of the future."[40] McManners further argues that "the failure of seminary teaching reflects the intellectual failure of the Ro-man Catholic Church in general in this period. There were no answers in

36. Ducomte, *La Laïcité*, 14–15.
37. Cabanel, *Les mots de la laïcité*, 8.
38. Magraw, *France 1800–1914*, 158.
39. McManners, *Church and State*, 13.
40. McManners, *Church and State*, 24.

the seminaries, because there were no answers to give. 'Scientific' unbelief met with no reply worth making."[41]

This period saw differences between Paris and the provinces in the strength and influence of the Church. In the provinces "the *curés* ruled their parishes as they had for generations, the ceremonies of religion were respected, even by those who did not attend mass, and the French Revolution was remembered in terms of Republican atrocities and Catholic martyrs."[42] Renan described the astonishment at the power of the clergy in provincial regions. The reason was simply that the Revolution had wrecked everything and broken all structures except the Church. The clergy alone remained organized outside of the State and in the provinces the bishop stood alone in the midst of a demolished society.[43] Initially anticlericalism was motivated by "a blend of practicalities and sullen resentments passed on from the Middle Ages, sardonic comments from Renaissance jest books, and the literate, intelligent hostilities of the Enlightenment."[44] However, not all anticlericalism was antireligious in nature and some of the opposition to the Catholic Church came from Protestants. Grévy maintains that authors connected with Protestantism, including the philosopher Renouvier, the historians Edgar Quinet and Ferdinand Buisson, contributed to the diffusion of the image of a Church inspired by contemporary events. These Protestants considered it their duty to demonstrate that it was not a matter of an accident of history, but the very nature of Catholicism which made it incompatible with liberty.[45] Grévy quotes the Protestant Quinet from his 1857 *La Révolution religieuse au XIX siècle*: "I have the honor to have never ceased, for forty years, not even for one day, to show the radical and absolute incompatibility of this form of religion with modern civilization, or with the emancipation of nationalities, or with political and civil liberties."[46]

The anticlericals looked to the Revolution which had freed the people from the tyranny of the Church, removed the repressive tithes to the Church, restored lands to the dispossessed, and was followed by great military victories under Napoleon. The Declaration of the Rights of Man and the Citizen was viewed as the epitome of liberty from oppression and there was no turning back to the times of religious domination. Anticlericals considered that the power of the Church had been broken and they would oppose any

41. McManners, *Church and State*, 28.

42. McManners, *Church and State*, 21.

43. Renan, *Questions contemporaines*, iv.

44. McManners, *Church and State*, 15.

45. Grévy, *Le Cléricalisme*, 43.

46. Grévy, *Le Cléricalisme*, 66.

restoration. "Against the Catholic myth of a Christian France had arisen the counter-myth of a revolutionary France, the standard-bearer of liberty."[47] The anticlericalism of the nineteenth century did not arrive in a vacuum. It was an attack on the Church, on tradition, on the aristocracy, and reflected the philosophical changes that had been in operation since the sixteenth century. The simple fact to be able to change religion, to be able to abandon any confession and to profess atheism or agnosticism without suffering the consequences which had resulted for centuries, constituted a transformation of the status of religion in secularized societies which is not always grasped.[48] Anticlericalism in the light of French history should not astound the unbiased observer. McManners succinctly summarizes the movement:

> The inherited fears of centuries, distrust of confession and of celibacy, love for the ideals of the Revolution and hatred of blind submission, the dream of a humanistic morality and the illumination of a new "religion" of science combined to create the anticlerical temper of the latter decades of the nineteenth century.[49]

There were other factors at work to undermine the teaching and authority of the Church. Darwin's *Origin of Species*, originally published in 1859, was translated and published in France in 1862 and undermined the biblical account of creation. Scientific knowledge was no longer beholden to theology. This period witnessed the secularization of knowledge which consisted in liberating knowledge from sacred writings. This redefinition of knowledge began during the sixteenth and seventeenth centuries with the affirmation of what was called a triple right. These were the right to freely exercise theoretic curiosity, the right of the spirit to submit all opinions to doubt, and the right of experience with its value opposed to the authority of the Scripture on non-essential teachings.[50]

Empirical verification became necessary for all truth claims and French Positivism provided the model. "The reverence once accorded to the pronouncements of theology was now revived, but transferred to those of scientists, and from 'science' something resembling a new 'religion' was born."[51] Science was freed from religious norms and what some saw as theological despotism. The sacred text became an obstacle to the progress of scientific investigation once science contradicted sacred propositions based on the

47. McManners, *Church and State*, 16.
48. Monod, *Sécularisation et laïcité*, 49.
49. McManners, *Church and State*, 19.
50. Monod, *Sécularisation et laïcité*, 35.
51. McManners, *Church and State*, 16.

limitations of knowledge of earlier times. The Scriptures were considered to be the source of knowledge of God, of ethics, and of eternal matters, while science treated those things subject to time. The two domains needed to be kept separate to prevent imposing norms from one domain on another in an act of tyranny.[52] Empiricism challenged all religious claims and divided Protestantism into two camps. In the eighteenth and nineteenth centuries Protestantism evolved between two major tendencies. Eighteenth-century Protestantism was divided between rationalism and pietism; nineteenth-century Protestantism was divided between followers of the Reawakening, who wanted to breathe new life into religion, and liberals, who granted science a status which led some to repudiate all transcendence.[53]

The Church and traditional theology were not only under attack by science; they were also under attack by those from within the Academy. In 1863, Ernest Renan, professor at the Collège de France, Chair of Hebrew, Chaldean, and Syriac, published his *Vie de Jésus* (Life of Jesus). The impact of this book cannot be exaggerated in which "the supernatural elements, the divine incursion were banished from the story."[54] Between 1863 and 1864 there were ten editions of the book. Renan had already provoked a scandal when he gave an inaugural lecture in February 1862 in which he was accused of denying and denigrating the Christian faith. Hundreds awaited the lecture and competing parties either supported him or called for his removal. He was opposed by the Church and received a letter from the Emperor himself which suspended the course he was teaching and announced the temporary suspension of his position as Chair of Hebrew. This was followed by a complete revocation in 1864 and only in 1870 would he be reinstated. The heart of the matter was considered to touch on the status of sacred texts in the study of religious science in France. The denial of miracles and the supernatural, his contestation of the divinity of Jesus, were rightly seen in contradiction to the Church's authority.[55]

In the 1880s, much of the energy of the Republicans was devoted to two major programs on their agenda—educational reform and the elimination of congregations providing education.[56] Throughout French history the Church had provided instruction in a framework in which authoritative religious teaching was associated with the formation of good citizens who would remain loyal to the Church. The anticlericals rightly understood

52. Monod, *Sécularisation et laïcité*, 37.
53. Montclos, *Histoire religieuse*, 108.
54. McManners, *Church and State*, 16.
55. Simon-Nahum, "Le scandale," 61–74.
56. Dansette, *Histoire religieuse*, 69.

that the control of education was fundamental to produce citizens loyal to the Republic. The 1801 Concordat had remained in effect and the Church's education of youth ensured its continued influence and domination if not politically, at least in the hearts and minds of the people. The laicization of education was proposed and implemented in order to undermine the Church's power and influence. "To break the hold of Catholicism over future generations and to unite the supporters of the Republic: such was the justification of the policy of laicization."[57]

The name Jules Ferry (1832–1893), a moderate Republican, remains forever attached to this period of educational turmoil. He is responsible for the law of 1882 which reformed and organized the system of free, obligatory, and laïque education.[58] For education to be obligatory it had to be free. The third point, laïque education, would take on greater importance. For Ferry the secularization of all institutions required the secularization of public schools. To have primary school students taught by teachers with different religious beliefs than the children would be a violation of their conscience. Ferry's project would replace moral and religious instruction with moral and civic instruction. The school needed to ignore religious affirmations when questions arose about God. There was pushback from political parties on the right who insisted that education must be catholic in conformity to the majority of the population and argued that non-Catholics could be excused from religious instruction.[59] The opposition to Ferry was to no avail. The government struck out at the religious teaching orders but without serious repression. The Jesuits were pursued with more vigor than other teaching orders with the forced closure of their unauthorized teaching establishments.[60]

While Ferry challenged clericalism, it appears that he was not an enemy of religion. Other Republicans, however, did not hide their desire to lead the battle of science and reason against the faith and to eradicate the Christian religion as well as all other religions.[61] With the arrival of Émile Combes (1835–1921) as prime minister in 1902, anticlericalism and the stigmatization of religious communities would reach their peak. Combes has been described as "one of those opponents of Catholicism whose hatred was rooted neither in unbelief nor skepticism, but in a

57. McManners, *Church and State*, 46.

58. Fontenay, "Un enseignement sur les religions," 37.

59. Dansette, *Histoire religieuse*, 87.

60. Dansette, *Histoire religieuse*, 83.

61. Gaillard, "L'invention de la laïcité," 30.

fervent deism."[62] He was violently anticlerical, a former seminary student whose ordination was refused by the Church.[63] Under him, more than 10,000 Catholic schools were closed, religious property was confiscated, and many religious workers were sent into exile.[64]

The Law Goblet in 1886 had proposed measures which opened the door for the idea of laïcité in the public mind. These measures included the repeal of the prohibition of working on Sunday, the cancellation of public prayers at the opening of Parliament, the priority given to civil marriage over religious marriage, new laws on divorce, the neutrality of cemeteries, and the liberty of funerals held without religious sanction. According to Machelon, at this point laïcité had acquired its modern sense. In what may have been a coincidence, Émile Littré, in a supplement to his *Dictionnaire de la langue française* (1877), added the neologism *laïcité* at the same time as the word *anticlerical*. For the following decades these two terms would remain associated.[65]

L'Affaire Dreyfus

One of the most fascinating historical events preceding the Law of Separation in 1905 was the Dreyfus Affair in the 1890s. It is considered a major trigger for the movement which led to the law of 1905.[66] Gildea notes,

> The Dreyfus affair was more than a question of miscarriage of justice; it involved a major political realignment, baptised the "Dreyfusian revolution" by George Sorel in 1909, which brought to power a broad political class from moderate Republicans to radicals and socialists. To prevent fracture, it constructed a political culture of the defence of revolutionary principles and the Republic, anticlericalism, Dreyfusism, and the shelving of most social legislation.[67]

This event shook France to its core and led to widespread reexamination of its republican values. It may be difficult to properly appreciate the importance of *l'Affaire* more than one hundred years after its occurrence. Yet modern historians continue to showcase this as a major contribution to

---

62. McManners, *Church and State*, 131.

63. Dusseau, "L'histoire de la Séparation," 17.

64. CNEF, *Laïcité française*, 15.

65. Machelon, *La laïcité demain*, 18–19.

66. Rognon and Weber, *La laïcité*, 41.

67. Gildea, *French History*, 311.

the necessity of the establishment of a laïque Republic in which liberty, equality, and fraternity might prevail for all citizens regardless of creed or without creed, where both belief and unbelief would be protected. *L'Affaire* "made possible a coalition of all defenders of the Republic on the basis of anticlericalism. . . . Even after Dreyfus was vindicated, the Affair continued to divide the nation."[68]

L'Affaire is connected to the intensified clerical and anticlerical struggle waged between Catholic and Republican forces following the crushing French defeat in 1870 at the hands of the Prussians which has been discussed above. The military loss was a blow to national pride, carried with it the annexation of Alsace-Moselle by Germany, and contributed to the low morale of the French military. Begley argues that "the erratic and lawless actions of successive French ministers of war and high-ranking officers on the army's General Staff in the course of the Dreyfus Affair can similarly be traced to a defining national trauma: the humiliating defeat suffered by the French army in the Franco-Prussian War of 1870."[69]

On one hand, those on the anticlerical, political left ascribed the defeat to the continued influence of the Church in institutions of higher learning. On the other hand, those who supported the Church and the monarchy saw the defeat as a sign of judgment on a nation that had turned from God and the divine right of kings. These two opposing forces would struggle for dominance and Captain Dreyfus (1859–1935) would become an unwitting pawn to galvanize both sides in the contest for the French form of government. French novelist and playwright Émile Zola (1840–1902) would issue his famous *J'accuse* (I accuse), an open letter written in 1898 to the French president and published in the newspaper *L'Aurore* in defense of Dreyfus. Dreyfus's arrest, trial, exile, exoneration and reinstatement would widen the gap between the political left and right. According to Brown, "Like Catholicism, nationalism had its ritual Judas. And these two forces converged as never before during the tumultuous nineties, in the Dreyfus Affair."[70]

Captain Dreyfus was a Jew from Alsace-Lorraine (Moselle), a long-disputed region which had returned to Prussian control after 1870. He became a convenient scapegoat to assign blame for France's inglorious defeat and revealed the divide between supporters of the Church and supporters of a laïque Republic. The story has often been told of the secret memorandum (*bordereau*) discovered by a cleaning woman in a wastebasket in the German Embassy and addressed to the German military attaché. The bordereau,

68. McManners, *Church and State*, 119.

69. Begley, *Dreyfus Affair*, 47–48.

70. Brown, *Soul of France*, xxv.

written in French, contained information on various aspects of the French army—French artillery, troop placements, and discussion on obtaining information about a field artillery operating manual.[71] Captain Dreyfus was assigned to artillery and suspicion fell upon him as the author of the bordereau in part because he was Jewish. He was arrested and accused of treason. The case early on received little interest but was inflamed by elements of the anti-Semitic press, including the Catholic publication *La Croix* "which called for the expulsion of Jews from France."[72]

The details of *l'Affaire* mesmerized not only the French public but reverberated internationally. Zola "denounced the framing of Dreyfus by the military hierarchy [and] constructed the affair as a struggle between liberty and despotism, light and darkness."[73] He penned his now famous elegant and scathing summary of the affair in his *J'accuse*. He addressed the president respectfully and with gratitude to inform him of what Zola considered would be a blemish on the President's name—"*cette abominable affaire Dreyfus*" (this abominable Dreyfus affair). Zola informed the president about the process and condemnation of Dreyfus. He spoke of "*le néant de l'accusation*" (the nothingness of the accusation). He described the plot with all the elements of a mystery novel needed to captivate the public—complicity at the highest military levels, conspirators in the shadows, forged documents, anonymous letters, mysterious women, fabricated evidence, and secret meetings. He warned the French of a looming dictatorship and recounted that Captain Dreyfus was condemned for treason, court-martialed, publicly shamed, stripped of his rank in the courtyard of the École Militaire, and exiled to Devil's Island with Church and military complicity. He revealed that only when Colonel Sandherr died and was replaced by Colonel Picquart (1854–1914) as head of intelligence did the truth come out and Commander Esterhazy found to be the real traitor. Even then, the military refused to reopen the investigation for fear that the condemnation of Esterhazy would lead to a review of Dreyfus's judicial process. Picquart was sent out of the country on missions to Tunisia and other places to silence his insistent voice and plea to clear Dreyfus. The crime had been committed. The general staff could not confess its crime since it would sully the military's reputation, a military still reeling from the defeat in the Franco-Prussian War. Losing face and public scorn was to be avoided at all costs.[74]

71. Cahm, *Dreyfus Affair*, 2.

72. Begley, *Dreyfus Affair*, 75.

73. Gildea, *French History*, 105.

74. Zola, "J'accuse . . . !"

The condemnation, degradation, and exile of Dreyfus would set in motion his defense by the Republicans. Zola named names beginning with the Lieutenant Colonel du Paty de Clam (1853–1916), judicial officer of the affair, who was identified as noxious, the one most culpable in the affair and who threatened Dreyfus's wife to remain silent. Zola accused other military officers (Sandherr, Mercier, Boisdeffre, Gonse) of committing judicial errors, of being accomplices in what he considered one of the century's most evil plots, of withholding proof of Dreyfus's innocence, of committing the crime out of Catholic fervor and biased investigation. He accused three graphologists of fraud in their analysis of documents, the war ministry of using the press to influence public opinion, and the first court-martial of introducing secret documents leading to the guilty person's acquittal. He admitted that he did not personally know those he accused and did not speak out of hatred. The enormous influence of Zola would contribute to Dreyfus's eventual exoneration and later provide support for the rationale and the defense of the law separating the Roman Catholic Church from the State.

Several references figure prominently in *J'accuse* which demonstrate the suspected underlying religious influences in how *l'Affaire* was conducted. General Boisdeffre (1838–1906), head of general staff, seemed to yield to his clerical views according to Zola. Lieutenant Colonel de Clam was accused of being involved with spiritism and occultism and speaking with spirit beings. The generals Gonse and Mercier were also suspected of yielding to their religious passions. De Clam is further accused of being part of a clerical milieu, hunting for "*sales juifs*" (dirty Jews). Zola described *l'Affaire* as a crime which hid behind anti-Semitism and a crime which exploited patriotism. The scandal was viewed as a threat to society and to the survival of the Republic in which Zola feared the "*droits de l'homme*" (human rights) would die.[75]

For his efforts Zola would be condemned for defamation and experienced self-exile in England for a year. However, there was no turning back as the Antidreyfusards and the Dreyfusards staked out their positions. The Antidreyfusards had the support of the Church and the army and were persuaded of the existence of a syndicate grouping anti-France, Jewish, Protestant, and Free Masonry forces.[76] The Dreyfusards had the support of writers, artists, and scientists. The radicals and free thinkers denounced the alliance of the Church and the army, "*le sabre et le goupillon*" (the sword and bottlebrush).[77]

75. Zola, "J'accuse . . . !"

76. Boyer, *La loi de 1905*, 72.

77. Dusseau, "L'histoire de la Séparation," 16.

There were more calls for the expulsion of all Jews from France. *L'Affaire* and its eventual resolution, including a second trial in 1899, left France shaken. In the minds of many, "since it was anticlericals, not churchmen, who rescued an innocent man from Devil's Island, the inference was drawn that the Catholics, in the last resort, put expediency before truth and order above justice."[78] This overlooked the fact that some churchmen, though relatively few in number, supported Dreyfus and that Colonel Picquart was Catholic. However, it fed the narrative that would continue to pit anticlerical forces against their clerical opponents. "Triumphant in the Dreyfus business, the anticlericals were in the mood for revenge."[79]

Pope Leo XIII (1810–1903) had previously "urged French Catholics to support the Republic but the effects of the Dreyfus case largely undid his efforts."[80] Montclos maintains that the policy of rallying Catholics to the Republic, extolled by Pope Leo XIII between 1890–1892, appeared for a moment to give a chance for a moderate Republic. But in 1898, following the Dreyfus Affair, many Republicans reinforced their anticlerical commitment.[81] According to Barzun,

> Like another piece of make-believe, but grimmer, the incredibly long-drawn-out Dreyfus Affair aroused passion and prejudice throughout the world. In France the chain of misdeeds—treason, coercion, perjury, forgery, suicide, and manifest injustice—re-created the cleavage of the 'two Frances,' always reoccurring at critical moments.[82]

Elected Prime Minister in 1899, Waldeck-Rousseau (1846–1904) "made a political decision against the Church because he had seen how the clergy played politics against the Republic."[83] Dreyfus was pardoned after the second court-martial with the consent of President Émile Loubet (1838–1929). At his first trial in 1894, Dreyfus's conviction had been pronounced unanimously. Since then, evidence for Dreyfus's innocence had become overwhelming. In 1899, Dreyfus was convicted once again but without unanimity among the judges and with extenuating circumstances.[84] The government justified its decision to pardon Dreyfus based on his deteriorating health after five years of exile and imprisonment on Devil's Island.

78. McManners, *Church and State*, 120.

79. McManners, *Church and State*, 125.

80. Walker et al., *History of the Christian Church*, 672.

81. Montclos, *Histoire religieuse*, 94.

82. Barzun, *Dawn to Decadence*, 630.

83. McManners, *Church and State*, 127.

84. Combarieu, *Sept ans à l'Elysée*, 37.

Both Loubet and Waldeck-Rousseau were called traitors and enemies of the Church. Dreyfus's supporters would continue their struggle for his full rehabilitation which the pardon did not provide.[85]

A first step would be taken against the Church in 1901 with the Law of Associations which required governmental authorization for religious teaching orders (*congrégations*). The refusal of authorization would lead to closure and confiscation of property and forced many religious workers into exile. It was only a matter of time before the Church came under more intense pressure. Émile Combes followed Waldeck-Rousseau and applied the law with a vengeance. Parliament rejected most of the requests by religious congregations for authorization and diplomatic relations with the Vatican suffered.[86] As a result, with Combes's policies in the ascendancy and "a vigorous, unyielding Pope newly elected, an open rupture between Church and State became a real possibility."[87] Finally, in 1905, "a radical republican legislature mindful of diatribes in *La Croix* and kindred publications (collectively christened "*la bonne Presse*") voted the separation of Church and State."[88]

1905 Law of Separation

At the end of the nineteenth century, the battle for the laicization of the State and public services had not ended and a decisive step had not been taken. Machelon contends that solemn measures, even brutal, were needed. The law of 1905 was prepared in a passionate climate and preceded by the rupture of diplomatic relations with the Holy See, which rendered the maintenance of the Concordat status quo impossible. The situation of ecclesiastical institutions throughout France was turned upside down. Often presented as an agreement, the law was in fact an act of force which destroyed the 1801 diplomatic convention. In exchange for an independence the Church was not seeking, the law deprived the Church of its patrimony and resources.[89]

Although presented in a pacifying form deemed beneficial for the institution targeted, the law's application led to violent confrontations. In time the law would undergo amendments to facilitate cohabitation between the separated institutions in a country with an overwhelming Catholic majority. Among these modifications was the creation of

85. Combarieu, *Sept ans à l'Elysée*, 39–40.
86. Gaillard, "L'invention de la laïcité," 32.
87. McManners, *Church and State*, 134.
88. Brown, *Soul of France*, 218.
89. Machelon, *La laïcité demain*, 19.

chaplain services in hospitals and the armed forces and the return of property to dispossessed institutions.[90] The law of 1905 terminated the 1801 Concordat (except in Alsace-Moselle) and provided the foundation for Church-State separation. Ended were both the attempt to establish the Church in political power and the attempt of the State to control the Church. The law was not negotiated with the Church, was opposed and condemned by Pope Pius X (1835–1914), and was perceived as an aggressive move against the Catholic Church. Protestants and evangelicals largely welcomed the Law of Separation which legally placed them on the same level as the Catholic Church. According to Boyer, at least since the Revocation of the Edict of Nantes, French Protestants defended the liberty of conscience. This was done on the philosophical level with Pierre Bayle, and on a concrete level with Marie Durand and the prisoners of the Tower of Constance at Aigues-Mortes, with the Huguenot galley prisoners for the faith, and with the persecuted assemblies meeting in the wilderness. The struggle for freedom did not end with the Edict of Toleration granted by Louis XVI in 1787, which provided legal existence and civil status to French Protestants. The battle continued with the involvement of Pastor Rabout Saint-Étienne in the Declaration of the Rights of Man and of the Citizen and for the rights of minorities which led to increased religious freedom for Protestants in 1789 and Jews in 1791. Protestants remained attached to the principles of 1789 and to the Revolution, even if they condemned the excesses of the Reign of Terror.[91] Boyer further contends that Protestants played a great role during this period in the separation. These Protestant leaders included historian Gabriel Monod, Raoul Allier, dean of a Protestant school of theology, and Francis de Pressensé, son of a Protestant pastor and author of the first draft of the Law of Separation in 1903. Louis Méjan, son and brother of pastors, wrote the law and had the task of applying it as the last director of the Ministry of Religions.[92]

These critical historical events and the acrimonious debates over the place of religion in France were fundamental to the formal introduction of the principle of laïcité in France in 1905. What emerged was not a grand plan with anticipated steps which finally produced the Law of Separation of Churches and State. Rather, there were centuries of struggle involving religion, religious dominance, religious controversy, and religious wars. It should not be surprising, given the place of religion in France, that many believed that a better society would be formed on another foundation which

90. Machelon, *La laïcité demain*, 20.
91. Boyer, *La loi de 1905*, 69.
92. Boyer, *La loi de 1905*, 74–75.

excluded religion and divine authority. It is not possible to judge all the motivations of those involved in the controversies and battles over the form of government under which the French people would live. What is clear is that there was disenchantment with religion and growing aversion to the divine right of kings. With the introduction of Cartesian doubt, the arrival of the Enlightenment emphasis on reason and the progress of humanity, and the rise of deism, atheism, and skepticism, winds of change were blowing from different directions. France, which had known centuries of upheaval, was forced to resolve the religious question which was at the root of clamor for revolutionary change and for societal stability.

In fact, three revolutions took place leading to the affirmation of a sovereign State and the exclusion of the Church from the political sphere of activity. The first was the religious revolution under Luther and Calvin during the first half of the sixteenth century. Reformation influences were not strong enough to win the day in France but were strong enough to impose a division of consciences within the kingdom. The second was the political revolution during the first half of the seventeenth century which was accompanied by the third, the scientific revolution. The second and third revolutions contributed to individualism, a questioning of the Church's authority, and a distancing from the established Church.[93] These revolutions were linked to religious controversy. The experience of interconfessional civil war contributed to the emergence of political authority as a peacemaking force, "Leviathan capable of protecting individuals with different beliefs and containing the violence brought about by religious division."[94] Monod follows Carl Schmitt in the opinion that the modern State was essentially the product of religious civil war which led directly to the neutralization and secularization of religious confessions.[95] The State sought to unite a nation long plagued with sectarian divisions. The rupture and fractiousness between competing religions led inevitably to the rupture between Church and State.

With this historical background in view, we can now turn to the contextual particulars of laïcité in France and the law of 1905 as found in documents, parliamentary debates, and essays. Laïcité both unites and divides France to this day. The documents provide a key for outsiders to understand the rationale for establishing laïcité as a principle in French society which continues to arouse interest, acrimony, and debate in the twenty-first century.

---

93. Gauchet, *La religion dans la démocratie*, 42–43.

94. Monod, *Sécularisation et laïcité*, 41.

95. Monod, *Sécularisation et laïcité*, 42.

4

Foundational Documents and Political Debates on Laïcité

THE DEBATES, SPEECHES, LETTERS, and events leading up to the 1905 Law of Separation furnish intriguing insights on competing agendas and personalities, on the concerns raised and addressed, and on the political process of the French Chamber of Deputies and Senate in the late nineteenth and early twentieth centuries. The historical events referenced in these documents reveal the extent to which the authors, orators, and polemists sought either the triumph of the ideals of the 1789 French Revolution in the separation of Church and State, or the repudiation of the Revolution in support of the union of Church and State and the restoration of the monarchy.

The politico-religious history of France provides the backdrop to understand the law of December 9, 1905. The law should be viewed through the lens of history as the culmination of centuries of struggle between the Church and State, monarchists and Republicans, Catholics and Protestants, religion and irreligion, and between clerical and anticlerical forces. The historical relationship between the Church and State in France has been described in three ways. The first most prominent and durable relationship was the alliance of the State and Papacy during the Ancien Régime and under the Concordats. The second and third were two short-lived relationships which occurred during the French Revolution. The first year of the revolutionary calendar (*calendrier révolutionnaire*) corresponds to 1792 (*l'an I*). During the Revolution, there was a national organization of religion from 1790 to 1796 (*1790–l'an IV*) and a separation of Church and State from 1796 to 1801 (*l'an IV–l'an X*).[1] The most important relationship for our purposes is that of the alliance of the State and the Papacy. This alliance included the Ancien Régime from Louis IX (1240–1270) to the French Revolution, then the Concordat under various empires, monarchies, and elected governments in the nineteenth century, until the Separation in 1905. Until 1875 the separation

---

1. Bire, *La séparation*, 27.

of Churches and State made only timid appearances in electoral programs. Beginning in 1881, momentum grew as serious propositions of law were presented and commissions were established to examine the conditions under which separation might take place.[2]

There were diplomatic crises, intrigues, and considerable controversies which took place in the two decades preceding the final enactment of the Law of Separation in December 1905. France went through successive governments in the nineteenth century which oscillated between support for and opposition to the Concordat. The discussions and debates accelerated in the final years and months leading to the separation of Church and State and the abrogation of the 1801 Concordat. There were several notable events and conflicts between the Vatican and the French government which hardened opposition toward the Church and played into the hands of anticlerical forces who sought the termination of the Concordat. The conciliatory posture of Pope Leo XIII, from 1878 until his death in 1903, was replaced by the rigidness of his successor Pope Pius X which resulted in the breaking of diplomatic relations between France and the Vatican.

The foundational documents in French discussed in this section were gathered in one volume in 2004 to mark the one-hundredth anniversary of the Law of Separation.[3] This section relies heavily on translated material from that book, much of which was drawn from archival material not readily accessible in other languages besides French. The book contains an introduction by Dominique Villepin (b. 1953), Minister of the Interior at the time of the book's publication. Villepin reminds us:

> The long path which led to the separation of Churches and State flows directly from the inspirational philosophy of the rights of man of 1789. . . . One principle is at the heart of the law of 1905: liberty. It established a direct line between laïcité and the revolutionary ideals affirmed in the Declaration of the Rights of Man and of the Citizen. Liberty, because no longer would any religious order be able to prevail in exercising any influence whatever on State decisions.[4]

These foundational documents include excerpts from books, journal and newspaper articles, and speeches. It is important to note that deliberations leading to the 1905 law constantly referenced earlier documents and events. These events include the Edict of Nantes in 1598 under Henry IV, which granted limited religious rights to Protestants in a Catholic nation,

2. Bire, *La séparation*, 27.

3. Bruley, *La séparation*.

4. Villepin, "Une certaine idée de la République," 8.

and the Revocation of the Edict of Nantes in 1685 under Louis XIV which led to large-scale persecution, bloodshed, suppression of religious freedom, and eventually to the French Revolution in 1789.

The documents begin with the 1789 Declaration of the Rights of Man and of the Citizen, particularly article 10 and its affirmation of religious freedom, which underpins modern politics in France and the ideal of a French Republic. The Civil Constitution of the Clergy in 1790 resulted in the loss of special privileges for the Church and clergy and the confiscation of Church properties. Priests were required to swear an oath to the king, to the government, and to the Constitution. The election of bishops and priests deprived the pope of the authority of confirmation. The refusal of many clergy to accept this Constitution, and its condemnation by Pope Pius VI, was at the origin of the conflict which led to civil war and religious persecution.[5]

During and following the French Revolution, France remained profoundly religious. In 1794, while the nation was threatened by civil war and *la Terreur*, Maximillian Robespierre defended the worship of a Supreme Being (*L'Être suprême*) and the immortality of the soul as an alternative to the Catholic Church. He held the conviction that the Republic could not be atheist.[6] An initial separation of the Church and State took place with the Constitution of the short-lived First Republic in 1795. Interpretations of the nature of this separation resurfaced in debates preceding the law of 1905. The Napoleonic Concordat of 1801 recognized the Catholic, Apostolic, and Roman religion as the religion of majority of the French but not as the religion of State. The Concordat also brought the nomination of bishops under the control of the First Consul, Napoleon and his successors, and provided subsidies for recognized churches and salaries for the clergy. Until its abrogation in 1905, the Concordat regulated relations between the Church and the State and was at the heart of the debates.[7]

Catholic Church and the Republic

In 1830, a minority group of liberal Catholics had proposed the separation of Church and State following the overthrow of the legitimate King Charles X (1757–1836) and the installation of Louis-Philippe d'Orléans (1773–1850). Under the new king, now known as Louis-Philippe I and regarded by many as a usurper, the political climate was less favorable toward the Church. The liberals considered that the Concordat needed to end in

5. Bruley, *La séparation*, 39–43.
6. Bruley, *La séparation*, 43–45.
7. Bruley, *La séparation*, 43–49.

order that the Church might regain its independence from the State. They demanded the liberty of conscience and freedom of religion. They saw no reason for the continuance of the Concordat if Catholicism was no longer the religion of the State. However, this group was disavowed by the Catholic hierarchy which remained committed to the Concordat.[8]

The *Syllabus* of Pope Pius IX (1792–1878) in 1864 was a condemnation of the errors of modern society and was used against the Church in the debates on separation by the Church's adversaries.[9] In December 1869, Pope Pius X opened the first Church Council since the Council of Trent in the sixteenth century. Hundreds of cardinals were in attendance.[10] The most noteworthy result of this Council was the proclamation of the dogma of papal infallibility on July 18, 1870. Ironically, this declaration, regarded as the apogee of papal authority, was soon followed by the pope's loss of temporal power on September 20, 1870, when Rome was seized by the Italian army and annexed to Italy. This event marked the end of the pontifical States and remained a source of contention between the Vatican and France, the Vatican's former protectors whose troops were withdrawn when war broke out between France and Germany.[11] The *Syllabus* and the claim of papal infallibility figure prominently in later discussions on separation as evidence of the Church's incompatibility with modernity and laïcité.

Léon Gambetta and Jules Ferry, both associated with laws related to educational reform, were influential in advocating for separation and a laïque State. Gambetta gave a speech in which he defined a laïque Republic on April 23, 1875. He sought to bring France back to her true traditions in guaranteeing the conquests and the principles of 1789, and most importantly, the principle according to which the State must be free from religious or transcendent claims of authority. The great design of the Revolution had sought to liberate politics and government from the yoke of diverse religious confessions.[12] Council President Ferry, on November 17, 1883, addressed his famous *Lettre aux instituteurs* (Letter to teachers) to explain the sense of a law enacted March 28, 1882, and to explain the principles and methods of teaching in laïque schools. He reminded them that religious instruction belonged to families and to the Church, and moral instruction belonged to the school.[13]

8. Bruley, *La séparation*, 53–54.

9. Robert et al., *Nouveau Petit Robert*, 2482.

10. Bruley, *La séparation*, 55–58.

11. Walker et al., *History of the Christian Church*, 671.

12. Bruley, *La séparation*, 59.

13. Bruley, *La séparation*, 63.

The Left and radical Republicans led by Émile Combes gained momentum at the end of the last decade of the nineteenth century and finally achieved power in 1902.[14] Many politicians were anticlerical to some degree or at least favorable to the separation of Church and State and were determined to settle the religious question. But they were not unopposed. There were moderate Republicans and monarchists who were wary of dissolving the Concordat. Some believed that the still-powerful Church needed the authority of State to retain a measure of control over the subordinate Church. Others held out hope that the monarchy would be restored and that the Church would once again occupy its place in alliance with the State.

Three documents have special value in understanding the relationship between the Catholic Church and the French Republic in the latter part of the nineteenth century leading up to the law of 1905.[15] McManners contends that "the political barometer of the Third Republic was set toward appeasement and compromise. Some conservatives were trying to escape the electoral consequences of their monarchial convictions, and some Opportunists were trying shake off the dependence on the Left involved in anticlericalism."[16] The Opportunists were moderates distinguished from the radical Republicans whose "political philosophy took its cue from the older, more moderate Gambetta and Jules Ferry whose republicanism was practical and cautious and whose reforms were mainly political in character."[17] French Catholics became "the right wing of a central conservative bloc in alliance with the moderate Republicans."[18]

The first document comes from a speech given on November 12, 1890, at what has been called the Toast of Algiers (Le Toast d'Alger). The occasion was a reception of officers of the French navy in Algiers, a former French department in Algeria. The archbishop of Algiers, cardinal Charles Lavigerie (1825–1892), had maintained links with the French government and remained active in the Vatican. Pope Leo XIII decided to use the cardinal to make known his decision to rally (le Ralliement) Catholics to the Republican regime. To many French Catholics le Ralliement was an act of betrayal which crushed monarchial aspirations. The cardinal became the spokesman for the pope in announcing a new political position desired by the pope. The cardinal believed that union was the greatest desire of the Church and of its pastors at every level of hierarchy, and was at that moment the greatest

14. Bruley, La séparation, 81.
15. Bruley, La séparation, 67–73.
16. McManners, Church and State, 65.
17. Keiger, Raymond Poincaré, 40.
18. McManners, Church and State, 69–70.

need in the presence of a bloody past and a threatening future.[19] Assurance was given that the pope was free from any preference for the French form of government, whether monarchy or Republic, and that the Church was not in sympathy with any of the monarchial parties fighting against the government. Many Catholics were still hostile toward the Republic and were supporting royalist movements. The pope wanted to encourage all Catholics to accept the regime in place. "In so far as the Ralliement was intended to create a new and influential Catholic line in politics, the monarchists were exasperated by the justifiable fear they were being asked to sacrifice a hopeless cause they loved for a hopeless cause they detested."[20]

The second document comes from a text written by Hippolyte Desprez (1820–1899), French ambassador to the Vatican from 1880 to 1882. In 1892, Pope Leo XIII had called upon French Catholics to accept the Constitution in order to influence republican institutions in a Christian direction and to recognize the established government.[21] Desprez concluded his memoir with his recollection of the call to *le Ralliement*. Most notable was his observation that the pope was not driven by any feeling of hostility against the form of government in France, and that the pope had often declared that he was free from any preference between the Republic or the monarchy.[22] However, "the immediate conversion of a majority of French Royalists into Republicans was neither possible nor credible, and by 1898 the Ralliement as a short-term expedient was manifestly a failure."[23]

The third document, a speech in Parliament, provides an understanding of the relationship between the Catholic Church and the Republic in 1894, two years after the pope's call to *le Ralliement*. Moderate Republicans, often called progressivists, were in power at the time and were in conflict with the anarchists and socialists. The moderate Republicans sought reconciliation with the Church and a pacification in the anticlerical battle. Eugène Spuller, Minister of Religions and an old friend of Léon Gambetta, pleaded for a new spirit of tolerance between the Church and State.[24] This new spirit soon failed because of the divisions created by the Dreyfus Affair and was followed by the electoral defeat of the moderates in 1899. They lost power to the radicals, and Catholics would once again distance themselves from the

19. Bruley, *La séparation*, 67–68.
20. McManners, *Church and State*, 72.
21. McManners, *Church and State*, 75.
22. Bruley, *La séparation*, 68.
23. McManners, *Church and State*, 79.
24. Bruley, *La séparation*, 71.

government. The arrival of the radicals to power would create the conditions to advance their agenda for the separation of Church and State.[25]

1901 Law of Associations

In 1899, René Waldeck-Rousseau was called upon to lead the government as Council President in the wake of political chaos brought about by the Dreyfus Affair. The Council President (*Président du Conseil*) was the head of the government during the Third Republic. Later under the Fifth Republic, this position became the office of Prime Minister (*Premier Ministre*). Waldeck-Rousseau's government lasted three years during which time he also held the position of Minister of the Interior and of Religions. He did not support propositions for the separation of Church and State and saw in the 1801 Concordat a means to control the clergy. To better establish the State's authority over the clergy, Waldeck-Rousseau proposed a law which would require religious teaching orders to request authorization within three months of the law's enactment to remain open. On October 28, 1900, he gave a speech at Toulouse where he outlined the project which was discussed in the following months. The law of 1901 concerning associations was designed as a crucial step in the battle against clerical influence and religious teaching congregations.[26] The law of 1901 concerned cultural (*culturelle*) associations. The law of 1905 concerned religious (*cultuelle*) associations. The distinction is important and many churches along with other religions chose then and choose today to operate under the law of 1901 which provides more flexibility but lacks the fiscal advantages of the law of 1905. The law was a half measure through which the State would continue the terms of the Concordat and enact restraints on religious teaching orders through State authorization.

In his speech Waldeck-Rousseau described himself as a man without a sectarian spirit.[27] He referenced the Concordat which governed the relations between the Church and State and was reserved for clergy in submission to the Church and subject to control of the State. He reminded his audience that under the terms of the Concordat the clergy was permitted to conduct worship and preach in the churches. His concern and the object of the proposed law was the religious orders. Teaching congregations had grown in number and in militancy and, in his opinion, risked dividing France into two groups of youth (*deux jeunesses*) if religious instruction

25. Bruley, *La séparation*, 72.
26. Bruley, *La séparation*, 77.
27. Waldeck-Rousseau, *Défense républicaine*, 155–59.

was provided by religious workers in their schools. He felt that this would lead to two societies: one becoming more and more democratic; the other influenced by doctrines that had survived the grand revolutionary and intellectual movements of the eighteenth century. Waldeck-Rousseau saw the rising influence of the Church as a powerful rival to the State. This state of affairs produced an intolerable situation against which all administrative measures had been powerless. He viewed the proposed Law of Associations as the solution to the educational problem in requiring teaching orders to be authorized by the State. He concluded his speech in announcing that the Law of Associations would be the departure point of the greatest and freest social evolution and, in addition, the indispensable guarantee of the most necessary prerogatives of modern society.[28]

The Law of Associations was adopted by Parliament on July 3, 1901. Abel Combarieu, secretary general during the presidency of Émile Loubet (1838–1929), published his Souvenirs to reflect on the political atmosphere of these crucial years of the Third Republic. The law gave the government freedom of action in choosing to show itself severe or tolerant toward religious teaching orders and workers' associations. Non-religious associations were permitted to freely organize as well but would enjoy civil recognition only if authorized by the government. Religious orders were not allowed to organize or exist without State authorization and teachers belonging to non-authorized teaching orders were not permitted to lead educational institutions. There was the expectation that religious orders would massively seek authorization, unlike the response to a decree in 1880 which provoked a crisis between the Church and State when Jesuits were expelled and teaching orders were required to request authorization.[29]

In June 1902, Émile Combes replaced Waldeck-Rousseau as Council President. Neither President Émile Loubet nor his secretary general Abel Combarieu expressed enthusiasm for Combes. In excerpts from his Souvenirs, Combarieu wrote that among the essential policies of Combes's cabinet were the firm application of the recent Law of Associations and upholding the Concordat.[30] Combes found in the writings of Anatole France (1844–1924), famous poet and novelist, a defense of his strict application of the Law of Associations. Anatole France, in the preface to Combes's book, Une compagne laïque, evoked the Dreyfus Affair and the anti-Semitism he claimed was orchestrated by the Church. The perpetrators of anti-Semitism were called missionaries of the Roman Church who

28. Combarieu, Sept ans à l'Élysée, 159; Bruley, La séparation, 80.
29. Combarieu, Sept ans à l'Élysée, 137–38; Bruley, La séparation, 80–81.
30. Bruley, La séparation, 84.

were joined by clericals.[31] He described the agitation which the 1901 law provoked, the surprise and indignation among the clericals (*noirs*) at the closure of unauthorized teaching institutions, the organized resistance to the law in Brittany, and the Church's exhortations which led to violence. Renan was quoted with approval to show that the tactic of the clerical parties was to push civil authority to the limit, then present action on the part of the authorities, which the clericals provoked, as shocking violence.[32] Renan's quote resurfaced again in 1905 during the debates on the Law of Separation. One parliamentarian cited Renan and claimed that the Catholic Church had constantly violated the Concordat, had pushed the Republican party to its limits, and when the Republican party turned against the Church and finally requested an accountability for the Church's actions, the Church only requested one thing—the upholding of the Concordat.[33]

Combes's policies did not go uncontested. Once again, Combarieu serves as an eyewitness to the intrigue and the tensions in the summer of 1902 produced by the application of the law of 1901 and the forced closure of religious establishments.[34] The news that nuns were expelled from unauthorized convents was reported to have saddened President Émile Loubet and his wife. His wife deplored the task undertaken by Combes as damaging for her husband and harmful for France. However, the policies of Combes appeared to have received the support of a majority in Parliament and the president found himself powerless to intervene. Waldeck-Rousseau remarked to the president that Combes was carrying out a stupid policy which was contrary to what had been understood at the time the law was adopted.[35] He reaffirmed that the object of the law had been to prevent further multiplication of religious teaching establishments and did not concern existing establishments.

Further opposition came from Bernard Lazare (1865–1903), described as a Jewish intellectual atheist and Dreyfusard. In a letter dated August 6, 1902, to the well-known poet and editor Charles Péguy (1873–1914), Lazare expressed his opposition to Combes and the laïque laws in the name of liberty of education.[36] He challenged the partisan exploitation of the Dreyfus Affair to tear down the religious teaching orders and the Church, and denounced the diversion of Dreyfusism in politics and in

31. Combes, *Une campagne laïque*, v.
32. Combes, *Une campagne laïque*, xxiii; Bruley, *La séparation*, 86–87.
33. Bruley, *La séparation*, 87n1.
34. Combarieu, *Sept ans à l'Élysée*, 209; Bruley, *La séparation*, 87–90.
35. Combarieu, *Sept ans à l'Élysée*, 210; Bruley, *La séparation*, 88.
36. Bruley, *La séparation*, 90–92.

Combist demagoguery.[37] Lazare made it clear that he was not defending the Church against which he had waged combat in the past. Yet he refused to accept either the dogmas formulated by the State or the dogmas of the Church and declared that in recent years the nation's most fervent enemies had not come from the chapels but from the lycées and the universities. One thing was demanded—complete liberty for reason—which did not require force to triumph.[38]

Émile Zola, who died in 1902, wrote his final novel entitled *Vérité* which was published posthumously in 1903. In *Vérité*, the third volume in his unfinished series *Les Quatre Évangiles*, he recalled the conflict of the Dreyfus Affair and the struggle against religious schools. He considered that if the nation suffered and was divided as enemies into two Frances [*deux Frances ennemies*], Rome was the cause. Zola described France as the last of the great Catholic powers who alone had the men and the money, the strength to impose Catholicism in the world, and that it was logical that Rome chose France to deliver the supreme combat in her bitter desire to reconquer temporal power, permitting her to achieve her secular dream of universal domination.[39] No words were minced in attacking the Church with reference made to the *le Ralliement* policy of Pope Leo XIII in 1882:

> Under the politics of Leo XIII, the Republic was accepted in order to be invaded. If the France of Voltaire and of Diderot has become the poor present-day France—troubled, misled, distraught, ready to return to the past rather than walk into the future—it is because the Jesuits and other teaching orders have put their hands on the children, tripling in thirty years the number of students, expanding their powerful places in the whole country.[40]

There were some who believed the Law of Associations prefigured an inevitable separation of Church and State. Louis Méjan, son of a Calvinist pastor, was one of the first to see separation on the near horizon.[41] He recounted conversations with politicians to whom he expressed his concern that the Law of Associations would lead to the separation of Church and State. In a conversation with Henri Brisson (1835–1912) in 1902, one of the founders of the Third Republic, Brisson told Méjan: "Before we might achieve the separation

37. Bruley, *La séparation*, 90.
38. Bruley, *La séparation*, 91–92.
39. Zola, *Vérité*, 187; Bruley, *La séparation*, 92–93.
40. Zola, *Vérité*, 188; Bruley, *La séparation*, 93–94.
41. Méjan, *La Séparation*.

of Church and State, France must live through forty years of happiness."[42] On another occasion, in conversation with Charles Dumay, Director of Religious Affairs, a post later occupied by Méjan, Dumay stated his opinion that the separation of Churches and the State would be a madness similar to that of a government which, having a place with ferocious animals in a cage, would open the bars to allow the beasts to rush into the crowd.[43] Whether the separation was madness or not, France never achieved her forty years of happiness and separation would soon become a reality.

Although Émile Combes severely applied the 1901 Law of Association, initially he continued to uphold the Concordat even if the door was left open for its later rescindment. His early support to maintain the Concordat is evident during a debate in January 1903 on State funds allocated to support the Church (*budget des cultes*) under the terms of the Concordat. He believed that the suppression of State funds for the Church would bring about confusion and that it was not possible with a signature to erase fourteen centuries of religious influences which had nourished the people.[44] Combes asserted that when he came to power he had promised to support the continuation of the provisions of the Concordat. He confessed that philosophically, and in his political sensibilities on the Left, he wished that free thought supported by reason alone might lead people throughout life, but realized that moment had not yet arrived. Since that time had not yet come, he needed to postpone the Left's desire for separation of Church and State and the abrogation of the Concordat.[45]

The historian Alphonse Aulard (1840–1928), a recognized expert on the French Revolution, weighed in and qualified his support for a necessary separation in articles published in *La Dépêche de Toulouse*, April 1903.[46] He referred to the above-mentioned speech by Combes on maintaining the Concordat which certain advocates of separation took as an encouragement toward eventual separation. Aulard addressed those on both sides of the issue—those who advocated separation and those who supported the maintenance of the Concordat. In a humorous manner, he named the two groups respectively *Tant-Mieux* and *Tant-Pis* (So Much the Better and Too Bad) to explain the arguments for and against separation. *Tant-Pis* accused Combes of seeking reprisals on the pope stemming from a quarrel on the interpretation of Concordat in the nomination of bishops. *Tant-Pis*

---

42. Bruley, *La séparation*, 82.
43. Bruley, *La séparation*, 83.
44. Combes, *Une campagne laïque*, 168; Bruley, *La séparation*, 97.
45. Combes, *Une campagne laïque*, 170; Bruley, *La séparation*, 98.
46. Aulard, *Polémique et Histoire*, 156–61; Bruley, *La séparation*, 98–103.

supported the Concordat in order to have the means to control the Church with financial support. *Tant-Pis* also feared that a free Church in a free State would soon lead to the Church as mistress and the State as slave.[47] *Tant-Mieux* did not understand how the Church would be freer if the clergy no longer received their salaries from the State and claimed that without State support the Church would no longer have the means to wage war against modern civilization. *Tant-Mieux* had no fear of the loss of diplomatic relations since the pope advises the clergy to take over the Republic to make it a Catholic Republic.[48] *Tant-Pis* concluded that it would be easier to maintain the Concordat. *Tant-Mieux* responded that the Concordat was outdated, that the regime needed to be changed in conformity with principles of the present-day French Republic.[49]

The first serious attempt to enact the Law of Separation took place April 1903 in a proposition by member of Parliament Francis de Pressensé (1853–1914), son of a Protestant pastor. He reiterated the necessity of a complete divorce between civil and religious society and considered that a treaty with a foreign head of a religious community constituted a flagrant exemption to the principle of the neutrality and the laïcité of the State, an attack on the liberty of conscience, and an advantage for recognized religious confessions.[50] In June 1903 a commission was established with the responsibility to study all the propositions on the future Law of Separation. The socialist Aristide Briand (1862–1932) was appointed the official spokesman of the commission. Louis Méjan wrote an account of Briand, future Council President, for whom the Law of Separation marked a decisive turning point in his political career. Méjan described Briand politically as the extreme left of the extreme left.[51] Briand had great political intuition and understood that the battle between the French government and the Holy See would end in separation. His conception of the impending separation won over a parliamentarian majority which led him to leave the Socialist Party and declare himself independent.[52]

Waldeck-Rousseau continued to vigorously oppose Combes in a June 1903 address to the Senate. Combes's government had rejected all the requests for authorization presented by the religious teaching orders and had forced the closure of thousands of religious schools. Waldeck-Rousseau

47. Aulard, *Polémique et Histoire*, 158.

48. Aulard, *Polémique et Histoire*, 159.

49. Aulard, *Polémique et Histoire*, 161.

50. Bruley, *La séparation*, 104.

51. Méjan, *La Séparation*, 90; Bruley, *La séparation*, 105–6.

52. Bruley, *La séparation*, 107.

accused Combes of transforming a law of control into a law of exclusion.[53] He restated his contention that the Law of Associations had taken into consideration the fact that Catholicism throughout the centuries and until the Reformation had the monopoly on education, and held a social status from which few departed. In his speech, Waldeck-Rousseau admired the United States as a young nation and attributed its success to the fact that it did not have to react to theocratic tyranny. The United States was compared to France, an ancient nation with a long history, which had conserved its ancient religious roots. He contended that wounds inflicted on those roots would affect the entire nation, and implored the members of the Senate to not go beyond that which was intended in the Law of Associations.[54]

Anticlericalism and the Vatican

Combes resumed his attacks on the Church in September 1903. At the inauguration of a monument to Renan at Tréguier, Combes claimed to follow the example of Renan and other freethinkers in their refusal to bow before any teaching or to hide their doubts behind any system of belief. He professed his conviction that he and others like him followed the light of reason without desiring to impose their method of reasoning on others. The Catholic priest was caricatured as someone who stands in the pulpit to anathematize those who think differently than him, and was contrasted with freethinkers and their largeness of spirit. Combes assured his audience that he was not attacking religion as such, but rather its ministers who seek to make religion an instrument of domination. He declared that all that was rightfully asked of religion was to enclose itself in its temples, to limit itself to the instruction of the faithful, and to keep from interfering in the civil and political domains. Combes appealed to public opinion which he thought shared his way of thinking. It was suggested that the enemy of religion was not the government, which wanted to separate religion from politics, but religious ministers who, in associating politics and religion, sought to place a despotic hand on both the conscience and the will of the nation.[55] Combes continued his attacks on religion in October 1903 at a festival marking the inauguration of a statue of Vercingetorix at Clermont-Ferrand.[56] The perils against which the nation needed to be defended were enumerated. The first three were royalty, empire, and nationalism. The fourth peril was

53. Bruley, La séparation, 108.
54. Péguy, "Waldeck-Rouseau," 85; Bruley, La séparation, 109–10.
55. Combes, Une campagne laïque, 354–55; Bruley, La séparation, 113–14.
56. Combes, Une campagne laïque, 369; Bruley, La séparation, 115.

clericalism, more threatening than the others, because it dragged in its wake all the opposition parties—royalist, imperialist, and nationalist—without counting a sizeable number of liberal Republicans who understood liberty in the terms of the *Syllabus*.[57]

During a speech at the Vatican to counter the aggressive stance of Combes's government, Pope Pius X inserted himself into the debate in November 1903. He declared it his duty to intervene in matters of power, justice, and equity. This duty extended both to private and public life, to social and political issues, and not only to those who obey but also to those who command. As supreme head of the perfect society, the Church, the pope desired to maintain good relations with princes and governors. Yet he clearly declared that it was necessary that the Church attend to politics and that no one could separate political matters from faith and morals.[58]

Later that same month, Georges Clemenceau reentered the political arena to both denounce the tyranny of a laïque State and to attack Catholics. The context was debate over whether to repeal the Law Falloux of 1850 enacted during the Second Republic. This law had granted greater liberty in primary and secondary school education and had benefited the Catholic Church. Catholics were called citizens of Roman society stuck into French society which found its origins in the Revolution and members of an international corporation in submission to a foreign sovereign. He also recognized the dangers of a laïque State and feared the totalitarian tendencies of socialism. In his speech, the State was described in these words:

> The State, I know well. It has a long history of murder and blood. All the crimes which have taken place in the world—the massacres, the wars, the stakes, the tortures—all have been justified in the interest of the State, for reasons of State. . . . Because I am the enemy of the king, of the emperor and of the pope, I am the enemy of the omnipotent State, the sovereign master of humanity.[59]

Clemenceau then rhetorically asked his audience if they had ever asked themselves why early Christians, who had been persecuted in the circuses, had later managed to pervert the precept to love another into torture, massacres, and the stake. His response was that Christians became victims of an illusion, the same illusion held by politicians, the desire to become the State. According to Clemenceau,

57. Combes, *Une campagne laïque*, 372–73; Bruley, *La séparation*, 116.

58. Bruley, *La séparation*, 117.

59. Clemenceau, "Discours pour la liberté," 42; Bruley, *La séparation*, 117–18.

Christianity was something admirable, one of the most beautiful movements ever seen in the world, until the day that Christians believed that they had found in the State a force for their propaganda. That day, Christianity foundered and has become only an institution of domination by iron and fire. It has been the worst tyranny that the world ever knew, and today, although murmuring words that come from tradition, Catholics aspire to nothing other than to reconquer political power and to refuse to others the liberties they request today, that is, to continue the oppression of the past.[60]

He believed that the true inheritor of conceptions associated with the Roman conquest was none other than the bishop of Rome who had made himself Caesar and took up again the dream of universal domination. Clemenceau's attack on the Church led to the denunciation of the State which, under the pretext of seeking national unity, had proposed changes to the education laws which would grant the State coercive authority. In other words, the nation would escape from the Church only to fall into the arms of the State.[61] Clemenceau declared that the solution was to secularize the nation and liberate it from the ancient Roman theocracy. This solution required the separation of the Church from the State. He hoped to see this separation accomplished in his lifetime, but in such a way that no French person would ever be hindered from attending public worship.[62]

Two of the most eminent archbishops of the Church wrote to President Loubet in January 1904 to protest another law being debated in Parliament, a law which would ban religious institutions responsible for training and providing teachers for private Catholic schools. In their letter, they quoted a supporter in the Senate, Catholic historian Henri Wallon, who declared that it was not peace but a deplorable religious war which ruled at that moment in France and it was the government which started it. The bishops objected to the proposed law which, according to them, had the goal not only to destroy religious teaching congregations in one stroke, but Christian teaching itself. They reminded the government that Catholics had opened private religious schools at their own expense, and they charged the government with wanting to destroy Catholicism in people's souls through antireligious instruction and education.[63]

60. Clemenceau, "Discours pour la liberté," 16; Bruley, *La séparation*, 119.
61. Clemenceau, "Discours pour la liberté," 37; Bruley, *La séparation*, 121–22.
62. Clemenceau, "Discours pour la liberté," 47; Bruley, *La séparation*, 122.
63. Bruley, *La séparation*, 123–24.

Socialist leader Jean Jaurès (1859–1914) pronounced a historical speech on March 3, 1904, in which he justified the proposition of law to ban religious training institutions. He reminded his audience that the law under discussion was the continuation of a policy begun twenty years earlier to provide free, compulsory, and laïque education. The method he chose to defend the proposed law was a survey of French history beginning with the 1789 Revolution which had removed and uprooted all teaching orders.[64] Teaching orders had not only been abolished. They had been removed from the legal system of a new society which proclaimed the incompatibility of the religious principle of subjection with the principle of individual liberty on which the new order was established. He further explained that at the time it had been imagined by some that the priests' preaching would be limited to conciliate the maxims of the gospel and the formulations of the Revolution and to propagate a kind of natural morality under the name of Christianity. He described the harmony between the revolutionary principle of the State and the revolutionary principle of individual liberty and held that human dignity was recovered in the Revolution. He affirmed that the new democratic State no longer laid claim to traditional principles and no longer appealed to a supernatural consecration or to historical legitimacy. The State was defined as an implicit contract of free and equal wills, seeking in its sovereignty the guarantee of their free development.[65] For Jaurès, the proposed law was a law of liberation and respectful of the integrity of the individual in the spirit of the Revolution. The law recognized that religious people had the right to liberty in their spirits and in their consciences, but the education of the State's youngest citizens required teaching that was free from any immutable doctrine or any other obstacle in order to develop the mind free from religion.[66]

Pope Pius X, who had previously asserted the Church's role in politics, once again spoke out to denounce the proposed ban on religious teaching orders. On March 18, 1904, shortly after Jaurès's speech, the pope addressed the cardinals at the Vatican. He expressed his happiness at the expressions of piety of French Catholics and his sadness at the barrage of attacks against the Church through legislative measures. The intention of the proposed law was detailed in forbidding all educational activity by teachers in religious institutions, even in those institutions which had previously been autho-rized. He lamented the fact that children would be educated contrary to the wishes of their parents without faith and without Christian morality, to

64. Bruley, *La séparation*, 125.
65. Bruley, *La séparation*, 126–27.
66. Bruley, *La séparation*, 128–29.

the peril of their souls. The law was seen as the means by which the State could confiscate the property of the Church, confiscations which would result in thousands of religious workers being deprived of their livelihood and resources, and others forced into exile. In the pope's opinion, the law, if enacted, would have the sad consequence of largely destroying Christian teaching, the principal foundation of every civil society.[67]

Events in the winter of 1904 would contribute to a rupture in relations between France and the Holy See. Secretary General Abel Combarieu recounted his recollection of events during this period with personal, eyewitness details.[68] The rupture originated with a voyage to Rome planned by President Émile Loubet. There had been rumors and discussion on whether or not the president would request a meeting with Pope Pius X who, by all accounts, was more traditional and inflexible than his predecessor, and who had defended the rights of the French Church. The president initially signaled his intention to request an audience with the pope. However, the pope tied any proposed visit to the necessity of discussing the expropriation of Vatican lands between 1860–1870 by the Italian government which led successive popes to consider themselves prisoners in the Vatican.[69] The president and the pope were resigned that a meeting might not take place and preoccupied with mitigating the effects of the distance between them. In March 1904 the pope addressed the cardinals at the Vatican and criticized the French government which took offense at the criticisms. With this new level of the deterioration in relations, the president resolved to cease any initiative for an audience, yet left the door open for the pope to indicate his desire for an audience with the president.[70] A stalemate ensued between France and the Vatican that was soon aggravated by the president's voyage which now excluded any audience with the pope.

The president's voyage to Naples and Rome, Italy, took place in April 1904 where he dined with King Victor-Emmanuel III (1869–1947). Together on the palace balcony they responded to the crowd's acclamation. There was the sense that the enthusiastic reception of the French president was not only to honor France, but also a little bit against brutal and domineering Germany, and much against the Vatican. At Naples, a rally was organized for the president at which there were signs posted with the words "*Vive Loubet, viva la Francia anticlericale.*"[71] The Vatican took offense at the presidential

67. Bruley, *La séparation*, 130.

68. Combarieu, *Sept ans à l'Elysée*, 276–82.

69. Bruley, *La séparation*, 134n1.

70. Combarieu, *Sept ans à l'Elysée*, 273; Bruley, *La séparation*, 136.

71. Combarieu, *Sept ans à l'Elysée*, 277–79; Bruley, *La séparation*, 136–37.

rebuff and indicated that a protest would be lodged against the president's visit. Three weeks after President Loubet's voyage to Italy, Rome sent a letter to foreign governments through their diplomatic representatives concerning the French president's visit to Rome. The letter might have remained an affair among diplomats had Jean Jaurès not obtained a copy which he had published in the newspaper *L'Humanité* on May 17.[72] The public revelation of the letter resulted in the recall of the French ambassador from the Holy See, the first major step toward the rupture of diplomatic relations, and the prelude to the Separation. The pope's letter revealed that he considered the French president's trip to Rome and visit with King Victor-Emmanuel III a serious incident over which he took great personal offense. He reminded his readers that Catholic heads of State had special ties with the pope and that government leaders should exercise toward him the same respect accorded to sovereigns of non-Catholic States.[73]

The pope's criticism of the French president and accusation of hostility toward the Vatican would not go unanswered. Jaurès contended that the letter was an insolent provocation to France and Italy. In his view, the pope had not hesitated to accuse the French Republic and its president before other governments. Jaurès further argued that the pope had issued a declaration of war in proclaiming that the king of Italy invited President Loubet to Rome with the intention to humiliate and offend the papacy. This was considered a declaration of war by the papacy on modern Italy and on the Revolution. As a result, Jaurès envisioned the necessity of breaking diplomatic relations between France and the papacy. He declared that the complete emancipation of France, finally rid of all political interference from the Church, now appeared as a national necessity.[74]

Georges Clemenceau joined the denunciation of the pope's letter in an article published May 18, 1904, in the newspaper *L'Aurore* with the title "*La guerre du Pape.*" With strong language he deplored the offensiveness of the letter toward France and Italy, announced that the conciliatory policies of Pope Leo XIII were dead, and that Pius X was a pope of conflict under the influence of a fanatical cardinal. Jaurès's assertion was reaffirmed that war had been declared and challenged the French government to respond in like manner. Clemenceau accused the Church of intransigence while living off the subsidies provided by the State. In his opinion, the subsidies provided the means for the Church to continue its war against the French Republic

---

72. "La Protestation du Pape."

73. Bruley, *La séparation*, 137–38.

74. Bruley, *La séparation*, 141; Jaurès, "La Provocation."

and France now needed to enter resolutely in the supreme battle of the Revolution against theocracy.[75]

Many politicians, particularly those of the extreme Left, clamored for an immediate termination of the Concordat following the publication of the pope's letter. Aristide Briand resisted acting rashly. He believed that the entire French Church should not suffer for the act committed by one man and that thoughtless action might be perceived as aggression against Catholics. In his speech before the Chamber, he called for a democratic debate, yet recognized that the conflict with the Vatican made clear in everyone's eyes the incompatibility which existed between the traditional Church and the democratic State. This incident presented the opportunity to liberate the State from all religious influence. In other words, liberation was now possible through these circumstances to break all resistance to the laicization of the State and the realization of confessional neutrality. Briand aligned himself clearly with those advancing the idea of a complete separation of Church and State. However, he comprehended the complexity of the problem and appealed to his fellow politicians to remain calm and exercise self-control.[76]

The pope's letter and its repercussions were followed by several conflicts which further strained relations between France and the Vatican. The conflicts were related to accusations against two French bishops known as "l'affaire des évêques."[77] These incidents are considered an important prelude to the separation of Church and State. In the first incident, the bishop of Laval was accused of an unspecified moral issue in contradiction to his vows. In the second incident, the bishop of Dijon was accused of being a Freemason. Correspondence was sent to the bishop of Laval from the Vatican advising the bishop's resignation. The correspondence violated the Concordat since it was not sent through proper governmental channels. The bishop turned for counsel to Combes, the Minister of Religions. Combes told the bishop that he did not have to obey the cardinal who sent the letter and informed the bishop that orders from the Vatican had no value. When the Vatican was challenged for this violation of the Concordat, the cardinal responded that he was giving advice, not an order. The French government considered this a typical, slippery response from Rome.

The matter might have been dropped except that the bishop of Dijon was threatened by a letter sent directly from the papal nuncio. On the pope's orders, the bishop was told that he needed to cease certain ministry functions and could not proceed with any ordinations in his diocese. The

75. Bruley, *La séparation*, 141–43; Clemenceau, "La guerre du Pape."
76. Bruley, *La séparation*, 143–45.
77. Bruley, *La séparation*, 146–49; "L'affaire des évêques."

French government viewed in this incident a double infraction to terms of the Concordat. The contentiousness continued when the bishop of Laval received a second letter which ordered his immediate departure for Rome under penalty of the loss of his episcopal authority. The bishop was then ordered by Combes to remain in France. The Vatican was given an ultimatum to immediately withdraw the incriminating letters under penalty of immediate rupture of diplomatic relations. There were suspicions that the pope would not yield, that the rupture of diplomatic relations would take place, and that the Concordat would be terminated.[78] The stage was being set for the final separation.

On August 2, 1904, Jean Jaurès published a speech in L'Humanité which he had given several days earlier. In the speech, he twice stated that democracy and laïcité were identical.[79] According to him, democracy assured complete and necessary freedom for all consciences, for all beliefs, for all religions, but no dogma becomes the rule and the foundation of social life. Jaurès explained that democracy did not require a newborn to belong to any confession, did not require citizens to belong to any religion to guarantee their rights, and did not ask the citizen to which religion he belongs, if any, when he votes. His conclusion was that if democracy was founded outside of all religious systems or religious institutions, if democracy was guided without any dogmatic or supernatural intervention, if democracy did not expect progress except from the progress of conscience and science, then it would be laïque in its essence and in its forms. The corollary to this reasoning was that education must be constituted on laïque foundations.[80] Later that month, on August 15, Jaurès published an article in La Dépêche du Midi maintaining that it was time for the problems between the Church and the State to be finally resolved. For the first time a timeframe was proposed for a vote on separation early in 1905. The separation would not be decided until December 1905, but the direction of the government and the urgency of action became clear.[81]

Impending Separation Announced

A speech considered decisive in movement toward separation was given by Council President Émile Combes in September 1904. He declared that the religious authorities had torn up the Concordat and he did not intend to

78. Bruley, La séparation, 147.

79. Bruley, La séparation, 149; Jaurès, "L'enseignement laïque."

80. Bruley, La séparation, 150–51.

81. Bruley, La séparation, 153.

patch it up.[82] It was made clear that his understanding of the political system consisted of the subordination of all bodies, of all institutions, whatever they may be, to the supremacy of the republican and laïque State, and in the end, the complete secularization of society. Combes explained the opposition the government had faced in the past seeking to achieve this goal. The year 1870 was invoked when the Republic had put an end to the Second Empire and he believed it was now the duty of the Republic to put an end to any dependence on religious authority. The opposition to the Republic was enumerated that had come from royalists, Bonapartists, nationalists who prostituted patriotism, and from clericals who he considered the most insidious and the most to be feared by all. He considered that when he and his party arrived in power, they found France invaded and partly conquered by religious orders. The Law of Associations had been a first step to free the nation from their control. It was claimed that of 16,904 religious teaching institutions, almost 14,000 had been closed, and Combes expected 500 more of the almost 3,000 which remained to be closed in 1905. He reiterated that he entered office with the sincere wish to maintain the Concordat but that the Church had routinely violated its terms. For the past century, according to Combes, the French State and the Church lived under a Concordat regime which never produced its natural and legal effects and had only been an instrument of combat and domination.[83]

The French government warned the Vatican of the serious consequences for continued violation of the Concordat, called on the Vatican to respect the treaty, and demanded that the Vatican confirm whether or not it would submit itself to the obligations of the Concordat as the government had.[84] When the government received no response from the Vatican, Combes informed the Vatican that diplomatic relations were broken and expressed his wish that the separation of Church and the State inaugurate a new and lasting era of social harmony in guaranteeing genuine liberty to religious communities under the uncontested sovereignty of the State. One final question was raised regarding France's position as protector of Christians in the Orient. Combes, however, did not consider this a significant problem. In a speech met with great applause and general approval, he explained that it was true that in the past, during a time of religious belief, France had placed great value on the idea of the Protectorate. Yet, he was convinced there were motives other than religious for which France had taken upon herself this glorious privilege which had sometimes been

82. Combes, "La Politique du Ministère."

83. Bruley, La séparation, 157–59.

84. Bruley, La séparation, 160.

more embarrassing than glorious. He asserted that France with her naval and military power had honorably discharged this duty and emphasized that the times had changed:

> We no longer have the same pretensions in respect to being the eldest daughter of the Church [*la Fille aînée de l'Église*], of which the monarchy made for itself a subject of pride, and we have the absolute conviction that our esteem and our influence depend today exclusively on our material power as well as on the principles of honor, of justice, and of human solidarity, which have value for modern France, heir of the great social principles of the Revolution.[85]

The State no longer wished to be the protector of the Orient and did not consider this issue as a hindrance to the forthcoming separation. Further, the State refused to endure more humiliation from the Church.

One notable minority Protestant voice was raised to challenge the idea of separation of churches rather than the separation of the Church in the singular. Historian Gabriel Monod (1844–1912) conceived the separation as a separation of the Catholic Church and the State. Protestant churches and the Jewish community were considered already separated from the State and a distinction was made between the Catholic Church of the Concordat and non-concordataire churches which did not have the same status. The separation was envisioned as taking place in a spirit of hostility and was the fault of both the Church and the State. He expressed his concern that the Catholic Church freed from the Concordat and in a sovereign State might continue to aspire to dominate society. For Monod, the very nature of the Catholic Church obligated it to aspire to direct all areas of public and private life. It was recognized that the State had been obligated unceasingly to wage resurgent warfare against the pretensions of the Church to usurp civil power. He clearly identified himself as a supporter of separation as necessary for a laïque State. Yet he was troubled by the rapidity of the prospect and noted with regret that most great changes in society had been accompanied by violence and disorder. Catholic pretensions, however, made an amical agreement difficult. The wish was expressed that the separation imposed on the Church would not be oppressive and that the Church would be allowed to freely organize itself.[86]

Albert de Mun (1841–1914), a Catholic deputy who had accepted *le Ralliement* of Pope Leo XIII in 1882, responded to a *Le Figaro* survey and

---

85. Bruley, *La séparation*, 162.

86. Bruley, *La séparation*, 163–67.

opposed the separation of Church and State.[87] As a staunch Catholic, he regarded the proposed law as contrary to the teaching of the Church. As a Frenchman, he deemed the law in absolute opposition to all the tradition of the ancient Catholic nation, and in consequence, destined to lead the nation to real interior and exterior decline. The separation was characterized as a divorce pronounced by the State for its own profit. There was fear that the separation would lead to persecution against the Catholic religion which had already suffered from the forced closure of religious teaching orders. Religious war was envisioned as a consequence of the law and the certitude expressed that in the end the State and the Church would need to enact another treaty. In the meantime, Mun exhorted Catholics to remain firm and to begin preparation for sacrifices required in a separation which was a mirage of liberty.[88]

A parliamentary storm began churning on October 28, 1904, which would lead to the downfall of Combes's government. A project of law on the proposed separation was adopted by the government's Council of Ministers which was contrary in some important points to the version proposed by the parliamentary commission. The major difference which surfaced was related to ecclesiastical properties. The commission recognized the difference between church properties built on state property and subsidized by the government and those built on land donated to the Church or bought with funds from church members. The former were declared property of the State or commune, the latter property of churches. The government's proposal made no distinction between these two types of properties. If the State retained ownership and control over church properties, there was fear that the State would continue to interfere in the administration of those properties. Another major issue was the organization of religious bodies. The commission's project proposed the authorization of national unions of religious bodies; the government's proposal sought to limit these unions to departmental boundaries in France. These issues would be at the heart of the debates to follow.[89]

The reactions to the government's proposal were swift. L. V. Méjan, among the first to respond, considered the government's text antireligious and contrary to liberty. Other Protestants were mobilized, in particular Protestant theology professor Raoul Allier, to write a series of articles which would have a great impact in shaping public opinion, and which have become an important source of the history of the Separation.

87. Bruley, *La séparation*, 167–69; Mun, "La séparation."
88. Mun, *Contre la séparation*, 62–64; Bruley, *La séparation*, 167–69.
89. Bruley, *La séparation*, 172–74.

Protestants viewed the project as harmful for Protestant churches, a project which for them would result in a new wave of persecution in forbidding their national unity by an official text.[90] Two Jewish rabbis weighed
in with their perspective on the proposed document. Rabbi Zadoc Kahn
(1839–1905) expressed his reservations on ending the Concordat. The history of Napoleon I was recounted, to whom Jews owed their existence as
a national religious entity. The reference was to 1831 when Jewish rabbis
gained equality with Catholic clergy in receiving salaries from the State.
The main concern was that the government maintained the unity of the
Jewish confession and authority over all the consistories and communities.[91] There was the fear that the abrogation of the Concordat would lead
to a crisis where national unity would be threatened. Rabbi J. Lehmann,
director of the Jewish seminary, expressed his concern for religious edifices
and religious traditions. Reference was made to the law of 1806, five years
after the Concordat, when the Jewish religion received official recognition. He further referenced the law of 1831 which assured the dignity and
the independence of ministers, but especially consecrated the principle of
religious equality. With only one hundred thousand Jewish adherents in
France and in French territories, the desire was conveyed to continue to
live peacefully under current laws as a minority religion.[92]

The bishop of Nancy, Monseigneur Turinaz (1838–1918), explained to
a journalist the reasons for which the Church would fight against the project of separation. Two projects were compared from the commission and
the government, Briand and Combes respectively, and Briand's project was
considered the least harsh of the two. Separation was preferable to present
hostilities. If it had to happen, Turinaz wished it would not take place according to the proposed conditions. Yet, he preferred the union of powers
for the happiness of the country. The possibility of the State taking over the
property of churches was disconcerting and appeared unjust. He spoke about
a church building which had been built at Nancy with voluntary gifts. The
bishop feared the State would take it without indemnification. The article
concluded in affirming that the form of government was unimportant to him
and that he did not fault the Republic. His opposition was toward governmental decrees and actions done in the name of the Republic.[93]

Public opinion included a Marxist point of view presented by Paul Lafargue (1842–1911), son-in-law of Karl Marx. Lafargue completely supported

---

90. Bruley, *La séparation*, 175–77; Allier, "A propos de la Séparation."
91. Bruley, *La séparation*, 176–78.
92. Allier, "L'Enquête du Siècle," 267.
93. Bruley, *La séparation*, 181–82.

the abrogation of the Concordat and the proposed separation of Church and State. He believed that the Church would be impacted in its prestige and economically. The brusque or progressive removal of the religious budget was advocated to complete the work which began in France with the Revolution. The idea was refuted that State subsidies for religious institutions and salaries for the clergy were the nation's debt to the clergy for confiscations of property and possessions during the Revolution. Lafargue claimed that it was not the nation, but the bourgeoisie which had dismembered and cornered for themselves the lands of the Church and that the revolutionary bourgeoisie, in seizing the possessions of the clergy, had only robbed the robbers. Christianity was described as a constitutional illness which the bourgeoisie had in its blood. He lamented that the revolutionaries of 1789, in the ardor of the battle, had pressed on too quickly in their promise to dechristianize France, and the bourgeoisie was victorious.[94]

Anatole France published *L'Église et la République* in January 1905 at the time Parliament was beginning its deliberations on the project of separation. In chapter 8 he raised and responded affirmatively to the question, "Must the State separate from the Church?" It was argued that the progress of civilization in nations determined a clear distinction between civil and religious spheres. In primitive societies, the priest was king. As they continued their development, people broke the bonds of theocracy which gripped them in their infancy. He considered that the pope had great power in France since most people no longer knew what a pope was. The Concordat was seen as a danger for the State since the State no longer knew what the Concordat was.[95] He related a story from his childhood when he was questioned about his religion for a census. France initially responded that he did not belong to any religion. The census taker prodded him to choose a religion anyway so the form would be complete. When France announced that he was Buddhist, the perplexed census worker replied that there were only three columns to choose from and Buddhist was not among them. For France, that response indicated that the State only recognized three forms of the divine and he regarded as unjust the fact that citizens had to subsidize a religion they did not practice. In reality, due to the Concordat, the laïque State believed and professed the Catholic, Apostolic, and Roman religion.[96]

Émile Combes resigned in January 1905 and was not able to see his project of separation come to term. Combes's resignation was connected to a scandal related to the War Minister, General André, and reports of

94. Bruley, *La séparation*, 183–84.
95. France, *L'Église et la République*, 91–93.
96. France, *L'Église et la République*, 99.

investigations and files documenting the political opinions of officers with information received from Freemasons.[97] A new government formed under Maurice Rouvier (1842–1911) and continued the march toward separation.[98] L. V. Méjan continued his documentation of the parliamentary commission's work and sensed that many proponents of separation sought a law which would be a decisive weapon in the anticlerical and anticatholic struggle.[99] The commission listened to many views on separation in seeking the most suitable solutions in order to confer all liberties and independence compatible with the rights of the State and public order. Since the Vatican opposed any reform or changes in the status of the Church in France, a considerable and often decisive power for action was given to sociologists, Jews, and especially Protestants. Protestants found themselves at the forefront of efforts to fight in the name of all churches. This influence included weekly articles by the Protestant Raoul Allier, which along with other publications, pursued the task to militate for a law as judicious and as liberal as possible.[100]

Confrontations in Parliament

The parliamentary commission, formed in 1903 and presided over by Ferdinand Buisson, adopted the project of law presented by the deputy Aristide Briand on March 4, 1905. The law moved to the next phase with further debate and opposition by those who continued to defend the necessity of maintaining the Concordat.[101] At the first deliberative session, a motion was made by deputy George Berry (1855–1915) to table the debate. Berry was described as a monarchist who rallied to the Republic and opposed the anticlerical politics of Combes. His speech was interrupted several times by partisans of separation. The Chamber of Deputies was reminded of the responsibility they were taking upon themselves to vote on this project of law without the consent of the people. The Chamber was accused of carrying out an antidemocratic project. It was argued that to deprive the Church of subsidies would have the greatest detrimental impact on the poor who could not provide for their places of worship. The effects of the separation which would strike the unfortunate were decried and would lead to disturbances of the peace in society.[102] He considered the Concordat as a peace

97. Bruley, *La séparation*, 172; Combarieu, *Sept ans à l'Élysée*, 297–98.

98. Bruley, *La séparation*, 191.

99. Méjan, *La Séparation*, 74–75.

100. Bruley, *La séparation*, 193.

101. Bruley, *La séparation*, 194.

102. Bruley, *La séparation*, 201–3.

treaty and claimed that all nations had found a way to live in peace with the papacy. The speech concluded with the warning that although not all Catholics followed the rites of their religion in an absolute way, that did not make them less wholehearted Catholics. It was feared that the day the State attacked their families, their wives, and their children in their religious devotion, they would become more Catholic than ever resulting in a revival of the Catholic faith in France.[103]

Aristide Briand responded immediately to Berry and reminded the Chamber of the incident concerning President Loubet's visit to Rome and the pope's response which initiated the diplomatic crisis. It was further asserted that Rome had never really acknowledged the terms of the Concordat and that the doctrine of the Church made it impossible for the Church to do so. Briand compared the present Pope Pius X with Pope Leo XIII. He considered that Pope Leo XIII had been reasonable and diplomatic and had known how to deal wisely with issues which arose during his reign. Pope Pius X was characterized as enamored with religious absolutism which made the rupture inevitable.[104]

Acrimonious interchanges among deputies continued that day with a second motion to stay the deliberations in order to negotiate with the Church. The motion was made by Abbot Hippolyte Gayraud (1856–1911) who had entered the Chamber as a Catholic Republican and was actively involved in religious educational issues. His speech demonstrated that the Church could not accept the diminution of its authority. Gayraud contended that this was the most important debate on religion since 1789 and articulated the Church's position regarding the separation of Church and State and the ideal of the union of civil and religious society. Another deputy, François Fournier, interrupted and interjected that this ideal union was in reality the domination of the pope and that the Church had never been at peace with civil power. Gayraud contended that the Concordat never was the faithful expression of Catholic doctrine in the rapports between the two powers. In the Concordat, the Church was recognized, not as the true religion—that which it was in their eyes—but simply as the religion of the majority of French people.[105] Gayraud reiterated the terms of the Concordat by which the government nominated bishops and through which priests were controlled by the government. He bemoaned the fact that the State had turned the Church into a beggar. Fournier riposted that this was a criticism of the Concordat and urged Gayraud to repudiate the Concordat. Gayraud

103. Bruley, *La séparation*, 209.
104. Bruley, *La séparation*, 211.
105. Bruley, *La séparation*, 212–13.

countered that the manner in which the Concordat had been applied, especially in recent times, had made it an instrument of oppression against the Church and against Catholic consciences.[106]

In Gayraud's opinion, the wisest solution to the present situation was to reconnect with the Holy See and return faithfully to the loyal and sincere practice of the Concordat. When he asked the Chamber if their goal was to destroy Catholicism in France, there were denials from the Left and insistence that they in no way sought to trammel the liberty of conscience of any religious confession. The assurances of the Left were unsatisfactory and Gayraud exclaimed that the great majority would not dare to respond clearly and frankly that they wanted to destroy Catholicism, wipe out religion, and hinder the liberty of conscience. The Right supported his call for a preliminary agreement with the Church and concurred with his historical references demonstrating that since the Revolution the government had always sought the advice of the Church. Fournier interrupted Gayraud with an ironic reference to the State seeking advice from the Church for the Revocation of the Edict of Nantes.[107] When Gayraud affirmed that the proposed laws of separation would never be accepted by Catholics or by the Church, a deputy from the Left responded that it was a declaration of war.[108] In alluding to the 1901 Law of Associations, Gayraud insisted that Catholics would never accept such laws and that above the laws of governments, there was the law of God and the liberty of Catholic consciences. The Right supported him with frequent applause and the Left opposed him with noisy outbursts. One deputy attacked Gayraud in saying that since Catholics obeyed only the pope, they were not good French citizens. In response Gayraud concluded that the separation of Church and the State, such as it was presented in the project of law, was an act of hostility against Catholics, not a project of liberty but a declaration of war.[109]

As deliberations continued, deputy Denys Cochin (1851–1922), in defense of the Concordat, requested permission to defend the church to which he belonged. Tyranny was defined as the confusion of two powers in the same hand and had its beginnings in England with Henry VIII (1491–1547) and kings who wanted to be popes and had mixed civil and religious powers. Cochin spoke glowingly of the United States where Catholics, Protestants, Israelites, freethinkers coming from old Europe had lived together and had

106. Bruley, *La séparation*, 214.
107. Bruley, *La séparation*, 215–16.
108. Bruley, *La séparation*, 217.
109. Bruley, *La séparation*, 219–20.

worked together for the prosperity of the new world.[110] The Concordat was seen as an instrument of peace between Church and State, a peace that had lasted for one hundred years, and a peace that should be maintained rather than risk the prospect of violence and exclusions if the law passed.[111] Alexandre Ribot (1842–1923), deputy from Pas-de-Calais, took a position against the Law of Separation.[112] He considered that in many respects the separation had already been accomplished. Under the Concordat, clergy were salaried by the State and were not allowed to participate in politics or meddle in elections. The termination of the Concordat would change that and the deputy wondered out loud if the nation was ready for this. He argued that the fact that the State subsidized clergy salaries did nothing to affect the independence of the State vis-à-vis the Church. His claim that the clergy were patriotic was met with a response that they were in fact Roman patriots. Negotiations with the Vatican were urged to discuss the terms of the separation. Lastly, he regretted that in France there was no longer a profound respect for religious beliefs or for the religious conscience and that there was now a kind of State irreligion which asserted itself and stood against the Catholic religion.[113]

One of the major issues faced by the Parliament was the disposition of religious edifices. Amendments had been proposed to allow churches to freely retain their properties for an undetermined period. There were reactions against those amendments by the anticlericals. Jean Codet (1852–1920) was deputy and later senator of Haute-Vienne. In his speech on March 21, 1905, he spoke of two societies which had existed side by side for a century, a clerical society based on the doctrines of the Church, and a laïque society, inspired instead by eighteenth-century philosophers and the principles of the Declaration of the Rights of Man and the Citizen of 1789. According to him, these two societies, founded on contrary doctrines, were engaged in combat and headed toward a divorce. The Church was accused of violating the Concordat which had already been torn apart by the Church. The one remaining scrap was the obligation of the State to pay a clergy which had become more and more Roman. For Codet, the rupture was necessary and inevitable and needed to be voted on. An advocate of the freedom of thought, he could allow anyone the liberty to believe and to practice and would vote to approve the project of separation without hesitation.[114]

110. Bruley, *La séparation*, 223–25.

111. Bruley, *La séparation*, 226–27.

112. Bruley, *La séparation*, 229–35.

113. Bruley, *La séparation*, 231.

114. Bruley, *La séparation*, 237–39.

Several speeches were made in Parliament on March 27, 1904, as deputies presented their arguments for or against the Law of Separation. Charles Benoist (1861–1936), deputy from Paris, took up the defense of religious teaching orders and opposed the Law of Separation.[115] He gave two reasons for which the Concordat needed to be maintained. The first reason concerned what was in the best interests for both Church and State:

> It is not in the interest of the State that the Church be abso-
> lutely independent; it is not in the interest of the Church that
> the State be absolutely master. Further, it is not in the interest of
> the Church to be absolutely independent; it is not in the inter-
> est of the State to be absolutely master. It is in the interest of
> both to discuss, to negotiate, and to mark out reciprocally their
> boundaries.[116]

The second reason was simply because as far as separation was really possible, it already existed. The Church and the State each fulfilled their own functions and no longer lived in the time when cardinals were ministers of State. The State had become perfectly laïque, completely secularized and there was no reason for a law to accomplish what was already a reality. If there was to be a separation it needed to be accomplished by the Church and the State together; otherwise the arbitrary authority of the State might lead to a police State. The 1801 Concordat was considered a sufficient act of separation. If the State voted the Law of Separation, which shared the same thinking as the repressive 1790 Civil Constitution of the Clergy, he warned that all roads lead to Rome, and predicted that the State would return there.[117]

Benoist was followed by the socialist Alexandre Bourson (1873–1953), deputy of Isère, described as a militant and anticlerical Dreyfusard. He alleged that the Catholic Church was locked in a battle against the laïque and social aspirations of the modern world and that the war of the Church against contemporary society, far from having been mitigated or pacified by the Concordat, had become constant.[118] For Bourson, the Church had never wanted to accommodate itself to the principles proclaimed by the Revolution in a society that since 1789 was no longer based on any dogma or religion. It was affirmed that in the Republic all were equal, all had the same rights, whether religious or with no religion, and that in a society founded on the very principle of laïcité and on the indifference of the State regarding all religions, all religious ideas could have a place. However, what was unacceptable

115. Bruley, *La séparation*, 239–45.
116. Bruley, *La séparation*, 242.
117. Bruley, *La séparation*, 243–45.
118. Bruley, *La séparation*, 245–46.

was that one religion enjoy a right, a particular privilege, and occupy a preponderant place in the State. These remarks were received enthusiastically by the Left and Extreme Left. He concluded that in the past century the State had laicized marriage, the family, institutions, and education. The hour had now come to proceed to the laicization of the State by this great reform, for which all the effort of the republican democracy was committed, and which was called the separation of Church and State.[119]

Boni de Castellane (1867–1932), described as an aristocrat, Antidreyfusard, and Catholic, was deputy of the Basses-Alpes and married to the wealthy American, Anna Gould. He opposed the project of the Law of Separation which he regarded as a project for the destruction of the Catholic Church by the State. The attempts of the French government to destroy the liberty of belief under the guise of separation were contrasted to the United States where the American democracy was not mixed with the divine. With strong words he accused the State of mutilating itself by recalling its governmental representative from Rome and of wanting to destroy the Church by the oppression of an enemy State. His final warning was that after this war declared against God, France would still be in danger.[120]

On April 8, 1905, one of the liveliest debates took place which captures the atmosphere of the debates and shows how the argumentation over the separation of Church and State led to debate on other burning issues connected with separation—education, morality, and faith.[121] Paul Perroche (1845–1917), deputy of the Marne, did not belong to any political formation and opposed the Law of Separation. He came to the defense of rural agriculturalists whose churches would suffer from the loss of government subsidies to the Church. A deputy from the Extreme Left mocked Perroche's constituents as "*bouilleurs de cru*" (moonshiners). Perroche predicted that if the separation took place religion would become a luxury that only those in cities and large towns would be able to procure. It was pointed out that even those on the Left still respected religious traditions and called upon the Church to bless their marriages, attend to the dying, and pray for the dead and that even the most indifferent wanted their children to receive moral instruction from the clergy that the laïque schools could not offer. Perroche was interrupted by another deputy who protested that these last remarks wounded him and exclaimed that his own children did not know any priests, had never been baptized, and were as moral as any other children.[122]

119. Bruley, La séparation, 247–48.
120. Bruley, La séparation, 249–50.
121. Bruley, La séparation, 251–55.
122. Bruley, La séparation, 252.

Perroche expressed his fears concerning laïque schools and contended that these schools were not neutral. He quoted from a document which a primary school supervisor had circulated among teachers. The document allegedly stated that the goal of the laïque school was not to teach to read, to write, and to count but was a war machine against Catholicism with the goal to train freethinkers. Perroche then criticized the State monopoly on education and stated that the laïque school was a mold in which one tosses a Christian's son and from which a renegade emerged.[123] His assertions were met with protests from the Left and support from the Right and Center. The authenticity of the document he quoted was questioned and he responded with the number and the date of the journal. Jean Jaurès interrogated Perroche on the word "renegade" he had used in order to know if that was how he considered former believers who changed their opinions to become freethinkers. Perroche concluded with an illustration from his experience, which was mocked as irrelevant, of a child who had written on the blackboard at school. The student wrote, "I believe in God," and the teacher wrote below, "I believe only in pretty women."[124]

Final Debates on the Modalities of Separation

By the spring of 1905 there was little doubt that the Law of Separation would succeed. The voices of opposition to the law and defenders of the Concordat remained in the minority. Their impassioned pleas were to no avail in a parliament controlled by the Left. The law would be voted. What remained were the details and the modalities of the law. One major question resurfaced concerning church properties belonging to religious confessions. Edifices constructed before the Concordat were considered property of the State. Edifices constructed after the Concordat became the subject of debate. Some of these edifices were built from the voluntary offerings of the faithful on property donated by cities or communes. Other edifices were constructed on property owned by churches but with financial aid from their localities. There were some politicians who sought the confiscation of all church property. There were others who saw confiscation as an injustice that would be remembered for generations. Voices of moderation arose to consider arrangements under which churches might retain their properties or at least retain the right to use these properties in perpetuity.

Paul Deschanel (1855–1922), deputy of Eure-et-Loir and future president of the Republic, was one of the most prominent voices of moderation.

123. Bruley, *La séparation*, 253.
124. Bruley, *La séparation*, 254–55.

On March 23, 1905, he pronounced a lengthy speech in which he argued for a broad interpretation of the Law of Separation to allow churches to retain their properties or the use thereof. He contended that the current debate, in putting aside the centuries-old mode of regulating relations between the Catholic Church and the State, and creating a new model, was the most serious debate since the Revolution. The manner in which the spiritual and the temporal were mixed was compared to the situation in the Islamic world. He asserted that the interference of religion in politics was detestable and corrupted both politics and religion and that a State invaded and subjugated by clerical power was condemned to perish. Mme. De Staël (1766–1817) was evoked who had expressed the wish of the French at that time to experience religious liberty as in America. Instead of religious liberty the nation was given the Concordat to fulfill the dream of Napoleon. The result was the clergy in the hands of the bishops, the bishops in the hands of the pope, the pope in the hands of the emperor.[125]

Deschanel admitted that the wish to prolong indefinitely the existence of a treaty, while all the circumstances which accompanied its appearance had been completely modified, would be an impossible challenge. He also maintained that it would be unworthy of France to make this great work an act of reprisals. The separation was necessary. However, whether the separation was good for all or a detestable adventure depended on the spirit in which it was done.[126] Religious liberty required that churches have the freedom to organize according to their teaching. The Vatican, under which the Catholic Church was guided spiritually, needed to assume the material and financial responsibility for the French Church. He closed his speech in calling the Revocation of the Edict of Nantes in 1685, decided at Versailles in the shadows without discussion, one of the greatest crimes ever committed against human conscience. The remarks were met by great applause throughout the Chamber. His fellow deputies were called upon to act in such a way that France, after the inevitable difficulties of those last hours, finally delivered from confessional battles which devoured and humiliated the nation, might give herself completely to the great works of life on which her power and her glory depended.[127]

Louis Barthou (1862–1934), deputy of the Basses-Pyrenees and anticlerical, spoke in support of the proposed Law of Separation on March 28, 1905.[128] He considered that the political provocations of the papacy had

125. Bruley, *La séparation*, 258–59.
126. Bruley, *La séparation*, 261.
127. Bruley, *La séparation*, 279.
128. Bruley, *La séparation*, 270–72.

made separation necessary. Nonetheless, he opposed what he perceived as the intolerance of the radicals. He preferred that the separation take place in a climate of tranquility and predicted that the rejection of the Law of Separation would entail the defeat of the Republican party. There was a clear refusal to entertain the restoration of diplomatic relations with the Vatican which would be a confession of powerlessness and an abdication of responsibility on the part of the government. His speech concluded in affirming the necessity of the separation of Church and the State following the example of the separation of the Church and the school. In these separations, he envisioned the fulfillment of the work of secularization begun at the Revolution, the Republic free of all confessional domination and tutelage.[129]

The task of summarizing the preceding discussions on the project of the Law of Separation and preparing for a parliamentary vote fell to Jean-Baptiste Bienvenu-Martin (1847–1943), deputy of Yonne, Freemason, current Minister of Religions, and founder of the radical, socialist Left.[130] In his remarks, he expressed the necessity of the abrogation of the Concordat since the Chamber had already voted for the rupture of diplomatic relations with the Vatican. One day earlier, Alexandre Ribot had invoked the necessity of negotiation with Rome on the conditions of separation. Bienvenu-Martin argued that the Church would never resign itself to separation without conditions that the State would judge unacceptable. He agreed with Louis Barthou that any negotiation with Rome would be an act of humiliation and that the government was not prepared to lower itself to that level. Bienvenu-Martin cited a recent pastoral letter from the bishop of Marseilles in which the bishop stated that there was not and there could never be a laïque State.[131]

The principle elements of the proposed Law of Separation were discussed. The first principle was that of the liberty of religion. Bienvenu-Martin charged that the Catholic party understood this principle in only one way in wanting liberty for itself but not for other religions. Further elaboration was provided by the Minister concerning regulations in the current penal code. The penal code sanctioned anyone allowing their house to be used for public worship without municipal authorization and forbade the opening of new places of worship without governmental authorization.[132] The Minister made the pledge that not only would no existing churches be closed, but that new ones would be granted the freedom to open without

129. Bruley, *La séparation*, 271–72.
130. Bruley, *La séparation*, 273–80.
131. Bruley, *La séparation*, 274.
132. Bruley, *La séparation*, 276.

any administrative authorization. The State intended to eliminate the official organization of religion and its character of public service which would require the removal of clergy remuneration after a period of transition. At the end of his speech, the Minister addressed the question concerning church edifices which were regarded as not belonging to Catholics. If they were cathedrals, they belonged to the State, or to the commune if local parishes. In his opinion, if Catholics furnished money to build churches, it was not so much as Catholics but as taxpayers. The assertion that most churches built after the Concordat were constructed largely with funds from the State and communes was loudly contested by some from the Right. The Minister was unmoved by the protestations and concluded that the great majority of churches were the property of communes and considered that the Law of Separation must respect this property.[133]

At this point in the parliamentary debates, there was little doubt that there were sufficient votes to approve the Law of Separation. The general discussion had closed. Albert de Mun, Catholic and adversary of the law, described the atmosphere of the Chamber as resigned to the "folly that everyone perceived, that everyone admitted in the halls."[134] Now it came down to the question of modifications and amendments to the law as presented by the commission led by Aristide Briand. The amendments came from the Left and the Right. The battle lines were clearly drawn. Some on the Left wanted the law to go further in suppressing the influence and prestige of the Church. Some on the Right sought to mitigate certain provisions and allow the State to continue providing funding for the Church.

One of the most vocal and articulate politicians on the Left was Maurice Allard (1860–1942), socialist deputy from the Var, who proposed a hostile alternate project of law. He did not mince his words or hide his intentions in affirming that for him separation meant nothing less than the lessening of the malignancy of the Church and of religions. He claimed to speak for Republicans who for thirty years had decided that the Church was a political and social danger that had to be fought in any way possible. The criticism was proffered that at a decisive moment Parliament would offer the Church a liberal project which was only a new regime of privilege to adopt in favor of the Church. It was maintained that the articles of the law as presented by the commission would not produce the separation he envisaged, a separation which would leave the Church broken, crumbled, dispersed, and left to its own forces. The goal of his alternative project of law was defined—that religion would become the abnormal thing and that nonreligion become

133. Bruley, *La séparation*, 277–79.
134. Mun, *Contre la séparation*, 199; Bruley, *La séparation*, 283–84.

the normal thing—in order to dechristianize the nation. Christianity was described as a permanent obstacle to the social development of the Republic and to all progress toward civilization, and as an insult to reason and to nature.[135] The idea of dechristianization was viewed as the work begun at the Revolution, interrupted by Napoleon, and in need of fulfillment. His words about Jesus provide remarkable insight into the antagonism toward religion as motivation to enact the separation of the Church and State and rid France of all religion:

> The day when the anthropomorphic god of the Jews left the shores of Jordan to conquer the Mediterranean world, civilization disappeared from the Mediterranean basin, and we should thank the Roman emperors who battled with all their forces the invasion of this childish and barbaric philosophy, and we should thank Julian the Apostate who marshaled all his efforts to combat this plague. . . . When Christianity left Rome and Greece, where it had smothered all civilization and where it left only ruins and rubble, and arrived in France, there existed in our country neither art, nor literature, and especially no science. . . . Under the influence of Judeo-Christianity all light disappeared; there was now only darkness.[136]

Many socialists did not go as far in their invective against the Church and religion although agreeing in principle with the sentiments. Édouard Vaillant (1840–1915), socialist deputy from the Seine, defended Allard's project of law which would treat the Church more harshly. In his opinion, the Church separated from the State would be like any other association supported by its members. The Concordat was deemed an obstacle to social democracy and the emancipation of the working class, and the Church was an instrument of error and moral domination for the profit of the upper class. He expressed his conviction that as long as the Church did not entirely disappear, as long as the laicization of society was not achieved, the task would not be accomplished.[137]

Aristide Briand, spokesman for the parliamentary commission, responded to the alternative project of law proposed by the group of socialists. In the end, the alternative project received only 68 votes in favor with 494 opposed. Briand called the proposal of Allard a project of elimination of churches by the State and warned that Allard turned toward the State in his haste to be done with religion. He protested that this project was not in

135. Bruley, *La séparation*, 285–87.

136. Bruley, *La séparation*, 288.

137. Bruley, *La séparation*, 289–91.

line with his own free-thinker conceptions of separation and called upon the parliament to resist the desire to make the Law of Separation a show of anticlericalism. Briand was convinced that in Allard's alternative project of law, he had sought an occasion before the Chamber to expound his own philosophical doctrine in religious matters.[138]

With the alternative project defeated, debates on the Law of Separation turned to an examination of the individual articles. The "*Loi du 9 décembre 1905 concernant la séparation des Églises et de l'État*" originally contained 44 articles. Modifications were made to articles 6, 7, 9, 10, 14 in 1908.[139] Article one stated that the Republic ensured the freedom of conscience and guaranteed the free exercise of religions with certain restrictions in the interest of public order as later defined. The debate on article one concerned the liberty of conscience and the liberty of the Church. The first deputy to express his concerns about article one was Abbot Lemire (1853–1928), deputy of Hazebrouck, who had favored *le Ralliement*. He contended that the liberty of conscience proposed was a liberty that could neither breathe, nor grow, nor flourish, a liberty without a future. He further complained that the conception of liberty in the Law of Separation was unlike anything found in other nations and would lead to a loss of liberty for the Church. Briand replied that this article would guarantee liberty of conscience for all beliefs and for all religions, liberty which only existed at the present time for certain privileged religions under the Concordat. Amendments to article one were proposed and rejected. Article one was approved by the Chamber as originally proposed.[140]

The next round of debates focused on article two and the removal of funds in the State budget for subsidizing authorized religions. Exceptions would be made to subsidize chaplains in public institutions including hospitals and prisons. There would follow changes regarding public places of worship with further elaboration in article three. The State would conduct an inventory of places of worship. Subsequent articles would deal with the disposition and distribution of properties to associations and the State. Jules Delafosse (1841–1916), deputy of Calvados, took the floor against article two to defend the usefulness of the budget subsidies for religious purposes. Support was voiced for the Concordat and the use of State funds for clergy salaries. The Chamber was criticized for their attitude toward French clergy, who he considered loyal to the Republic, even if there were some exceptions. For Delafosse, the Concordat made priests bureaucrats who did not revolt

138. Bruley, *La séparation*, 291–93.

139. Bruley, *La séparation*, 452.

140. Bruley, *La séparation*, 295–96.

against the State. He imagined that the loss of State funds for the clergy would result in the loss of religion in thousands of communes throughout France. Briand responded that in a Republican regime there needed to be full and complete confessional neutrality of the State. He added that the Church would adapt to the new regime which would do nothing to protect it nor anything to destroy it.[141]

Further discussion ensued to amend the second paragraph of article two. One amendment was proposed to allow departments and communes to subsidize religions. Another amendment, related to the removal of the religious budget, was lodged to reestablish diplomatic relations with the Vatican. The rupture which had taken place in 1904 had been followed by the removal of funds for the French embassy representation to the Vatican. The proposed amendment was declared necessary in recognition that the pope was not only the head of French Catholics but the head of Catholics around the world. For those supporting the reestablishment of diplomatic relations, the prestige of France was at stake.[142]

Maurice Allard, who had earlier openly acknowledged his hostility toward the Church and animus toward all religion, proposed an amendment to laicize the calendar and remove all religious references. While Sunday would remain a day of rest without religious signification, all holidays with religious connotations would be eliminated and replaced by civil holidays. The purported objective of the amendment was to guarantee the neutrality of the State in religious matters. Allard regarded as illogical, once the separation took place, the observance of the day of the resurrection of Christ, the day of his birth, and the day of his ascension to heaven. In his mind, since the Church had borrowed from pagans to establish holidays, the State should borrow from the Church to establish its own civil holidays. In his proposal, instead of Christmas, winter solstice would be celebrated; at Easter, instead of celebrating the miraculous resurrection of a mystic named Jesus whose very existence is hypothetical, the renewal of organic life would be celebrated. French parliamentarians, who were representatives of the French people, were not prepared to throw out all religious tradition. The proposed elimination of Christmas and Easter, rooted in centuries of religious observance, went too far. The amendment was rejected with 60 for and 466 against. All other amendments were rejected as well.[143]

The conclusion of the debates took place on July 3, 1905, with a speech by Aristide Briand. He reminded the Chamber that in France there were

141. Bruley, *La séparation*, 299–300.

142. Bruley, *La séparation*, 305.

143. Bruley, *La séparation*, 307–8.

millions of Catholics who practiced their religion, some with real conviction, others by habit, by family tradition. He judged it unwise to introduce
a law which might provoke the indifferent, those who might suspect that
the Church was treated unjustly. He emphasized that the project of law as
conceived would give to Catholics, to Protestants, and to Jews that which is
theirs, granting them the free and unlimited use of their religious buildings,
offering them full freedom to practice their religion.[144] He insisted that the
law must show itself respectful of all beliefs and allow the religious the option to express themselves freely. In conclusion, returning to the question of
State subsidies for religion, he stated that if the Church could not manage
without subsidies from the State, the Church was already dead.[145] Following
his speech, the Law of Separation was approved with 341 deputies for the
Law of Separation and 233 opposed. From the Chamber of Deputies, the
law passed to the Senate on July 9, but not before a final salvo from Albert
de Mun who called July 3 one of the most sorrowful and humiliating days
of their generation which marked for France the opening of a dreadful era.
He considered that 341 deputies denied the secular traditions of France and
announced its moral degradation.[146]

Protestant theologian Raoul Allier (1862–1939) had penned several
articles during the debates on the Law of Separation. Following the vote in
the Chamber of Deputies, Allier wrote another article, which later appeared
in the *Cahiers de la Quinzaine*, with his opinion on how the Senate might
receive the law and whether there would be another round of battles. He
wrote that the law, although not perfect as a work of humans, had great
merit. The law was considered a powerful effort to reconcile the rights of
churches and the rights of the State in the accomplishment of a difficult
reform. With a few modifications, he felt the law would be without reproach
and anticipated the discussions on the law in the Senate. The general consensus was that for the law to take effect the following January 1, the Senate
would need to adopt the text without modification.[147]

Charles Péguy (1873–1914), journalist and founder of the *Cahiers de la
Quinzaine*, gave his impressions of the law in an article published on October
22, 1905, one day before the debate in the Senate. He considered that the influence of Émile Combes on the law had betrayed the Republic which Waldeck-
Rousseau had tried to save. Yet he conceded that even if the separation was
ill-conceived under Combes, under his successors the separation would take

144. Bruley, *La séparation*, 340–41.
145. Bruley, *La séparation*, 343–44.
146. Bruley, *La séparation*, 346.
147. Allier, "La Séparation au Sénat," 111–12; Bruley, *La séparation*, 347–48.

effect in a more republican spirit. Sorrow was expressed at the departure from power and the death of Waldeck-Rousseau and criticism voiced at the domination which Combes had exercised over the Chamber. He decried Combes's rise to power and accused him of exercising a ruthless Caesarism in the Republic. However, he expressed relief and gratitude that the final law adopted by the Chamber was not Combist and anticatholic but revealed a sincere effort of mutual liberation between the Church and the State.[148]

The debates in the Senate in the fall of 1905 were uneventful and did nothing to modify the Law of Separation as received from the Chamber of Deputies. Charles Dupuy (1851–1923), a moderate Republican and senator from Haute-Loire, deplored the absence of relations with Rome and denounced the socialist threat. An amendment was rejected as irrelevant concerning the guarantee of the liberty of conscience for government bureaucrats and military personnel.[149] Clemenceau expressed his dissatisfaction with article four and the disposition of Church properties since the properties belonged neither to the State nor to the Church, but belonged to the faithful.[150] There was discussion and opposing amendments on the application of the law in French territories according to article 43. In response, the government would later decide the conditions under which the law would be applied outside of France, but the amendments were rejected.[151]

New Status Quo

On December 6, 1905, Combes, former Council President and now senator from Charente-Inférieure, spoke for the Democratic Left in expressing their decision to vote for the law as received from the Chamber in the interest of the law's implementation taking effect on January 1, 1906. The Senate proceeded to the vote and approved the law 181 for and 102 against. There was brief discussion and an amendment to modify the title of the law, which was rejected. The original title was retained: *Loi du 9 décembre 1905 concernant la séparation des Églises et de l'État*. The Law of Separation was signed by President Loubet on December 9, 1905.[152]

Over the next few days, newspapers took various positions on the law. Some were neutral and sought moderation in the application of the Law. Others were enthusiastic and congratulatory at the Church's separation

148. Péguy, "Notre patrie," 12; Bruley, *La séparation*, 349–52.

149. Bruley, *La séparation*, 354–55.

150. Bruley, *La séparation*, 357.

151. Bruley, *La séparation*, 362–65.

152. Bruley, *La séparation*, 367–69.

from the State. *La Justice* simply reproduced the text of the law.[153] *Le Constitutionel* raised the challenges of the law's application. There was speculation on whether the pope would accept the law. The article quoted opinions that the Law of Separation would weaken religious sentiments.[154] *Le Journal* wrote that its readers were not interested in theoretical discussions of a text, but its application. The article went on to discuss the questions asked by nominal and practicing, bourgeois and peasant Catholics, who numbered 37,800,600 in the 1881 census: How will I get married? How will I baptize my children? How will they do their first communion? How will I be buried when I need to ask the Church for this service? And will it cost more for these different services now than under the Concordat? How will my bishop and priest be chosen? What will happen to my church building? These questions could not yet be answered in detail and everyone was awaiting the response of the pope.[155] Yet the questions themselves reveal that religious impulses are not easily extinguished and that laws separating the Church from the State could not remove religious aspirations. *Le Petit Parisien* advised the government to exercise moderation in applying the Law of Separation during a period of transition when changes might trouble the nation. There was also the wish expressed that the clergy would respect the law and not use their freedom to attack the Republic's institutions. The wish was accompanied by a warning that the Republic would need to assert its indispensable supremacy in the event the clergy rebelled.[156] *Le Siècle* remarked that for the past thirty-five years the Church and the State had lived like cat and dog and that the law was a sign of progress. The author related a conversation with a friend who said, "I was brought up on the Church's knees. I stopped practicing long ago. During the Dreyfus Affair, when I saw the Catholics and their priests rush in judgment against the hapless Jew, I stopped believing, because it seemed impossible to me that Jesus the Jew would deliver his people to the fury of his worshipers."[157] *Le Radical* quoted Combes who described the law as "a law of liberty, of social peace, and of moral freedom."[158] Finally, *La Lanterne* went further than other newspapers. It recounted that ten years earlier the Church almost seized control of the Republic and gloated that the Church now found itself stripped of its privileges. The article

153. "La Loi de Séparation."
154. "Au jour le jour."
155. "Après la loi de séparation."
156. "La Séparation votée" (*Petit Parisien*).
157. "La Séparation votée" (*Siècle*).
158. "Une Date."

concluded, "Finally, the Republic prevailed. Down with the Church and long live the Republic!"[159]

Although the Law of Separation settled the religious question juridically, religious questions did not go away. As a matter of fact, the application of the law created unforeseen issues, diverse interpretations, and did not end the contentiousness between the Catholic Church and the State. We have seen that Protestants generally welcomed the law and the abrogation of the Concordat. Yet, the majority of French citizens remained Roman Catholic, if only in name and by tradition. Albert de Mun later wrote that the Law of Separation did not have the support of the French people.[160] Yet, according to McManners, "He meant the Catholic laity. The people of France generally, or at least the male voting population, had a chance to declare their attitude to the Law of Separation in the parliamentary general election of May [1906], and voted overwhelmingly in favour of it."[161]

The twentieth century and the aftermath of the Law, to which we now turn, presented challenges to the Law of Separation, modifications of the law, new laws to clarify the law of 1905, a long period in which the Church appeared to have accepted and adapted to its new status, and the rise of Islam to contest established principles of laïcité. However, there was no turning back to the former state of affairs. The battle for a laïque State had been won. The Church would never again share power with the State. Rulers would never again rule by divine right. The Republic would control the public education of its youngest citizens. The twentieth century would see the ramifications of the law on French society as Church and State settled uneasily into their new relationship.

159. "Enfin."
160. Mun, "La lettre aux évêques."
161. McManners, *Church and State*, 162.

5

Laïcité in the Twentieth Century

THE LAW OF 1905 enacted during the Third Republic (1870–1940) provides a major historical reference for changes in the relationship between government and religion in France. We have seen historically that beginning in the sixteenth century there was an intellectual revolution, with important implications for religion, which progressively removed God from the life of the mind and shrank his presence in the public sphere.[1] The Republic proclaimed the separation of Churches and State all the while thinking especially of the Catholic Church.[2] The law today represents a fundamental aspect of laïcité in the nation's history.[3] Laïcité during the Third Republic, at different times and places, had been either an instrument in the service of religious liberty or a weapon directed against religions.[4] The Third Republic achieved the ideals of the French Revolution in establishing a new form of religion with its belief in the progress of humanity, intellectual and social freedom, and salvation offered to everyone through the public school. This new religion's heroes ranged from Joan of Arc to Voltaire with new tables of the law and the Declaration of the Rights of Man with a categorical imperative inscribed on hearts.[5] Secular religion did not develop by chance at the time when the separation of religion and the State took place. The two movements were correlated.[6]

The Law of Separation of 1905 in France was the outcome of the long process and multiple attempts to disestablish State religion, a process introduced with the arrival of the Protestant Reformation. There was clear progression from one official, recognized religion before 1789, to four recognized religious expressions under the 1801 Concordat—Catholic,

1. Yacoub, "Islam politique," 85.
2. Cabanel, *Les mots de la laïcité*, 3.
3. Rognon and Weber, *La laïcité*, 71.
4. Machelon, *La laïcité demain*, 21–22.
5. Cabanel, "La question religieuse," 177–79.
6. Gauchet, *La religion dans la démocratie*, 80.

Lutheran, Reformed, and Jewish—to religious plurality and the liberty of conscience in 1905.[7] Gauchet summarizes the essence of the law: God is separated and does not meddle in the political affairs of men. He no longer requires society to be directed by looking to "eternal bliss" since salvation is an individual matter.[8]

Religious confessions responded differently to the law of 1905. The first half of the twentieth century was certainly a time where the freedoms to believe and speak were formally accepted, but great obstacles remained to the expression of these freedoms.[9] The law led to the founding of the Fédération protestante de France (FPF) in 1905. For most Protestant confessions, the change of churches' legal status brought about by the Law of Separation was received without hostility.[10] According to Sébastien Fath, the separation of Church and State had little impact on evangelical French Protestant churches who saw an act of Providence in the law of December 1905. These churches, few in number, emphasized conversion and a regenerate church membership and were distinct from French Reformed churches which had a *"sensibilité* évangélique."[11] Patrick Cabanel traces the influences of prominent Protestants, among them Ferdinand Buisson (1841–1932) and Pierre-Félix Pécaut (1828–1898), from the 1880s and their enormous contribution to educational reform in the name of laïcité. He recounts the ebb of Protestant influence, the rise of an antireligious laïcité, and "the laïque silence" around the name of God which reached its pinnacle early in the twentieth century.[12] Protestant leaders would be attacked, not by the Catholic Church, but by their former allies and considered politically useless, abandoned by the progress of history, where "the champions of personal morality, of conscience, and of interior religion, would appear more and more as dinosaurs."[13]

For Judaism, there was no opposition between French laïcité and the faith. During WWI Jews paid with their blood the debt owed to France for according them citizenship in 1791.[14] The law's application, however, would create a tumultuous state of affairs and encounter opposition from the Catholic Church for several years while issues were addressed and eventually

---

7. Fetouh, "La laïcité," 47–48.

8. Gauchet, *La religion dans la démocratie*, 83–84.

9. Carluer, "Liberté de dire," 40.

10. Prévotat, *Être chrétien*, 195.

11. Fath, "De la non-reconnaissance," 151–52.

12. Cabanel, *Le Dieu de la République*, 239.

13. Cabanel, *Le Dieu de la République*, 213.

14. Korsia, "La laïcité français," 80–82.

resolved. World War I would turn people's attention to more serious external threats and serve to unite the country. A period of pacification would follow as the nation adapted to the changes. The end of the twentieth century would witness a reemergence of laïcité corresponding to demographic changes and the rise of Islam's influence.

The law of 1905 was not static. To address new questions in the twentieth century, the law has been modified multiple times.[15] It is argued that there has not been a consistent, reliable, and proven application of the law of 1905 from which one can construct political and religious discourse. The law of December 1905 only had the goal to organize the deconfessionalization of the State and remove financial subsidies to recognized religions. No reference was made in the law to the laïque form of political and administrative institutions and it was not viewed as immutable.[16] Over the last century, everyone has been able to read the key articles their own way, and if the Republic does not officially recognize any religion, it still acknowledges them.[17] Churches destroyed during WWI were rebuilt with loans from the State which was contrary to the law of 1905 which ended subsidies to churches. Churches were built in new suburban areas in the 1920s and 1930s with government assistance. As soon as there was a consensus in a community, the law of 1905 was not a definitive obstacle to the solution of problems raised.[18]

The twentieth century would also experience challenges in the application of the law of 1905 as French society became less homogeneous with the arrival of immigrants of religions either not present or not considered in the law. Changes included urban cemeteries with confessional sections where burials took place according to religious confession, the orientation of the body, and kosher and halal meals served in the armed forces. These examples are often offered to show that laïcité is not an intangible dogma and that the Republic has known how to adapt its practices.[19] The legislators in 1905 did not foresee the sociological upheavals which transformed France in the twentieth century. Yet the law of 1905 continues to occupy a fundamental place in France's public law.[20]

We should be reminded again that there was no explicit reference to the word laïcité in the 1905 Law of Separation, although the concept

15. Gauchet, *La religion dans la démocratie*, 55.

16. Koubi, "La laïcité," 48–49.

17. Machelon, *La laïcité demain*, 12.

18. Rognon and Weber, *La laïcité*, 92–93.

19. Cabanel, *Les mots de la laïcité*, 18.

20. Boussinesq, *La laïcité française*, 57.

informed the content in the quest for a laïque Republic. We will see later how the word itself has evolved with multiple definitions and with different opinions on whether to describe it as a value, concept, or principle. The law originally contained forty-four articles, of which several were subsequently abrogated. Two grand governing principles emerged in the law's first two articles which remain at the heart of discussions on laïcité: (1) the liberty of conscience and the free exercise of religion along with restrictions elaborated in other articles in the interest of maintaining public order; and (2) the elimination of funds budgeted by the State for minister salaries or religious subsidies, except for chaplains (*aumôniers*) when necessary for the free exercise of religion in schools, hospitals, prisons, and asylums. Since laïcité was neither mentioned nor legally defined, the door was left open to various ideologies and interpretations of the law.

This chapter will attempt to understand the religious landscape in France following the law of 1905 and how the nation adapted to change in the twentieth century. We will focus on the first hundred years of French history following the law of 1905. This period covers several changes of government in France beginning with the remainder of the Third Republic (1870–1940) and the Catholic Church's accommodation to the law. The Third Republic ended with France's defeat by Nazi Germany and the establishment of the Vichy government (1940–1944). The short-lived Fourth Republic (1946–1958) was established following WWII and replaced by the Fifth Republic (1958–present).

Catholic Accommodation to the Law of 1905

The Law of Separation was not well received in all quarters and became a point of division within the nation. The crisis began with a decree on December 29, 1905 to inventory Church properties and possessions with the intention to liquidate them and distribute them to authorized religious associations (*associations cultuelles*). The inventory decree followed from the law's provisions to eliminate public establishments of worship and the removal of funds from the State budget previously allotted for religious purposes. Aristide Briand explained the rationale behind the decree and presented it as the liquidation of the patrimony of public establishments formally under state control, and their distribution to private associations. The inventory was seen as a necessity once the law separating the Church from the State was enacted. Regardless of the justification offered, some viewed this action as State confiscation of church properties.[21]

21. Bruley, *La séparation*, 375–76.

The beginning of the inventories was uneventful until one detail of the inventory became public and provoked an uproar. The inventories included the opening of the altar tabernacles in Catholic churches to inventory the contents. This action was considered sacrilegious and scandalous by the majority of Catholics and many regarded it as religious persecution. The first confrontation took place at the church Sainte-Clotilde in Paris on February 1, 1906. Catholics barricaded the streets around the church to prevent entry. The forces of order broke through the barricades, broke down the church door, and entered the church under a flurry of projectiles. A similar incident took place the following day at the church Saint-Pierre-du-Gros-Caillou also in Paris. The resistance was led by lay people, among whom a number of royalists were found, and did not have the support of all the clergy. The vicar at Sainte-Clotilde declared that this Catholic anarchy was foreign to the gospel.[22] Albert de Mun wrote in the daily newspaper, *Le Figaro*, that for three days there was civil war in Paris. The government of the Republic had besieged the churches and its representatives had stormed churches. Soldiers had been dispatched, blood flowed and there were many wounded. He lamented that honorable citizens, guilty of demonstrating their faith, were condemned more harshly than criminals.[23]

Pope Pius X issued an encyclical on February 11, 1906, *Vehementer Nos*, in which he condemned the Law of Separation. He asserted that the Concordat, a treaty between two entities, could not legally be annulled by one party. He accused the French government of a great insult inflicted on the Holy See and a lack of courtesy practiced between States. The separation was considered unjust and disastrous for France. It was asserted that under this law the Church would not be free in France. The pope called for unity among French Catholics in the face of attempts to decatholicize France. He expressed the prayer that God would restore peace to France through intercession to Mary.[24]

The Law of Separation returned to center stage before the Chamber following the death of a man during protests against the government and the continuing inventories on March 7, 1906. This incident led to a vote of no confidence for the government of Maurice Rouvier, successor to Émile Combes, and the formation of a new government under Ferdinand Sarrien and George Clemenceau. One of the first measures of the newly-formed government was the temporary suspension of the inventories. It inaugurated an era of tranquility in France and a thaw appeared in relations between the

22. Bruley, *La séparation*, 377.
23. Bruley, *La séparation*, 378–79; Mun, "La guerre religieuse."
24. Pius X, "*Vehmenter Nos*"; Bruley, *La séparation*, 382–83.

Roman Church and the French State.[25] This pause in inventories would allow time for Catholics and proponents of separation to prepare for when the law regarding Church properties would be implemented on December 12, 1906. The delay also provided further opportunity for the Catholic Church to organize associations for the transmission of properties inventoried. During the stay of inventories, Pope Pius X, who had already condemned the Law of Separation, issued a new encyclical, *Gravissimo Officii*, on August 6, 1906, condemning the law's stipulation that churches organize into *associations cultuelles* with authorization from the State. He refused to accept the legitimacy of the State's authority to demand that the Church organize into *associations cultuelles* if the State did not recognize the irrevocable rights of the Church and the authority of the Roman Pontiff over properties considered as essential for the functioning of the Church.[26]

Abbot Gayraud, as an elected deputy, had played an important role in the 1905 parliamentary debates. He wrote to Aristide Briand on August 20, 1906, in search of a solution to the problem of the *associations cultuelles*. He explained that Catholics found it impossible to submit to the Law of Separation without clarification on article four concerning the *associations cultuelles*. He emphasized that the pope was not requesting that the State negotiate with him, but was only seeking legal guarantees concerning the rights of the religious hierarchy. In effect, Gayraud suggested an addition to article four which would clearly state that the *associations cultuelles* would be established under the authority of bishops.[27] Gayraud's letter was followed by a letter of information (*circulaire*) from Briand sent to departmental prefects. The letter provided clarification and guidance in the application of the law concerning the formation of *associations cultuelles*. He reminded the prefects that the law had conferred on religious establishments the right to proceed to the attribution of their properties within one year after the Law of Separation was enacted.[28] Briand informed the prefects that it was not up to the prefects to determine the legality of an *association cultuelle* in refusing to accept the declaration made by their representative.[29]

The Catholic Church initially refused to form *associations cultuelles* within the one-year deadline offered by article four of the law of December 9, 1905. As a result, the State took possession of Church properties. The stalemate between the Church and the State led Aristide Briand to propose

25. Briand, *La Séparation*, 17; Bruley, *La séparation*, 399–400.

26. Bruley, *La séparation*, 409–11.

27. Méjan, *La Séparation*, 335–36.

28. Méjan, *La Séparation*, 316–17.

29. Bruley, *La séparation*, 414.

another law to allow churches to continue the use of edifices for public worship. Discussions on the law were held December 26 and 28, 1906, and the law was promulgated January 2, 1907.[30] The new law was condemned by Pope Pius X on January 6 in a letter entitled "*Une fois encore*" (once again) in which he accused the proponents of separation of wanting to destroy the Church and dechristianize France.[31]

Despite the pope's opposition to the new law, the Church's intransigence eventually began to soften. French bishops met in Paris from January 15 to 19, 1907, and decided, with the Vatican's approval, to accept the new law on a trial basis so that churches might continue to worship in properties under the control of the State. Deputies hostile to the Catholic Church decried what they perceived to be an ultimatum from the bishops. Clemenceau and Briand were at odds to the point where Briand was ready to resign. Briand succeeded in passing a new law on March 28, 1907, which stipulated that public gatherings may take place in churches without prior authorization. This law was a decisive step toward pacification.[32] One major modification of the law of 1905 took place on April 13, 1908, to settle the contentious issue of church properties. The new law stipulated that local communes and departments would be responsible for the upkeep and conservation of religious edifices. Briand defended the law which faced opposition from anticlericals who considered the law too favorable toward the Church.[33]

With the law enacted, the Church would now need to survive in a new context stripped of political influence. Méjan wrote an article entitled *Psychologie de la séparation de l'État et des Églises* in which he reported the feelings and responses of French bishops after December 1905.[34] Although the consequences of the separation were less tragic than during the French Revolution, the bishops' lives were shaken by what they perceived as a moral and social revolution. Méjan received many moving letters from bishops, some which he preserved, in which the bishops revealed their anguish at what they viewed as a divorce. They suffered in their religious conscience and in their undeniable patriotism from the separation of *la Patrie et la Papauté*, a separation accomplished with a forced agreement and with animosity. They did not believe that many French people understood the tragedy of this drama for them. They indicated that even though Combes's politics were not in the interest of France or the church, the Holy See and its faulty

---

30. Briand, *La Séparation*, 174–75; Bruley, *La séparation*, 417.
31. Pius X, "Une fois encore."
32. Bruley, *La séparation*, 419.
33. Bruley, *La séparation*, 422–25.
34. Méjan, *La Séparation*, 294–98; Bruley, *La séparation*, 425–29.

pontifical decisions were responsible for the divorce. They believed they
had suffered because of the haughty intransigence of Pope Pius X and his
nonce. It was also noted that all the bishops protested energetically against
the pretention on the part of the State's representatives to unilaterally break
the Concordat.[35] In Méjan's opinion, one reason for the Pope's implacability
was to prevent the independence of the French Church from the Vatican as
was the case in the Gallican tradition.

This change of status for the Church and its political defeat left wounds
that many believe began healing during WWI (1914–1918) in what has been
called the "*fraternité de tranchées*"[36] (brotherhood of the trenches) between
clergy and civilians. For many, it was the war of 1914 which marked the
change because of the position of the French clergy who supported national
unity.[37] French people of all political persuasions fought alongside one another to protect and preserve the Republic. The vast majority of Catholic
bishops sided with the patriotic cause. The defense of the nation came first
and helped extinguish, at least for a time, ancient quarrels.[38] McManners
states it well in describing this period of French history:

> The heroism of the clergy and the Catholic soldiers, especially
> the officers of right-wing inclinations, and the sense of the
> overwhelming need for unity annihilated the vicious, routine
> Republican anticlericalism of the previous generation. . . . No
> recriminations between politicians and churchmen followed the
> war of 1914–1918. Catholics had proved that they accepted the
> Republic by fighting for it and dying for it.[39]

Not all historians agree with this assessment. Nicolas Mariot refutes
the idea that WWI became a patriotic melting pot. He sees the *fraternité de
tranchées* as a myth. He admits that there were acts of heroism and a sense
among many in the trenches that there was neither Catholic, nor Protestant,
nor Republican, nor rich, nor poor. Yet he believes that the myth of osmosis
between the lower classes and the elite lingers today to support a democratic
dream.[40] In any case, the wartime rapprochement experienced between the
Church and the Republic was more a truce than genuine reconciliation.[41]
The time in the trenches also opened the eyes of priests who discovered the

35. Bruley, *La séparation*, 429.
36. Gaillard, "L'invention de la laïcité," 36.
37. Dusseau, "L'histoire de la Séparation," 19.
38. Prévotat, *Être chrétien*, 13–14.
39. McManners, *Church and State*, 175.
40. Bastière, "La grande illusion."
41. Prévotat, *Être chrétien*, 17.

religious ignorance of soldiers who did not understand even basic religious concepts. For the first time the phenomenon of dechristianization appeared in all its magnitude.[42] The Church experienced an upsurge in the hearts of people and at the end of the war, patriotic manifestations were inconceivable without the physical presence of the Church and most bishops celebrated the victory and discerned in it the finger of God.[43]

Following WWI, Pope Benedict XV (1854–1922) sought a thaw in troubled relations with several European nations, including France. There was a growing desire for normalization of relations between France and the Vatican following the return of many Catholic clergy and teachers to France after the war. Diplomatic relations between France and the Holy See were restored in November 1920.[44] The principle of *associations cultuelles*, rejected by Pope Pius X, would finally be accepted by the Vatican in January 1924 under Pope Pius XI (1857–1939). The acceptance was not without controversy. Many bishops considered the acceptance of laïque laws as shameful compromise. Politicians on the extreme left denounced any negotiation with the Church. Politicians on the extreme right believed the Church was humiliating itself by negotiating and demanded the repeal of laïque laws.[45] The issue was finally settled with the creation of *associations diocésaines* dependent on the ecclesiastical hierarchy and respecting its rights.[46] One of the thorniest problems of the application of the law of 1905 was found in its resolution by negotiation and compromise which satisfied both parties.[47]

The Church entered progressively but slowly into an historical horizon where democracy and laïcité were structural givens of society.[48] The Second Vatican Council (1962–1965) demonstrated just how well the Catholic Church adapted to the new order. The Council incorporated the concept of laïcité in its deliberations in declaring laïcité as a guiding criterion for the formulation and the proclamation of the faith.[49] At the beginning of the Council, Pope John Paul XXIII (1881–1963) confirmed that Vatican II needed to be in continuity with the teaching of the Church, but a continuity which would neither be foreign to the evolution of history,

42. Prévotat, *Être chrétien*, 20.

43. Prévotat, *Être chrétien*, 26.

44. Jeantet, "L'école et la laïcité," 33.

45. Prévotat, *Être chrétien*, 36–37.

46. Boussinesq, *La laïcité française*, 35.

47. Bruley, *La séparation*, 429.

48. Coq, *Laïcité et République*, 313.

49. Alberigo, "Facteurs de laïcité," 211.

nor obsessed by the notion of error.[50] There was the recognition that in the history of the Church there had been a gap between a Church identified with the clergy and the Christian people who were left aside. The discovery of the Church as the people of God would permit the Church to survive and fulfill its vocation in society.[51]

Etymological Evolution of Laïcité and French Exceptionalism

Since 1905, and especially toward the latter half of the twentieth and early twenty-first centuries, the meaning of laïcité has evolved as a subject of debate. The word laïcité itself did not appear in dictionaries until 1873 although associated words like laïque had been in use for some time in French history. As mentioned earlier, Émile Littré added the word in 1877 as a neologism in a supplement to his *Dictionnaire de la langue française*. At the same time, he added *cléricalisation*, *cléricaliser*, *cléricalisme*, and *anticlérical*. Pierre Fiala writes that in the following decades all these terms would provide lexical support for the great polemical debates between Republican laïcisateurs and conservative clericalists.[52] Littré was followed by Ferdinand Buisson in an article in the *Dictionnaire de pédagogie et d'instruction primaire* (1887). Over twenty years later, in his *Nouveau dictionnaire de pédagogie et d'instruction primaire* (1911), Buisson explained that the word was correctly formed but not in general use, and that the neologism was necessary to clearly communicate the idea behind the term.[53] Until the nineteenth century, the French language knew only the word *laïc* to designate someone distinct from the clergy who did not exercise religious functions.[54] Still others find it paradoxical that the struggle against religion's clutch on public life was made with words borrowed directly from religious language.[55]

Fiala provides an interesting analysis of French dictionaries to demonstrate the morphological changes which have taken place during major phases of laicization in France. He explains that there is a whole family of words associated with laïcité, some no longer in use (*laïcal, laïcation, laïcocéphale*), and other neologisms (*laïcard, catho-laïcité, ultra-laïcité*),

50. Alberigo, "Facteurs de laïcité," 217.

51. Alberigo, "Facteurs de laïcité," 225.

52. Fiala, "Les termes de la laïcité," 48–49.

53. Esteve-Bellebeau and Touzeil-Divina, *Laï-cité(s)*, 13n2.

54. Machelon, *La laïcité demain*, 15–16.

55. Rognon and Weber, *La laïcité*, 11.

which together bear the traces of the great steps of laicization in France.[56] He analyzes definitions of laïque in dictionaries from the seventeenth to the twentieth century and asserts that the word originally simply defined a distinction of a religious nature between clergy and laypersons to which was later added a radical opposition between laïque and religion.[57] Buisson had contrasted *laïque* with *clérical* and defined the clerical spirit as the pretention of a minority to dominate the majority in the name of a religion and the laïque spirit as the aggregate of aspirations of the people, from the Greek *laos*, the democratic and common spirit. Fiala concludes that this semantic reinterpretation highlights the profound nature of ideological conflict that one meets in the evolution of definitions.[58]

There are difficulties in translating laïcité into other languages. English-language writings often speak of secularism or the secular state. The word *laïcité* is now being used by some writers for the American situation of church and state relations and the neologism *laicity* has appeared. However, the word *laïcité* is virtually untranslatable without a false meaning in any foreign language relatively close to French.[59] For the theologian, the word *laïcité* resonates strangely to the ears and echoes the ancient tensions between lay persons (*laïcs*) and clergy (*clercs*) in Catholicism before the modern distinction was made between the Church and State. The word was traditionally associated with anticlericalism and the specificity of French laïque ideology as elaborated in the nineteenth century which tends to overshadow the traces of its origin.[60] In the end, recognizing the difference in words used for laïcité and secularization in other languages, many retain a differentiation in the terms and processes. At the same time, the interactions between the terms laïcité and secularism must be considered with the reality that laïcité as a political regulation applies to groups and individuals who have a different rapport with secularization.[61]

These challenges involved in definitions complicate any discussion on laïcité. Anyone studying the concept of laïcité must observe how the word has evolved in meaning. This evolution has required the addition of adjectives with attempts at clarification. In the course of the twentieth century, and specifically in the 1989 headscarf affair (see below), the Conseil d'État, which advises the French government for projects of law and serves as the

56. Fiala, "Les termes de la laïcité," 41.
57. Fiala, "Les termes de la laïcité," 45.
58. Fiala, "Les termes de la laïcité," 53.
59. Machelon, *La laïcité demain*, 59.
60. Lefebvre, "Origines et actualité," 64–65.
61. Baubérot and Milot, *Laïcités sans frontières*, 14–16.

supreme administrative judge to settle litigation related to government agencies, referred to the principle of laïcité and reignited the debate on the Law of Separation's application. At that time, the socio-political definitions, while still underrepresented, took on a more important place and the notion of laïcité at that point seemed established.[62] In Bowen's opinion, "In France's very recent history, laïcité has become one of those 'essentially contested concepts' such as 'freedom' and 'equality,' that provide resources for arguments, not starting points of agreement."[63]

The question then arises whether laïcité is a French exception and if so in what way. The Conseil National des Évangéliques de France (CNEF) recognizes that France is often presented as one of the champions of laïcité.[64] It is argued that laïcité is a French specificity, incomprehensible in Great Britain, where customs agents can wear the veil, as well in the United States, where elected officials publicly invoke the name of God.[65] Because the law of 1905 settled chaotic historical relationships which often led to violent wars of the two Frances, there are therefore real reasons for this French specificity.[66] Gauchet speaks of the prism of French singularity by which one sees democratic society in both the obvious problems and in hope for renewal.[67] In official documents the Conseil d'État recognizes that the term laïcité is untranslatable outside of Latin languages and considers any *exception française* as relative. The Conseil raises the larger question of how relations between churches and the State are organized to ensure the liberty of conscience and freedom of religion.[68]

Machelon defines laïcité as a legal principle of separation of which the word and the idea come from Christianity—to render to Caesar that which is Caesar's and to God that which is God's.[69] He understands that laïcité *à la française*, which aims in a general manner to free the civic life from the control of religious institutions, is the product of a multi-secular history.[70] France has been compared to the situation of the United States, Canada, England, and Germany, and the argument advanced that laïcité as a doctrine and as an ideology is a phenomenon linked singularly with French

---

62. Fiala, "Les termes de la laïcité," 55.

63. Bowen, *Headscarves*, 2.

64. CNEF, *Laïcité française*, 17.

65. Roy, *La laïcité*, 29.

66. Rinnert, "Le principe de laïcité," 132.

67. Gauchet, *La religion dans la démocratie*, 12.

68. "Un siècle de laïcité," 245.

69. Machelon, *La laïcité demain*, 11.

70. Machelon, *La laïcité demain*, 15.

republican history, to an unusual mode of governing in the Western world in its relations with civil society, and in its centralized, methodical organization of cultural, social, and economic activity.[71]

Political modernity and a Copernican revolution took place in all of Europe and on the American continent, but it took on a particular form in France. Likewise, there is truly a French exception in the process of exiting the wars of religion which bloodied Europe of the sixteenth century and marked the end of Christian unity. The Edict of Nantes in 1598 is the historical reference which allowed the cohabitation of two religions, Catholic and Protestant. Gaillard advances a French exception in the matter of the separation of Church and State since French laïcité, of which the fundamental text is the law of December 1905, led not only to the disassociation of citizenship and religion, but also to the negation of any official role of churches in civil society.[72] Ducomte asserts that French exceptionalism is partly true but views laïcité as a universal principle and as an instrument of social harmony.[73] Jean-Jacques Queyranne, regional president of Rhône-Alpes since 2002, prefers the descriptor French singularity (*singularité française*) to French exception (*exception française*). Along with Gaillard, he recognizes the importance of the Edict of Nantes and views it as the origin of the law of 1905 and the law itself as the crowning of a movement of laicization begun long before and which became a law of pacification and serenity.[74] Regarding French exceptionalism, Bowen affirms that "the history of relations between the state and religions in France is one of frequent conflicts and temporary resolutions, but to the extent that the historian can discern underlying continuities, he or she can claim to find a distinctive French approach to the issue, that because it is part of French history, should be maintained."[75] Others take some exception to the notion that French laïcité is the model to use to compare other national situations and assert that the United States early on put into practice the reality of laïcité without designating it as such.[76]

One of the principal characteristics of laïcité in France was emancipation from religion which in its first stage retained the notion of duty according to Kantian and republican patriotic traditions. The notion of duty was completed with the ideas of self-sacrifice and anticlericalism and

71. Zylberberg, "Laïcité, connais-pas," 37.

72. Gaillard, "L'invention de la laïcité," 20.

73. Ducomte, *La Laïcité*, 3.

74. Queyranne, "Ouverture des rencontres," 9.

75. Bowen, *Headscarves*, 20–21.

76. Baubérot and Milot, *Laïcités sans frontières*, 9.

although freed in appearance from theological reference, an element of religiosity was preserved. In effect, moral obligations toward God were transferred to moral obligations toward others in human spheres. This phase, characterized by the obligations of duty and sacrifice, lasted into the 1950s when the "it is necessary" yielded to the spell of happiness, the categoric obligation of the stimulation of the senses, and the right to be true to oneself, freed from all imposition of values outside of oneself.[77] This emancipatory separation was considered necessary since the State serves all the people (*laos*) and religious conceptions of existence are affairs of the conscience and cannot be imposed on others.[78]

It should be noted that some have questioned whether laïcité is better described as a universal principle rather than merely as a value. This recognizes the emergence of the particularity of laïcité in French history while also exploring the universal importance of laïcité as a principle alongside democracy and human rights with their accompanying values. Laïcité is spoken of as a fundamental principle of democracy and thus universal as a principle.[79] The Republic constitutes an ancient ideal, a historical remembrance from which emerged principles of life in community, or values capable of providing societal coherence. The role then of laïcité is a rupture from a society built on religion. Laïcité does not create the necessary new social tie. The Republic defines the new social bond which citizens acquire through education. The survival of laïcité, in its necessary connection with the Republic, assumes a robust education.[80]

There seems to be a general consensus among these writers that, even if laïcité as a concept or principle is found in other societies, there is a sense in which the form it takes is particular to France and that linguistically it captures a specificity inseparable from its historical context. The various ways in which laïcité is used requires knowledge of the context and the perspective of those using the term. The references to laïcité are used with ambivalence which corresponds to a underlying ambiguity.[81] The complexity and the confusion cannot be completely avoided, especially by those looking in on French society from the outside. The concept of laïcité over time has been associated with various adjectives with different nuances according to the speaker's perspective (*latitudinaire, globalisée, apaisée,*

77. Ferry, *L'homme-Dieu*, 115–17.

78. Haarscher, *La laïcité*, 9.

79. Coq, "Un principe universel," 6–7.

80. Coq, "Un principe universel," 11.

81. Machelon, *La laïcité demain*, 9.

ouverte, de combat, républicaine, antalgique).[82] Queyranne exemplifies those who understand laïcité in an enlarged sense, stating that it is not a simple legal and constitutional principle but a value of civilization supported by a "living together" ethic.[83] It is critical to understand this distinction. As a legal and constitutional principle, laïcité was primarily concerned with liberty of conscience and freedom of religion or non-religion, the State and the Church occupying separate spaces without interference or control. Once laïcité becomes a value of democracy or civilization then it can be applied to a host of issues unrelated to its origin and perhaps even unrelated to religion. Some of these will be discussed later.

For our purposes, these adjectives might be condensed to two adjectives which encompass the rest—*laïcité libérale* and *laïcité anticléricale*. The first, *laïcité libérale*, seeks a peaceful (*apaisée*) coexistence between believers and non-believers, liberty of conscience, tolerance of all systems of belief or unbelief, the neutrality of the State in religious matters, and the exclusion of religious influence in State matters. The second, *laïcité anticléricale*, is more aggressive (*de combat*), does not claim neutrality, views religion as oppressive, and seeks to further marginalize or remove all religious influence in society. Both perspectives were proposed and debated leading up to the law of 1905. The first more liberal and tolerant perspective seems to have won out and reflects the law as enacted. The second more combative and anticlerical perspective has vigorously reentered the debate with the emergence of Islam as the second largest religion in France.[84]

In the minds of some, the term *laïcité-combat* was completely justified in the late nineteenth and early twentieth centuries in opposition to a dominant Church. Only a forceful separation succeeded in removing the Church from influence and interference in the political realm. A legal measure was necessary to guarantee liberty of conscience and equality among religious confessions. During the twentieth century *laïcité-neutralité* came to the forefront because the Catholic Church had been conquered and it was no longer necessary to attack it head-on.[85] For others, the diachronic evolution of the laïque discourse and the synchronic coexistence of diverse interpretations underscore the inappropriateness of the formulation "laïcité" in the singular. The plural form "laïcités" stresses diverse understandings and interpretations, whether French or foreign.[86] The addition

---

82. Esteve-Bellebeau and Touzeil-Divina, *Laï-cité(s)*, 13–18.
83. Queyranne, "Ouverture des rencontres," 9.
84. Tavoillot, "Les deux laïcités."
85. Viguier, "La laïcité," 80.
86. Orange, "Laïcités dans le monde," 29–30.

of an adjective to the noun laïcité often signifies the meaning one wishes to ascribe to laïcité.[87] The contention is made that many who defend or contest laïcité, as well as those who want it to evolve, either misunderstand or interpret laïcité according to their personal biases and conceptions of laïcité. This has led to the development of philosophies and ideologies of laïcité which appear to have little or no legal basis.[88]

Émile Poulat distinguishes three facets of laïcité—the idea, the program, and the regime laïque—which permit everyone to live together without resolving any differences, without pretending there has been resolution, and without demanding it. He identifies the difficulties French laïque society confronts since the ancient Christian culture is now submerged by the new modern, laïque culture, and both now must confront foreign cultures, particularly Islam.[89] Poulat insists that laïcité cannot be reduced to a religious question, or to the confrontation between the Church and State which ended in the triumph of the State. He understands laïcité fundamentally in its legal aspect as the separation of Church and State and the principle of religious neutrality. He recognizes that laïcité arose in opposition to the catholicity of the monarchy up until the French Revolution and what remains today is a wound of the violent history which accompanied laïcité. In essence, he views laïcité broadly as the principle which guarantees the liberty of conscience for everyone.[90]

Some consider it an error to narrow the concept of laïcité to the law of 1905. In this view, neither positive nor negative laïcité exist, neither tolerant nor intolerant laïcité, neither open nor plural laïcité, neither rigid nor closed laïcité. All public space is laïque and experiences the same application of the principle of laïcité.[91] In summary, laïcité might be seen in both a broad and narrow sense. Its broad sense carries the respect of the liberty of conscience in that the State belongs to all people without discrimination regardless of belief system. In its narrow sense, the term refers to the struggle against clericalism and the separation of the State from any religious confession.[92]

The definition of laïcité remains blurred with multiple interpretations and adjectives. The Conseil d'État defines laïcité as both a juridical concept and a political philosophy while recognizing that few concepts

---

87. Rinnert, "Le principe de laïcité," 129.
88. Boussinesq, *La laïcité française*, 13–14.
89. Poulat, "Culture laïque," 60–62.
90. Poulat, "Culture laïque," 64–65.
91. Koubi, "La laïcité," 57.
92. Haarscher, *La laïcité*, 3.

have received such diverse interpretations.[93] The original juridical sense of laïcité in the separation of Church and the State has been enlarged. Daniel Beresniak contends that laïcité rests on the recognition of the primacy of the person over the group, and what flows from it, the recognition of free choice and the negation of the principle of authority.[94] Meaning often depends on the agenda and ideology of the speaker and its application is part of the larger debate to this day. This will become more evident in clashes over laïcité in the twenty-first century.

Relation of Secularization and Laïcité

The preceding section demonstrates divergences on the meaning of laïcité. To further complicate matters, there is also disagreement about the term laïcité and its English equivalents, secularism or secularization. We saw earlier in the introduction the distinction between secularization as a phenomenon of society that does not require any political implementation, and laïcité as a political choice which defines the place of religion in society in an authoritative and legal manner.[95] This is echoed by Luc Moyères who holds that laïcité à la française is the product of French history and the fruit of a local evolution.[96] François Boucher argues for the use of secularism as an English translation for laïcité. He claims to follow "well-established practice in the English-speaking world" and asserts that "it is possible to distinguish the political concept of secularism from the sociological notion of secularization."[97] He may be correct in his assertion of established practice in the English-speaking world. In this writer's opinion, however, French authors largely understand laïcité as a French specificity and consistently distinguish laïcité from secularization and secularism. The Conseil d'État describes secularization as a process which is progressively accomplished in all Western democracies. However, in its narrow, more French sense of laïcité, it is the transformation of relations between religion and the State. Laïcité signifies the refusal of subjugation of the political to the religious, or vice-versa, without denying some overlap between them.[98]

Gauchet prefers to speak of the departure of religion (*sortie de la religion*) in order to avoid the terms laicization and secularization. He views

93. "Un siècle de laïcité," 246.
94. Beresniak, *La Laïcité*, 109.
95. Roy, *La laïcité*, 19–20.
96. Moyères, *Laïcité, Islam*.
97. Boucher, "Open Secularism," 23.
98. "Un siècle de laïcité," 245–46.

the two terms as a process which has affected all Western societies in different forms. Its form in France is unique and the word laïcité well summarizes its specificity which particularity needs to be appreciated today if one wants to understand the relativization it is undergoing today.[99] This *sortie de la religion* does not signify a complete abandonment of religious belief in society. It describes a world where religion no longer determines the structure. In this world religions continue to exist, only now at the interior of a political order that they no longer determine or dominate.[100] The descriptive relevance of the terms laicization and secularization is not denied, but they find their origins in the ecclesiastical world and do not go to the heart of the upheaval brought about by the elimination of religious dominance.[101] Gauchet also makes a distinction between a Europe of laicization in Catholic countries characterized by a confessional unicity, and a Europe of secularization which prevailed in Protestant lands, where following a break with Rome, national churches continued their influence in the political sphere.[102] The former required a political intervention to release society from the grip of the Catholic Church; the latter often has a place for a religion of State. In general, laicization is associated with countries of Catholic tradition and secularization is more characteristic of Protestant countries. In other words, secularization took place as a phenomenon of evolving societies in Protestant nations apart from State intervention. Laïcité, however, required an act of legal intervention from the State in order to force the separation of religious and state domains.[103]

In his oft-referenced book, *Sécularisation et laïcité,* French philosopher Jean-Claude Monod notes that the word "secularization" was born as a French neologism (1553) in the legal field. Initially used in a limited way juridically, the term received its first political consecration with preliminary discussions regarding the Treaty of Westphalia in 1648.[104] He presents three points for elucidating the relation between secularization and laïcité. He writes that laïcité is the political product of the historical process of secularization, the institutional result or at least one of the institutional results; laïcité is a variant of secularization as the general form of modern western societies; and French laïcité has its specificities, written

---

99. Gauchet, *La religion dans la démocratie,* 9.

100. Gauchet, *La religion dans la démocratie,* 13–14.

101. Gauchet, *La religion dans la démocratie,* 17–18.

102. Gauchet, *La religion dans la démocratie,* 19–20.

103. Haarscher, *La laïcité,* 45.

104. Monod, *Sécularisation et laïcité,* 80.

in a unique history.[105] He further distinguishes between the general process of secularization found in Western societies and its specific forms in
different national contexts.[106]

Historically speaking, the origin of the term secularization is the process by which a monk leaves the convent (prefiguration of eternity) in order
to live in the present age (*saeculum*).[107] In France, one finds that the term
secularization initially came into prominence in relation to the acquisition
of Church possessions by the State. Properties were considered secularized
when transferred from the Church to State ownership. The law of November
2, 1789, declared that all ecclesiastical assets were placed at the disposition of
the Nation. The revolutionaries sought to rid the country of clergy, regarded
as begging vagabonds and parasites, who had obtained their wealth in ex-
ploiting the powerless. These possessions included monasteries which were
considered unseemly places of inactivity and divorced from concerns for the
public good. The secularized possessions allegedly provided relief to those
in distress. However, the secularization of Church possessions during the
French Revolution went beyond merely nationalization of properties. The
scope was much grander and pointed to a vast recasting of society based on
the foundation of the rights of man and the citizen.[108] Not all expressions of
secularization were fundamentally antireligious or antichristian and semantic plasticity and the variety of its levels of application remain.[109] Some vari-
ants of secularization concentrated on the rational essence of Christianity
and its moral precepts which were convergent with the well-being of society.
Yet the term laïcité characterized the institutional achievement of secularization, and linguistically in French the term and the notion of secularization
preceded those of laïcité in the political lexicon.[110] Along this same line of
thinking, there remains confusion between laïcité, which is the separation of
the State and religion, and secularization which is the natural and progressive detachment of society from religiosity.[111] Lefebvre portrays laïcité as that
which rendered reason sovereign and freed it from transcendent authority.
Secularization is viewed as another concept which signifies the emancipation of societies from religious guardianship, where Christianity ceases to
be the source of a common world vision. One of the principle consequences

---

105. Monod, *Sécularisation et laïcité*, 7.

106. Monod, *Sécularisation et laïcité*, 13.

107. Baubérot, *Les laïcités*, 114.

108. Monod, *Sécularisation et laïcité*, 81–83.

109. Monod, *Sécularisation et laïcité*, 14.

110. Monod, *Sécularisation et laïcité*, 85.

111. Fetouh, "La laïcité," 48.

of secularization appears in the fact that a society can now be freed from religious legitimization for the definition of its values.[112]

Laicization and secularization are often associated and these controversial expressions are sometimes taken as symbolizing multiple interpretations of the same reality—the arrival of a laïque universe in the midst of which belief in the existence of God no longer structures political and public space.[113] During the decade of the 1960s there was a search for authenticity which claimed the eradication of all dogmatism whether of moral or religious origins in the name of respect for the individual. This period marked the ultimate outcome of the long process of secularization which since the eighteenth century led toward the attainment of laïcité. In the ancient world, the political universe from which the Revolution intended to break, was completely dominated by the notion of hierarchies. In this view, every democratic movement in the two centuries following the Revolution sought to dismantle hierarchies and insisted on the necessity to further promote equality and laïcité, an absolute equalization of values and conditions.[114]

In whatever way these two concepts may be viewed with their nuances, and there is no consensus, Baubérot makes a stunning observation in stating, "Contrary to the fears of many, secularization and laicization have not led to the disappearance of Christianity."[115]

Laïcité in the French Constitutions and Alsace-Moselle

Although the principle of laïcité in Church-State separation was established in the law of 1905, the word laïcité was officially and explicitly enshrined in the Constitutions of the Fourth and Fifth Republics in 1946 and 1958 respectively. In the Constitutions the word laïque took on its truly modern value.[116] The two Constitutions repeat word for word that France is an indivisible, laïque, democratic, and social Republic. The French Revolution's *Déclaration des droits de l'homme et du citoyen* of 1789 was reaffirmed in both Constitutions. The preamble of the Constitution of 1946, enacted following the end of WWII and the Allied victory, declares that every human being, without distinction of race, or religion, or belief, possesses sacred and inalienable rights. The Fifth Republic's 1958 Constitution was

112. Lefebvre, "Origines et actualité," 63–65.
113. Ferry, *L'homme-Dieu*, 37.
114. Ferry, *L'homme-Dieu*, 111–12.
115. Baubérot, *Petite histoire du christianisme*, 76.
116. Fiala, "Les termes de la laïcité," 50.

established under the leadership of General Charles de Gaulle.[117] The shorter preamble of the Constitution of 1958 refers to the 1946 Constitution but makes no explicit mention of "sacred" in relation to rights contained in the 1946 preamble. Added to article 1 in the 1958 Constitution were two phrases which guaranteed equality before the law of all citizens without distinction of origin, of race, or of religion, and respect for all beliefs. Interestingly, according to Machelon, for General de Gaulle the Republic was laïque, but France was Christian.[118]

It is worth asking what changed since 1905, with movement from legislative laïcité to constitutional laïcité, and how opposition to the law gave way to accommodation if not consensus. According to some interpretations, the transformation was due to the Catholic Church's changed perspective. The Church had experienced the separation as an aggression and in particular as an infringement on both its dominant position as the guardian of true values on which to construct a just society, and on its hierarchical principle (until the formation of diocesan associations in the 1920s). The Church began to view laïcité more in terms of neutrality rather than strict separation. In other words, the laïcité-separation progressively gave way to laïcité-neutrality.[119] Additionally, since neither the 1946 nor the 1958 Constitutions defined the concept of laïcité, the Church was able to defend the principle by connecting it to the idea of religious liberty. The rise of communism and the destitution of national churches also gravely concerned the Catholic Church. Haarscher writes,

> Communism provided the example of overthrow that the Church had to avoid if it wanted to exist in civil society: the domination of a secular religion at the place of a transcendent religion, the repression of Catholics (and of churches in general) in place of non-Catholics, as was the case during the Ancien Régime. . . . Faced with the dangers of totalitarianism, the excesses of political separation (quickly corrected however by the will of compromise by Briand and Jaurès) appeared relatively benign. Thus, the Church sided with human rights, which permitted it to plead in favor of a neutral State, respecting all beliefs, guaranteeing religious liberty, including educational liberty.[120]

There are departments of France exempt from the law of 1905 owing to historical circumstances which existed at the time the law was promulgated.

117. Magstadt, *Understanding Politics*, 170.
118. Machelon, *La laïcité demain*, 25.
119. Haarscher, *La laïcité*, 21–22.
120. Haarscher, *La laïcité*, 23.

They are Alsace (Haut-Rhin and Bas-Rhin) and the department of Moselle. To understand the exception, one must go back to the Concordat governing the Church in France signed between Napoleon and Pope Pius VII in 1801. The law of 1905 abolished the Concordat. However, Alsace and Moselle were part of Germany in 1905 as a result of the French defeat in the 1870 Franco-Prussian War. After the defeat of the Central Powers (Germany, Austria-Hungary, the Ottoman Empire, and Bulgaria) in 1918 at the end of WWI, these departments returned to France and the Concordat was maintained with provisional status. The return of this region to France was not without its complications. After over forty-five years under German rule (1871–1918), the initial euphoria of the war's end was soon replaced by disillusionment. And the reality was that the majority of the population had never lived under French sovereignty and some of the German social legislation was more favorable than French laws.

These departments, with their marked linguistic and religious differences, resisted the pressure of the French government to introduce the French language (spoken at the time only by the upper-class), to remove instruction in German from schools, and to apply the law of 1905. The French government finally yielded on the religious question but remained intent on introducing French and eliminating German as the language of instruction. Then in 1924, a coalition of radicals and socialists (*Cartel des gauches*) won the legislative elections and sought to reverse the religious policies of the more conservative coalition of right and center parties (*Bloc national*).[121] As a result, the government Herriot attempted the introduction of laïcité in the three departments of Alsace-Moselle.[122] In spite of this attempt, the Concordat was legally confirmed in 1925 by the Conseil d'État. This status was disrupted again when these regions were annexed by the Germans in 1940 and once again reestablished in 1945 after the defeat of Nazi Germany.[123]

In these regions, the State officially recognizes four religions which existed in the early twentieth century—Catholic, Lutheran, Reformed, and Jewish. While the State has legal authority to appoint church leaders, in practice the State endorses those elected by Protestant or Jewish organizations and those chosen by the Pope. The bishops of Metz and Strasbourg are nominated by the president after consultation with Rome. All ministers are also accredited by the State which is now considered a formality. In return, the State takes responsibility for the remuneration of ministers of these four faiths. Municipalities provide a place to meet, assume the costs for

121. Prévotat, *Être chrétien*, 38.
122. Machelon, *La laïcité demain*, 22.
123. Guénois, "Pourquoi le Concordat."

these communities to function, and consider them public establishments. Religious teaching is regulated according to the Law Falloux of 1850 and is obligatory in public schools although parents may receive an exemption for their children.[124] Crucifixes can still be found in public schools which has troubled many advocates of strict laïcité especially since wearing clothes or symbols with religious signification was banned by law in 2004.[125] One of the issues presently debated concerns religions, for example Islam and Evangelical Protestants, which do not enjoy the same status as the recognized religions. There have been calls for the Concordat to be revoked in these regions with no religion any longer receiving special treatment.[126] However, polls show that the Alsacien population remains attached to regional rights on religion.[127] The next chapter will treat more recent attempts to change the concordataire status of Alsace-Moselle.

Any attempt to compare the French concept of constitutional laïcité with the secularism of her European counterparts and non-European nations must take into consideration both common factors and differences. These variations are specific to each nation's history and the place of religion in society. Indeed, there are nations with state churches where various faiths dominate—Catholic, Protestant and Orthodox. The difference in forms and application of laïcité can be attributed to the historical departure points. In France there was Gallican independence from Rome and the absolute predominance of the Catholic Church. The situation in the United States is largely the result of an exile of those persecuted for their religion in the Old Continent, in particular the Protestants. From the beginning they sought to establish a new society on the basis of the liberty of conscience. These differences influenced how politico-historical problems were treated and relationships between governments and religion.[128]

Jeroen Temperman differentiates between declared secular states and those states which might be considered secular without explicit constitutional reference. He demonstrates that "many states constitutionally establish themselves as secular states, many states constitutionally separate religion from the state, whilst some states, in fact, do both."[129] Temperman considers secular states as those whose authority and actions are not justified by religious commitments. He further states that declarations of secularity most

124. Haarscher, La laïcité, 34–35.
125. Rognon and Weber, La laïcité, 93.
126. Baubérot, "La laïcité absolue."
127. Cabanel, Les mots de la laïcité, 6.
128. Monod, Sécularisation et laïcité, 92–93.
129. Temperman, State-Religion Relationships, 111.

often address impartiality in religious matters and are not necessarily indicative of official atheism or anti-religion.[130] Temperman does find parallels
between France and the United States as examples of "official state secularism as the innovative endeavor to legitimize state authority precisely by *not*
anchoring it in the dominant religious doctrine."[131] Others see similarities
between the United States and France, that although the United States lacked
the word laïcité, they put it into practice early on. They laicized the federal
government earlier than a number of European States, including France, in
making it independent of religious confessions.[132]

However, the similarities which Temperman and others rightly observe must also be contrasted with differences. Perhaps no one has better
or more elegantly described the contrast between the America he visited in
the nineteenth century and the France of his upbringing than Alexis de Tocqueville expressed in his book *De la Démocratie en Amérique*. Tocqueville
marveled at the immensity of the land and the freedoms he perceived to be
enjoyed by the American people. He commented on the lack of historical
memory as one of the reasons for the apparent superiority of the American
political system and for the absence of religious conflict. He observed that
the democratic basis for citizenship was born without internal revolution.
A further comparison is made between nations with an aristocratic past
and those whose origins were democratic. De Tocqueville asserted that individuals in aristocratic societies with a Catholic culture tended to confine
people to a well-defined social stratification which hindered social mobility.
The lack of differentiation between political and religious identity legitima-
tized the segmentation of society.[133]

Machelon provides a French perspective and analysis on the differences between France and the United States:

> Seen from Europe, the American model of religious rights shows
> a biblical simplicity. The United States, wrote de Tocqueville,
> were established that it might be possible to pray to God in free-
> dom. Since then, its society and its institutions are bathed in an
> atmosphere of religiosity with a permanence and warmth that
> impresses the observer. Not less striking is the absolute neutral-
> ity of the powers that be in religious matters.[134]

130. Temperman, *State-Religion Relationships*, 111–12.
131. Temperman, *State-Religion Relationships*, 112.
132. Haarscher, *La laïcité*, 3.
133. Déloye, "La laïcité française," 24–26.
134. Machelon, *La laïcité demain*, 57.

He further observes that the quasi-religious respect of religious liberty, coming from the rupture with established churches and consecrated in the first amendment to the United States Constitution, imposes on public authorities strict obligations against public subsidizing of religion, direct or indirect, being rigorously forbidden by the establishment clause.[135] Americans adopted the separation framework, yet the atmosphere which surrounded it was largely colored by religiosity. The president takes an oath on the Bible even if all other great religious confessions and religious movements are protected and have their established place.[136]

Another French perspective compares religious decline in France with the apparent intensification of religion in the United States. The author, Jacques Soppelsa, professor at the Sorbonne and president of l'Académie Internationale de Géopolotique, writes with some forgivable hyperbole about the depth of religiosity in the US where no official act, throughout all the United States, is enacted without the Lord's assistance.[137] In his opinion, even with a 25 percent Catholic population, the country is fundamentally marked by a spectacular surge of fundamentalism.[138] Individuals are considered fundamentalists (Charles Fuller, Aimee Semple McPherson, Pat Robertson, Benny Hinn) or neo-fundamentalist (George W. Bush). This might come as a surprise to both them and to many fundamentalists, but demonstrates the problem with religious perceptions from other contexts. For some, the rise of fundamentalism is worrisome for underdeveloped nations because the prosperity gospel supposedly affirms that God does not love the poor and blesses only true believers. The ominous conclusion is that Protestant fundamentalism has become the major element, not only of the American religious landscape, but of North American society itself, the complete opposite of the very notion of laïcité.[139]

Religious Decline in France

French historian Adrien Dansette, writing mid-twentieth century, affirmed that the French possess a rational spirit and are more skeptical than other people. Several reasons are enumerated which contribute to this assessment. He claims that ancient religious beliefs were more readily received in remote areas where traditions preserved elements of social hierarchy.

135. Machelon, *La laïcité demain*, 58.
136. Robert, "Fondements juridiques," 9.
137. Soppelsa, "États-Unis," 48.
138. Soppelsa, "États-Unis," 49.
139. Soppelsa, "États-Unis," 51.

In his assessment, beginning in the nineteenth century, skepticism toward transcendental beliefs and religious authority increased for various reasons. These reasons included expanded educational opportunities for boys and girls and teaching content under the control of the State; the increased distribution of printed material; the progress of means of communication; obligatory military service since 1872; and more generally with transformations in the modern world and greater socialization among people from different horizons.[140] Beresniak comments that all religions claim to propose the only right way, although for the last two centuries it is generally acknowledged that faith is a private matter. When the idea of salvation by faith disappeared, it created an emptiness which was filled in the eighteenth century by the idea of salvation by society, that is, by a temporal social order guaranteed by the State.[141] In addition, Ferry affirms that after the relative retreat of religion, and after the death of the grand utopias which placed human actions in the forefront of historical progress, the question of sense in life has lost a place to be expressed collectively.[142] Yet, however one may analyze the perceived skepticism of an allegedly rationalistic people, there remains a persistent belief in God in France. Historians of religion hold that the frequentation of places of worship does not necessarily correlate with belief or unbelief.[143] Even Ferry recognizes that belief has not completely disappeared but has become for many a personal matter, relevant for the private sphere with a strict neutrality in the public sphere.[144]

The decline of the established Church in France began long before the 1905 Law of Separation and it continues today. This decline began in 1792 when the Church lost its administrative control over official civil activities—birth, marriage, death—and lost its religious monopoly under the 1801 Concordat. In 1881–1882, the laws of Jules Ferry created obligatory, free, and laïque public education and weakened the Church's influence. In 1905, the Catholic Church lost its position obtained under the Concordat and a much more level playing ground was provided for other religions.[145] The Catholic Church remains influential in France but has had to accommodate itself to a new order. From the Revolution to Vatican II the Roman Catholic Church refused to accept the principle of political autonomy. For the Church, public authority found its origin, not in human will, but in the

---

140. Dansette, *Histoire religieuse*, 33

141. Beresniak, *La Laïcité*, 145.

142. Ferry, *L'homme-Dieu*, 19.

143. Chassaigne, "Laïcité," 190.

144. Ferry, *L'homme-Dieu*, 38.

145. Simon, *France païenne*, 44–45.

divine order. The Church continued to defend the priority of religious identity both individually and collectively and refused to accept the reality that it was no longer the exclusive matrix of the social bond in society. The Catholic Church needed to adapt to a France where it was considered a religious orthodoxy in competition with others in a pluralistic religious market.[146] Habermas writes that "until the 1960s, Catholicism had great difficulties in understanding the secular thinking of humanism, the Enlightenment, and political liberalism."[147] Viguier believes that with the influence of the ideals of 1968 concerning individual liberties, and with opposition to all power structures or violations of the freedom of thought, the Catholic Church was abandoned.[148] Ferry, comparing premodern and modern people, explains that the fundamental values of Moderns truly contain nothing original, nor very modern. What was new, however, is the fact that these values were conceived beginning with man and not deducted from a revelation which precedes and encompasses him.[149]

The decline begun in the eighteenth and nineteenth centuries accelerated in the twentieth century. Hippolyte Simon, bishop of Clermont since 1996, archbishop emeritus since 2016, does not contest that sociological studies agree in pointing to a crumbling, sometimes even a collapse of the religious practice of Catholics in France.[150] The concern is that cultural and moral values are undermined in the opposition of French culture to the Catholic Church. Although many French people continue to have Catholic funeral services, Catholic marriages and baptized/catechized children have steeply declined. Statistics are one measure of decline and speak for themselves. In Basse-Normandie, for example, the percentage of Catholic marriages dropped from 90 percent to 64 percent from 1960 to 1990, almost 1 percent a year. In all of France only 50 percent of marriages were Catholic in 1992. The number of baptized children in France dropped from 80 to 60 percent from 1962 to 1992. In 1994, it was estimated that only 42 percent of French children were catechized.[151] From 1986 to 2004 the number of declared Catholics in France declined from 81 percent to 64.3 percent while the number of Protestants remained stable at about 2 percent. Yet religion has not disappeared in France. The number of French

146. Déloye, "La laïcité française," 32–33.

147. Habermas and Ratzinger, *Dialectics*, 37.

148. Viguier, "La laïcité," 80.

149. Ferry, *L'homme-Dieu*, 44.

150. Simon, *France païenne*, 9.

151. Simon, *France païenne*, 31–32.

people married, baptized, and catechized in the Catholic Church remains significant even if diminished.[152]

Simon, writing in 1999, saw several future possibilities for the Catholic Church in France corresponding to three categories—Catholic burials (80 percent of French), Catholic catechism (42 percent of French children in primary school), and monthly Catholic attendance at Mass (15 percent): (1) The Church retains its influence because of the strength of tradition. Many who distance themselves from the Church return at the time of their death, (i.e., President François Mitterrand). The lack of Catholic education among the youth, however, makes this scenario unlikely. (2) In thirty years, France will no longer have a Catholic majority. The Church will remain linked by history to Christianity but will need to adapt to being in a pluralistic nation. He does not discount the possibility of a Catholic revival but is not optimistic. (3) Since the majority of parents of children catechized do not attend mass, there is little reason to believe that their children will attend when they reach adulthood.[153]

In 2005, the Pew Research Center and Council for Foreign Affairs organized a roundtable discussion in connection with the 100th anniversary of secularism in France. The topic focused on the differences between Europe and the United States in attitudes regarding the place of religion in society. The 2002 Pew Global Attitudes survey was cited to demonstrate "striking differences in public opinion between the US and European countries on issues such as the importance people attach to religion in their lives and the linkage they perceive between belief in God and morality." It was found that "the majority of Americans consider religion important in their personal lives and closely associate religion and morality," and that "Americans are generally more comfortable with religion playing a major role in public life." Europeans, however, "generally place much less importance on religion in their lives, and general indicators show that major churches in Europe are declining in terms of membership, recruitment of clergy, financial contributions and overall public influence."[154]

One of the speakers at the event was Peter Berger, professor of sociology and theology at Boston University. He commented on the religious presence in much of the world including the United States and designated Western Europe as the exception in the lack of religious influences. He noted that "separation of church and state in France is now exactly 100 years old." He debunked the idea, one which he held earlier in his career, that

152. Fath, *Du Ghetto*, 322.

153. Simon, *France païenne*, 10–11.

154. Pew Research Center, "Secular Europe and Religious America."

"modernity necessarily leads to a decline in religion." He now believes that modernity leads to pluralism which he defines as "the coexistence within the same society of very different religious groups." Berger recognizes that "there are millions of Americans who are born-again Christians of one sort or another—there is nothing like this in Europe except in very small groups." He closed his speech in answering the question of why the difference exists between Europe and the United States. His response is enlightening: "When you deal with historical or social phenomenon of that magnitude, you can be sure of one thing: there's not going to be a single cause. There's going to be a complexity of causes. I've come up with seven. And I'm still not sure."[155] One thing is sure. People now have a choice in Europe which had been denied them for centuries. The implication is that the United States has had centuries of choice without the memory of institutionalized state and organized religious coercion. Europeans have exercised their choice to no longer belong to religious structures by exercising the right of the principle of voluntary association. According to Émile Poulat,

> If the influence of churches in [French] society is diminished it is not because the law excludes them from public life, but is above everything else a matter of society and culture. Science is laïque, the economy is laïque, the media, leisure activities, sports are laïque, and they are what shapes the mind not only more but also differently than catechism. . . . Churches still have authority but no longer have power.[156]

Yet the Church has not completely lost its place in French society, and religion and belief in God did not die. Certainly, there has been quantitative dechristianization when compared to times of obligation, conformity, and hereditary Christianity as seen in the reduced number of those practicing religion. French Catholic historian Delumeau summarizes the decline of Christianity in France in that the God of Christians was in times past much less alive than one might have believed and today much less dead than one might think.[157] He concludes his book with a probing question. In the end, is dechristianization simply the withering away of a model of Christianity that another is already perhaps in the process of replacing?[158] What remains to be seen is what model or models of Christianity in France God might use to re-evangelize this nation.

155. Pew Research Center, "Secular Europe and Religious America."
156. Poulat, "Culture laïque," 72–73.
157. Delumeau, Le christianisme, 149.
158. Delumeau, Le christianisme, 211.

Laïcité and Public Education

The law of 1905 was not greatly preoccupied with public education although the original concept and application of laïcité had its roots in separating the Church from public education. The public school had been one of the principal areas of battles between the "two Frances" all during the nineteenth century.[159] By 1905, much conventional wisdom had long assumed that religious instruction in public schools was in contradiction to laïcité. There had been a steady decline in religious influence in the removal of religion from public school curriculum in the nineteenth century where a laïque, obligatory, and free education was viewed as an essential element of forming citizens in the Republic. In the 1880s, Jules Ferry was influential in enacting laws concerning public and laïque education.[160] The separation of Church and school was settled in 1881–1882 under the educational laws associated with Jules Ferry abrogating the 1850 Law Falloux which had allowed religious instruction.[161] Under the law of 1882, in place of religious instruction in school, schools had to allow parents one day a week, aside from Sunday, to provide religious instruction for their children. In 1886, religious personnel were no longer permitted to teach in public elementary schools. Religious and moral instruction were replaced with moral and civic instruction. In 1905, all mention of God and the future life were removed from higher education in the *écoles normales*. However, it was only in 1923 that the mention of "duties to God" (*devoirs envers Dieu*) was finally eliminated and all religious references abandoned in primary schools.[162] The left-leaning Herriot government intended to prevent the Church from seeking a hold on society and on French youth, a hold judged prejudicial to the free awakening of the mind.[163] The "duties to God" were briefly reinstated in 1940 during the Vichy government (1940–1944) of Marshal Pétain (1856–1951). Religious instruction was added in 1941 with State subsidies for private schools. At the end of WWII, the principles of the laïque republican school were reestablished.[164]

Laïque instruction was seen as necessary both from an epistemological and sociopolitical standpoint and necessitated the removal of religious instruction. It was in the context of education that Monod concluded that

159. Rognon and Weber, *La laïcité*, 16.

160. Fontenay, "Un enseignement sur les religions," 37.

161. Gauchet, *La religion dans la démocratie*, 57.

162. Willaime, *Europe et religions*, 177.

163. Prévotat, *Être chrétien*, 38.

164. Jeantet, "L'école et la laïcité," 34.

laïcité can be understood as the complete secularization of institutions, as the institutional and juridical crowning of diverse processes of secularization and that laicization was a difference of degree—secularization taken further to its final consequences—the separation of Church and the State. Monod cites Quintet who in his *L'enseignement du people* (1850) expressed the conviction that modern science had been established in separating it from the science of the Church and that constitutional politics were made possible in the separation of religion from the State. For those who contended that teaching separated from religion would lead to moral chaos, Quintet contended that only in a laïque society would be found the principle of respect for the liberty of belief or unbelief.[165]

Just as laïcité loomed large in the debates on education in the nineteenth century, it resurfaced during the twentieth century and both adversaries and proponents marshaled laïcité to their cause. Voices arose to challenge the status quo and argued that religion was an important element in the history of France and should not be ignored. The argument was advanced that over the past century knowledge concerning religious phenomena had increased which should not be excluded from education. In 1982, La Ligue de l'enseignement proposed the non-confessional and pluralistic teaching of religions in schools in the name of multiculturalism. The idea was advanced that religions could be studied from a sociological angle with a historical and cultural perspective.[166] In support of this proposal, laïcité was defined as the total opening to knowledge. The theory was advanced that religions could be studied rationally and there was the duty to exercise reason in all domains and to refuse ignorance and fear.[167]

In 2002, Régis Debray authored a report for the Ministry of National Education which again raised the issue of religion in education. According to Debray, French opinion, in its majority, approved the idea of strengthening religious study in public schools for a reasoned approach of religions as realities of civilization. He rued the flattening and fading of daily life when the Trinity is only a metro stop, when religious holidays, vacations at Pentecost, and sabbaticals, are only accidents of the calendar. Assurance was given that the goal was not to put God back in school, but to prolong the human itinerary with multiple views, and the conviction expressed that one cannot strengthen the study of religion without strengthening studies overall. Debray was persuaded that apart from the knowledge of Wahhabism, of the Quran, and of monotheism, one could not understand the events of September 11,

165. Monod, *Sécularisation et laïcité*, 86–89.
166. Willaime, *Europe et religions*, 179.
167. Lambert, "Laïcité et religions," 41–42.

2001; without knowledge of the *filioque* and ancient confessional divisions in the Baltics one could not understand the breakup of Yugoslavia; without knowledge of Protestantism, one could not understand jazz and Martin Luther King. Non-confessional religious instruction would provide students additional means to escape from the prison of the present, then return with understanding to the world of today.[168] The report acknowledged the merits of the concerns of those who saw religious instruction as a Trojan horse or as a wolf in the sheepfold. His response was simply that teaching about religion is not religious teaching and he encouraged the passage from a *laïcité d'incompétence* to a *laïcité d'intelligence*.[169]

Debray made an instructive comparison between the situation in France and other European nations to show that there was no European model which France should follow. He emphasized that a laïcité written in the Constitution was more demanding than a legal separation of Church and State, more ambitious than a simple secularization and that the application in France constituted a singularity in Europe.[170] According to Debray, the Constitution of Ireland pays tribute to the Trinity; in Greece, where the Orthodox Church and State are connected, confessional teaching is obligatory; in Spain catechism is taught by professors approved by the diocese; in Portugal the Catholic Church provides instruction; in Denmark, with the Lutheran national church, there is a non-obligatory course on Christianity; in Germany, depending on the region, Christian education is officially part of instruction; and in Belgium students can choose between a religious course or a non-confessional course on morals. These examples were presented to demonstrate the difference between teaching a religion and teaching religious culture.[171]

In the realm of education, it is noteworthy that confusion about the meaning of laïcité remains widespread even among school students. A survey in 2015 revealed that 13 percent of students in junior high school (*collège*), living in troubled urban areas (*zones sensibles*), did not know the meaning of laïcité, in spite of the fact that posters are displayed at the entrance of schools with the principles of laïcité. To round out the survey, 42 percent of students defined laïcité as the acceptance of all religions, 30 percent as the right to not believe, and 9 percent the rejection of all religions (with 6 percent "other").[172]

168. Debray, "L'enseignement," 3–6.
169. Debray, "L'enseignement," 22.
170. Debray, "L'enseignement," 22.
171. Debray, "L'enseignement," 23–24.
172. "Sondage: La laïcité à l'école."

Protestant Evangelicalism in Catholic France

The history and development of evangelicalism in France must be understood in the larger historical context of religion in France. According to
Sébastien Fath, however, French specialist in the study of Evangelical Protestantism, evangelical Protestants have not yet benefitted from sufficient
investigation for an overall synthesis to be feasible.[173] Allen Koop adds that
the work of American evangelical missionaries in France has been largely
ignored by both secular and religious scholarship.[174] The development of
evangelicalism was severely limited by politics and the existence of the State
church. Jean-Yves Carluer writes that France, which claims along with others the paternity of the Rights of Man, had for a long time multiplied the
obstacles to complete religious liberty.[175] Even after the 1801 Concordat,
evangelicals were not part of the recognized religious confessions. Carluer
asserts that the liberty to believe granted by Bonaparte was not liberal but
was a means to govern. The first article of the law prohibited ministry in
France to all foreigners, which severely hindered evangelical expansion in
the country. Further, the Napoleonic penal code harshly sanctioned all possibility of gatherings apart from official religious confessions.[176] The status
gained by the recognized religious confessions was not granted to other
confessions who were repressed as unrecognized confessions. In speaking
of the Mennonites, Carluer contends that these descendants of Anabaptists
of the sixteenth century lost a great deal when the Concordat was signed
compared to their situation under the Ancien Régime and under the Revolution.[177] Evangelicals experienced repression and persecution during the
nineteenth century with a succession of regimes and revolutions until the
Third Republic. France experienced a long and difficult transition toward
religious liberty. This arduous struggle undoubtedly explains the weak development of evangelicals in France.[178]

Fath has made a significant contribution in his works on Baptists in
France and French Protestantism and sketches historical periods in the
emergence of French Protestant Evangelicalism. He documents the early
period under the Concordat (1800–1849) when non-concordataire evangelical churches were first considered neutral then later treated as outsiders

173. Fath, *Du Ghetto au réseau*, 15.

174. Koop, *Evangelical Missionaries*, 14.

175. Carluer, "Liberté de dire," 35.

176. Carluer, "Liberté de dire," 42–43.

177. Carluer, "Liberté de dire," 49.

178. Carluer, "Liberté de dire," 71.

and even deviants. On several occasions he explains that evangelicalism has often been perceived in France as foreign or American yet in reality is rooted in French history and culture. His massive study on the Baptists describes the obstacles they faced in entering a society with strong Catholic influences in the period from 1810 to 1950. Part of the difficulty was that these Protestants did not resemble French Protestants in the Lutheran and Reformed churches.[179] Evangelical Protestants, at the beginning of the Third Republic, experienced a turning point even more important than 1905 that led to what he calls a *"lune de miel"* (honeymoon) between evangelicals and the Republic.[180] This happened at the time when Reformed churches experienced a schism in 1872 between an orthodox majority and a liberal minority. Several evangelical Protestants were involved in politics and evangelicals were considered anticlerical, advocates of individual liberty, democracy, and laïcité. The new-found status of evangelicals was reinforced by the support of many evangelical leaders for Captain Dreyfus during *l'Affaire* which shook French society. Among these leaders was Protestant theologian Raoul Allier, who had been active in advocating for a liberal, more moderate version of the law of 1905.

In 1907, in the context of the separation of Church and State, Allier reaffirmed the commitment of the Union des Églises évangéliques libres (UEEL) to the authority of Scriptures. The UEEL adopted a new Declaration of Faith in 1909 at the Synod of Sainte-Foy in light of the new political reality under which churches lived.[181] Evangelical churches experienced momentum with evangelistic campaigns widely held. There was an emphasis on morality and economic justice which resulted in an acclimation without precedent of Protestant evangelization in France with the Catholic Church viewed as hostile to the Republic. The Baptists and independents (*libristes*) were the most active in politics leading up to 1905 with several influential senators. Fath writes that on a small scale, Evangelical Protestants fully profited from the deficit of elites at the summit of the Republic because of the temporary quarrel with the Catholic Church.[182]

Fath also describes the growth of evangelicalism in France, the growing urgency of biblical training, and the founding of evangelical training institutions:

> At the mid-point of the 60s, it was difficult to not be struck
> by the popular dimension, at times even populist dimension,

179. Fath, *Une autre manière*.
180. Fath, *Du Ghetto au réseau*, 128.
181. Baty, "Églises évangéliques," 296–99.
182. Fath, *Du Ghetto au réseau*, 128–29.

of French evangelical churches. Within the Protestant minority, there was considerable contrast between the Reformed and Lutherans, on one side, and evangelicals on the other side. The former had a rich intellectual tradition, a well-honed and efficient system of training, and a prestigious cultural legacy. The latter lacked serious training, few cultural connections, and a heavy deficit of credibility in the area of reflection.[183]

The founding of Faculté Libre de Théologie Évangélique in Vaux-sur-Seine (FLTE) in 1965 is viewed as the culmination of an emphasis on theological education. Samuel Bénétreau, André Thobois, Jules-Marcel Nicole, and Jacques Blocher were among the well-trained and highly regarded professors. This new school did not replace l'Institut Biblique de Nogent-sur-Marne (IBN) founded in 1921 which had been the primary training center for evangelicals. The FLTE distinguished itself from IBN with a rigorous academic curriculum which included biblical languages, a four-year program, and an emphasis on research. Fath notes that the establishment of the FLTE marked a turning point in the history of evangelical Protestants in France which contributed to evangelicalism's growing credibility.[184] The importance of this school becomes clearer in the context of a crisis in French Protestantism when the majority of Lutheran and Reformed churches minimized individual salvation and emphasized ideologies of social progress. To counter the inroads of liberal theology, the Faculté libre de théologie réformée (presently La faculté Jean Calvin) was founded in 1974 in Aix-en-Provence in a return to the teaching of Calvin and the Confession de la Rochelle. The founders considered that the truth of the gospel was challenged and replaced by humanism.[185] Under attack in Protestant circles was the very definition of evangelization:

> The task of Protestant churches in the presentation of the offer of salvation changed in content. The traditional definition of evangelization insisted on the explicit proclamation of the message of the Gospel, that one might summarize as a call to faith in a divinity which was incarnated (Jesus Christ), to reconcile, by his death and his resurrection, repentant sinners with their heavenly creator, God the father.[186]

In 1956, Jean Séguy wrote to expose the problem of Protestant sects in France. A distinction was made between Protestant sects which

183. Fath, *Du Ghetto au réseau*, 189.
184. Fath, *Du Ghetto au réseau*, 190.
185. Berthoud, "La faculté libre de théologie reformée."
186. Fath, *Du Ghetto au réseau*, 191.

regarded the Bible as the only inspired book with a Reformation lineage and other sects with additional authoritative writings. Among the former were included the Quakers, Methodists, and Salvation Army. Among the latter were Christian Science, Church of the Latter-Day Saints, and other sects which did not find their origins either in Catholicism or the Reformation.[187] On the origin of Protestant sects, according to Séguy, geographically they came to France from England or the United States and genealogically from churches emerging from the Reformation.[188] Now over fifty years later it is acknowledged that evangelicalism is now at the heart of debates on the future of religion and champions a model with which religion and the Republic must reckon.[189]

Three evangelical movements from Protestant England faithfully preached the gospel and contributed to the growth of evangelicalism during the twentieth century. These movements were the Salvation Army, Popular Evangelical Mission, and the Assemblies of God. Collaboration grew among these movements and some Reformed churches for the organization of large-scale evangelistic meetings.[190] In 1946, the Annuaire Protestant counted only twenty-five evangelical churches in the Paris region apart from Lutheran and Reformed churches.[191] Pownall documents church planting efforts undertaken by the Église Reformée, Assemblées de Dieu, Fédération Baptiste, Alliance des Églises Évangéliques Interdépendantes, Assemblées de Frères et de France Mission, Églises Évangéliques Libres, Alliance Baptiste, Églises charismatiques, and Églises ethniques.[192]

Ethnic churches began to multiply in the early 1980s with African churches in the lead. However, few ethnic churches have succeeded in integrating into the French Protestant landscape. One exception is several African churches affiliated with the Fédération des Églises et Communautés Baptistes Charismatiques. The Annuaire Évangélique from 2002 to 2003 listed two hundred seventy-two evangelical churches in the Paris region. Of those, about thirty-eight churches are explicitly ethnic and another twenty-five churches possibly ethnic but unsubstantiated. The difficulty in gathering information on churches has led to the conclusion that the numbers of ethnic churches are underestimated.[193] Thus, the statistics may be seen

187. Séguy, *Sectes protestantes*, 7–8.
188. Séguy, *Sectes protestantes*, 13.
189. Fath, "Protestants évangéliques français," 361.
190. Pownall, "Un demi-siècle d'implantation," 54–55.
191. Pownall, "Un demi-siècle d'implantation," 57–58.
192. Pownall, "Un demi-siècle d'implantation," 58–66.
193. Pownall, "Un demi-siècle d'implantation," 67–68.

in different lights. Certainly, the growth of evangelicalism and the progress made in the twentieth century is encouraging. However, it should not mask the reality that evangelicals remain underrepresented in France. Pownall concludes in reflecting on the wisdom of the strategy of targeting the Paris region. He notes that results, with different strategies, have been modest among a population largely closed to the gospel and wonders if it is time to target those more open to the gospel.[194]

One indication of the lack of influence and presence of evangelicals in France comes from a gathering led by the Minister of the Interior in April 2011. The theme was "*Une laïcité respectée pour renforcer la cohésion nationale.*" The press communiqué stated that the purpose of this reunion was a reminder of the importance of laïcité affirmed by the 1958 Constitution as one of the organizational principles of the Republic. This reunion sought to further national cohesion and rally France to its fundamental values. Among the participants invited to this gathering were representatives of the Catholic, Jewish, Muslim, Buddhist, Orthodox, and mainline Protestant confessions. Notably absent was any representative from the evangelical community such as the CNEF.[195]

We might also ask how the Catholic Church views evangelicals. Michel Mallèvre's introduction to his book on evangelicalism provides a response. He recognizes that evangelical communities were often ignored and treated with contempt as cults. They have now become the focus of numerous articles and television coverage which highlight their impressive growth, while at the same time denouncing proselytism, the enrichment of some of their leaders, and strange behavior during worship.[196] He provides a further assessment in observing that all in all, many Catholics and the press present evangelicals under unflattering aspects which are far from representing the whole movement.[197] Yet he laments that the evangelical movement is characterized by militancy and that its members appear more occupied with the individual salvation of their neighbors, to whom they announce salvation in Jesus Christ with zeal, than with an engagement in the world.[198]

Koop provides a sobering analysis of the American contribution to evangelicalism in France between WWII and 1975. In Koop's opinion, until World War II, "most American Christians assumed that European churches were capable of carrying out the task of evangelism in their respective

194. Pownall, "Un demi-siècle d'implantation," 72.
195. Guéant, "Une laïcité respectée."
196. Mallèvre, *Les évangéliques*, 5.
197. Mallèvre, *Les évangéliques*, 99.
198. Mallèvre, *Les évangéliques*, 71.

countries."[199] American missionaries established a post-war presence in France but the lukewarm welcome by the French hindered missionary work with misunderstandings about identity and intentions.[200] In addition, many French Protestants resented being considered a mission field and were surprised by the presence of missionaries.[201] The difficulty of engaging in ministry was complicated by the backgrounds and unpreparedness of the missionaries. Koop observes that most missionaries worked in urban areas but had been raised in rural communities and few had converted from Catholicism. He further notes that most missionaries lacked the training needed for ministry in France. Many missionaries arrived in France with enthusiasm and lofty evangelistic goals and soon learned how badly prepared they were for the challenges of ministry in another culture.[202] Koop describes the dramatic growth of the American evangelical movement in finances and personnel which met with little success and great discouragement. American missionaries also learned to their dismay that even in secular France the Catholic Church exerted great influence.[203]

Late Twentieth-Century Resurgence of Laïcité Debate

Throughout much of the twentieth century, even with the changes in relations between the State and religion, laïcité appeared to be an unchallenged reality especially once it was enshrined constitutionally in 1946 and 1958. Cabanel designates the 1980s as a pivotal turning point in France. He describes the emphasis on individual rights, the secularization of the laïque ideal, the growing visibility of Islam in public space and debates, the place of religions newly recognized by the State, and the concern to teach the religious dimension of society in public schools. He concluded that a new landscape was put in place in the 80s, very different and distant from the France both Catholics and non-Catholics had known in previous generations.[204]

The year 1989 was decisive with Islam emerging as a threat to French laïcité. The emergence of Islam as a visible phenomenon was brutally perceived by public opinion with the Islamic headscarf affair (*l'affaire du foulard*

199. Koop, *Evangelical Missionaries*, 7.
200. Koop, *Evangelical Missionaries*, 10.
201. Koop, *Evangelical Missionaries*, 24.
202. Koop, *Evangelical Missionaries*, 11–12.
203. Koop, *Evangelical Missionaries*, 23.
204. Cabanel, "La question religieuse," 182.

islamic) in 1989 in the school at Creil.[205] At the beginning of the school year, two students of Moroccan origin arrived at school with headscarves. After refusing to remove them, claiming their fidelity to Islam, they were expelled from school. The principal justified his decision on the basis that religious manifestations of belief were prohibited in public schools. The question of the headscarf instantly took on a national dimension which made it a State matter.[206] It was at this moment that the advocates of laïcité divided. The issue was whether the introduction in public schools of religious symbols belonging to the private sphere might be equated with a recolonization of the public sphere. Some argued that wearing the headscarf was benign. Others argued against it from a strict interpretation of separation which confined religion to the private sphere. The headscarf was seen in a larger context of struggle as only the beginning of religious claims which would lead to more demands especially from Muslims.[207]

Also, in 1989 Ayatollah Khomeini issued his fatwa against the novelist Salmon Rushdie, accused of blasphemy in his treatment of the Prophet Mohammed in the book *Satanic Verses*. It was a time of international tension and fears related to the rise of militant Islam. According to Bowen,

> The Rushdie incident brought together several related fears about Islam: that it was intolerant, that Muslims, once in power, would kill those who left the religion and would cut off the hands of thieves; and that the relative success of the Iranian mullahs meant that Islam was on a worldwide roll, certain to come to power elsewhere. . . . Religion, but particularly Islam, seemed to have crossed into politics in places very close to France.[208]

Over the next few years *l'affaire du foulard* continued to divide opposing camps of laïcité. The terms *foulard* (headscarf) and *voile* (veil) are both employed for this incident and the choice of word is probably not neutral.[209] There was a split between supporters of a *laïcité ouverte* (open), advocating integration through education, and proponents of a *laïcité fermée* (closed) who were opposed to all signs of religious identification in public schools, particularly in dress. Baubérot affirms that until this incident the headscarf was worn unchallenged in France by students and teachers, visible but without social importance, and that it was not seen as a Muslim headscarf

205. Jeantet, "L'école et la laïcité," 35.
206. Rémond, *L'anticléricalisme*, 377.
207. Haarscher, *La laïcité*, 35.
208. Bowen, *Headscarves*, 83.
209. Rémond, *L'anticléricalisme*, 375.

(*foulard islamique*).[210] French philosopher Finkielkraut disagrees and states that this was not a foulard but a veil and one of the Islamic devices for subordinating and putting women in their place.[211]

The fracture between advocates of different concepts of laïcité gave birth to the Comité Laïcité et République (CLR) and prompted debates with La Ligue de l'enseignement. Both organizations agreed that laïcité was an ongoing combat carried out against all forms of extremism, against injustice, and for human dignity.[212] They were not in agreement, however, on all points and their disagreements are found in French society today. The CLR took a stronger stand against religious symbols and raised the specter of *communautarisme*, which developed the formation of communities along ethnic, religious or cultural lines to the detriment of integration.[213] They also viewed with suspicion the support of the Catholic Church for the religious rights of Muslims. The Ligue regarded as unfounded the fears of the CLR and did not consider seriously that individual freedom in religious identity might somehow shake the foundations of a society which had been evolving toward the protection of individual rights for ten centuries. The Ligue also believed that the majority of Muslims wished to integrate a French society which provided equal rights for all. These rights included the free exercise of worship and the liberty of expression.[214]

The changed landscape of France during the twentieth century, and specifically the issues of the late 1980s and early 1990s, contributed to the revival of interest in laïcité. Maurice Barbier identified this ten-year timeframe when laïcité became the object of new debates with multiple issues which needed to be addressed.[215] After decades of accommodation and relative calm, an embattled end-of-century was ushered in with ancient, unresolved questions on the relation between religion and the State. As Rinnert notes, issues surrounding Islam were the catalyst for the renewed debate on laïcité. She argued that to speak of Islam when it was a question of laïcité was neither Islamophobic nor stigmatizing. From young girls wearing veils in Creil in 1989 to the wearing of burkinis on French beaches in the summer of 2016, there was no need to deny that it was essentially these events that brought the debate to the forefront of the nation's concerns.[216]

210. Baubérot, "L'affaire des foulards," 9.

211. Finkielkraut and Lévy, *Le Livre et les livres*, 33.

212. Kessel et al., "Ni plurielle, ni de combat," 64.

213. Robert et al., *Nouveau Petit Robert*, 478.

214. Kessel et al., "Ni plurielle, ni de combat," 68–69.

215. Barbier, "Esquisse d'une théorie," 73.

216. Rinnert, "Le principe de laïcité," 130.

Likewise, while the decline of organized religion was undeniable, there were unmistakable signs of religious inquiry in the wake of world wars, terrorism, economic uncertainty, and failed governmental systems. Ferry reviewed the twentieth century and concluded that all serious sociological studies disclosed the magnitude of the movement of secularization winning over the democratic, European world which resulted in a veritable dechristianization.[217] Yet Finkielkraut, who wrote toward the end of the twentieth century, affirmed that today God seemed to have had his revenge and the universal fiasco of secular revolutions had offered a completely new legitimacy to religious radicalism.[218] Gauchet sees the failure of religious substitutes which filled the vacuum created by the decline of Christianity. For him, the great spiritual event at the end of the twentieth century had been the death of revolutionary faith in earthly salvation.[219] He saw a paradox in the weakening of religion and the return of religion to center stage as an overturning of laïcité as it was traditionally understood. Yet, in his assessment, any apparent religious resurgence which comes from outside France had nothing in common with the Pentecostal fever active in third world cities, or with evangelical fundamentalism at work in the Bible Belt in the United States.[220] He interpreted the demand of public recognition of private religion as the focus of changes in Europe and in challenges to laïcité. This demand was perceived as less troubling for secularized Protestant nations but as a major rupture with French culture.[221] Finally, Prévotat wrote from a Catholic perspective that some worrying aspects of religious decline, like the reduction of the number of regular religious practitioners, did not signify the end of Christianity, but rather inaugurated a new mode of existence or a period of retreat momentarily necessary for the recovery of missionary momentum.[222]

We conclude with Robert that the dechristianization of France in the twentieth century led to substitutions for life in community outside the organized Church.[223] Dechristianization has also given rise to other more radical forms of religion to fill the vacuum and has dashed the hopes of secular religion to fill the void left by the marginalization of transcendental religions. The question concerning religion in the public sphere remains

217. Ferry, *L'homme-Dieu*, 65.

218. Finkielkraut, "La laïcité," 54.

219. Gauchet, *La religion dans la démocratie*, 23.

220. Gauchet, *La religion dans la démocratie*, 36–38.

221. Gauchet, *La religion dans la démocratie*, 40.

222. Prévotat, *Être chrétien*, 261.

223. Robert, "Fondements juridiques," 6.

unresolved as well as "the compatibility of the progress of humanism with the idea of divinely revealed moral truth."[224] The twenty-first century, to which we now turn, gives evidence that laïcité in France remains uncontested as a concept, value, or principle. The ongoing struggle resides in its meaning and application according to each disputatious voice.

224. Ferry, *L'homme-Dieu*, 66.

6

Twenty-First-Century Challenges to Laïcité

FRENCH SOCIETY ACCOMMODATED ITSELF to religious changes in the twentieth century following the disestablishment of concordataire state churches. The arrival of the law of 1905 ended decades of harsh combats between political and laïque powers.[1] The law was both a law of rupture and a law of conciliation. The rupture was considered justified by many since the Church was a threat to the Republic. The conciliation was a guarantee of the free exercise of religion and the liberty of conscience.[2] Jean-Michel Bélorgey describes French laïcité as a response to confrontations between the Catholic Church and political powers and to several centuries of religious quarrels which profoundly marked and bloodied French society, and as an attempt to battle the imperialism of the Catholic Church of France, the eldest daughter of the Church.[3]

We saw previously that by 1924, the Catholic Church accepted its new status and adapted accordingly to its diminished prestige, influence, and numbers. The Catholic Church waited until the twentieth century to recognize the freedom of conscience, the autonomy of scientific inquiry, and the equality of all people, believers or not—all the things that Pope Pius IX still anathematized in his 1864 *Syllabus*.[4] The Church continued to believe that the Law of Separation was contrary to the order willed by God, but could be accommodated from the moment the State respected the rights and the liberties of the Church.[5] Radical transformation in the Catholic Church in France followed in the fifty years after Vatican II.[6] Both

1. Soppelsa, "De la laïcité," 2.
2. Rognon and Weber, *La laïcité*, 91.
3. Bélorgey, "Terroirs de la laïcité," 53.
4. Pena-Ruiz, *Qu'est-ce que la laïcité?*, 181.
5. Prévotat, *Être chrétien*, 30.
6. Korsia, "La laïcité," 84.

the Catholic Church and its adversaries came to accept the idea of a State serving all citizens and no longer subject to religious belief.[7] There was optimism that the Church had in itself the spiritual resiliency to remove itself from the nostalgia of an idealized past in order to put itself without reserve at the service of a laïque society, to contribute along with all others, to invent a better humanity in the present civilization.[8]

The law of 1905 evolved in the twentieth century, particularly between World War I and World War II, and mostly in relation to questions of education. It was understood that the public school was both the realization of a particular political organization and of specific religious and moral options.[9] The public school's primary purpose remained the formation of young citizens according to republican values. Soppelsa argues that the evolution of the concept of laïcité was modest for most of the twentieth century and that its structure, its coherence and its objectives were not fundamentally questioned.[10] Matthew Kaemingk maintains that "the utter dominance of secular liberalism in Europe during the twentieth century created the impression that the question of faith and public life had all been laid to rest and that the problem of public religion had been solved."[11]

Toward the end of the twentieth century, the concept of laïcité began to develop beyond its traditional sense of separation of Church and State and the concept of State neutrality. Laïcité was conceived in a new manner and generally in terms of freedom. Traditional laïcité appeared outdated and inadequate.[12] The opening years of the twenty-first century in France presented contemporary challenges for laïcité and applications of the law of 1905. For that reason, in 2006 laïcité could be described as a modern idea requiring systematic promotion because it remained more than ever the prerequisite for economic, social, and political progress at the beginning of a new millennium.[13] Indeed, in the last few decades the subject of laïcité returned to prominence in French society. What began as a trickle of books on laïcité in the late 1900s became a torrent in the early twenty-first century. The multitude of studies which have been consecrated to laïcité led to blurring the notion rather than clarifying it.[14]

7. Haarscher, *La laïcité*, 24.

8. Coq, *Laïcité et République*, 330.

9. Billard, *De l'école à la République*, 1.

10. Soppelsa, "De la laïcité," 3.

11. Kaemingk, *Christian Hospitality*, 6.

12. Barbier, "Esquisse d'une théorie," 71.

13. Soppelsa, "De la laïcité," 3.

14. Barbier, "Pour une définition," 129.

Many of the concerns and questions raised in the twenty-first century are far removed from issues debated and resolved at the time of the law of 1905. It has been noted that within a year or two of the centennial of the law of 1905 there was an extraordinary upsurge in laïque debate in France concerning a question—the wearing of symbols or clothing by which students ostensibly manifested a religious commitment—which certainly was nothing new but which was hardly an issue in the debates of 1905.[15] Islam presented the problem of laïcité in a different manner to French and European society. The problem was not the long presence of Muslims in France, but the radicalization of Islam in the 1990s.[16] The issues now included employees in the public sector who are obligated to be neutral in religious matters, hospitals where women refused to be treated by male doctors, and school debate on displaying religious symbols in dress and accessories. To add to the tensions, social conflict arose in much of Europe where Muslims often lived in unfavorable conditions and overcrowded neighborhoods beset by crime.[17]

Among the questions raised concerning Islam and its place in French society, perhaps none is more important than the question of Islam's compatibility in Western democracy. The writer Ghaleb Bencheikh claims that the incompatibility of Islam and laïcité is one of the most tenacious prejudices in the minds of French people.[18] Cesari asserts that "the crucial question for scholars of Islam, which recent events have done nothing to change, is that of Muslim integration in European societies."[19] Her approach does not deny the ability of Muslims to acclimate to a new context and she distinguishes between Islam as found in majority-Muslim nations and as a minority in non-Muslim countries.[20] In fact, she observes that among immigrant Muslims, "more and more, religious practice tends to become a private matter, freed from the social conventions and standards of Islam as practiced in officially Muslim countries."[21] However, the critical and unanswered question remains: "How can Islam and Muslims be integrated into Western culture while still maintaining the latter's principles of equality and individual freedoms?"[22] This question is crucial if, as Cesari claims, "the most divisive question among religious authorities is to what extent

15. Rognon and Weber, La laïcité, 89.

16. Dusseau, "L'histoire de la Séparation," 22.

17. Cesari, Islam and Democracy, 23.

18. Bencheikh, "L'Islam au risque," 87–88.

19. Cesari, Islam and Democracy, 3.

20. Cesari, Islam and Democracy, 44.

21. Cesari, Islam and Democracy, 45.

22. Cesari, Islam and Democracy, 63.

the obligations of *Shari'a* can be fulfilled in the West."[23] She emphasizes that "certain underlying assumptions of *Shari'a*, such as the inequality of men and women, the unequal status of different religions, and the status of the apostate in Islamic tradition, must all be reexamined in light of the Western conception of human rights."[24] Fontenay compares the issues of kippa and Saturday absences for Jewish students, which have been resolved amicably, with the radical demands of a combative Islam which become obstacles to education. She considers it essential to respond to the question of the compatibility between extreme forms of Islamic allegiance and the non-obsolete demands of the French school system.[25]

The question of the compatibility of Islam with republican values was raised one hundred years ago regarding Catholicism. We saw earlier that the fraternity of World War I trenches united a divided French people in a common cause in defense of the Republic. There are skeptics who doubt that Islam can imitate Catholicism's accommodation and renounce its global vision of world domination. One important difference is that Catholicism was not a foreign religion introduced into the nation by an immigrant population. Others consider that Islam can accommodate itself to Western society once purged of its political ambitions. To that end, there is a call for boundaries to be established without excessive demands which might be judged as intolerant.[26]

Saad Khiari attempts to demonstrate that the French values of *liberté*, *égalité*, and *fraternité* are found in a proper reading of the Quran. He questions the qualifications of most intellectual and political detractors of Islam who do not know Arabic and who use mediocre French translations of the Quran, and he doubts their objectivity in their critique of Islam. He likewise questions whether it is legitimate to place Islam, as a revealed religion, and as such the work of God, opposite a construction imagined by men, the Republic, in order to determine its destiny.[27] Further, while recognizing the laïque character of the French Republic, he accuses the far right of using the issue of laïcité to sow doubt on the compatibility of Islam with the values of the Republic.[28] Catholicism adapted to the laïque Republic in the twentieth century. In a similar vein to Islam today, Catholicism of yesteryear claimed the status of a revealed religion in a struggle against

23. Cesari, *Islam and Democracy*, 146.

24. Cesari, *Islam and Democracy*, 169.

25. Fontenay, "Un enseignement sur les religions," 39.

26. Bélorgey, "Terroirs de la laïcité," 58–59.

27. Khiari, *L'Islam et les valeurs*, 10.

28. Khiari, *L'Islam et les valeurs*, 12.

human institutions. In time, following the law of 1905, Catholicism grudgingly accepted the loss of its influence in the political sphere. It remains to be seen whether the same will be true of French Islam in the twenty-first century or what laws might bring that to pass.

Rognon and Weber provide a thoughtful analysis of French society one hundred years after the introduction of juridical laïcité in 1905 to show that changes in French society cannot be separated from global changes and challenges. They assert that one of the major challenges for laïcité comes from globalization and its multiple effects on national societies. They recognize that a century after the law of 1905 societies have become multicultural. Immigrants have encountered discrimination in which employment, housing, and respect are often refused to those who do not look European. However, there is the concern that attempts to grant collective rights, beyond the individual rights granted to every citizen, lead to an identity defined by membership in a group rather than as an individual. In their opinion, this group identity results in the fragmentation of society and creates a profound crisis for laïcité.[29]

The understanding of French laïcité continues to expand from its original conception and intention under the law of 1905. This is unsurprising since the French religious, political, and demographic landscape has been radically altered during the past one hundred years. A public debate, held in 2005 to celebrate the one-hundredth anniversary of the introduction of the law of 1905, recognized these changes and the new challenges associated with them. The conference was entitled, "La Laïcité: Une question au présent." The texts were compiled in a book of the same name which examined the significance and the signification of laïcité in contemporary times.[30] Once again it became evident that there were divergent conceptions of laïcité itself.[31] Rognon and Weber explained that from the law of 1905 there remained especially the grand principles. The difference was their application in concrete situations, more precisely in the conflicts taking place due to interpretation.[32] We agree with Cabanel that laïcité is one of the most difficult words in contemporary French language.[33]

29. Rognon and Weber, La laïcité, 101–3.
30. Birnbaum and Viguier, La Laïcité.
31. Haarscher, La laïcité, 24.
32. Rognon and Weber, La laïcité, 91.
33. Cabanel, Les mots de la laïcité, 64.

Islam and the Clash of Cultures

The resurgence of interest in laïcité is unquestionably linked with the emergence of Islam as the second largest religion in France.[34] Jenkins notes that "some observers see Europe making a wholesale transition into the Muslim world, becoming part of Eurabia, a word that provides a concise shorthand for an array of cultural and ethnic nightmares."[35] The centenary celebration of the law of 1905 and the presence of a large Muslim community in France combined to relaunch the debate on laïcité in a pressing manner.[36] The relatively homogeneous France of the early twentieth century was replaced with the pluralistic, heterogeneous France of the early twenty-first century. In 2004, France's Muslim population was estimated at over four million.[37] Cesari writes, "It is a significant fact that throughout Europe, the arrival of Islam has reopened the file—up to now considered 'case closed'—the relationship between Church and State."[38] It has been asserted that the laïcité of the nineteenth century fought against religious imperialism and against the pretentions of hegemony of the Church, and the laïcité in contemporary times is locked in a struggle with religious fundamentalisms which threaten democracy.[39] In the late twentieth and early twenty-first centuries, laïcité reappeared in contentious debates particularly regarding the place of Islam in French society.[40] Cesari makes the following observation:

> Islam's approach to the concept of democracy was turned upside-down once Muslims began to establish communities in the West. The changes that are currently taking place are even more remarkable in that for the majority of Muslims, the concepts of democracy and secularization are associated with Western domination, both colonial and postcolonial.[41]

In addition, as Roy notes, "In the West secularization is seen as a prerequisite for democratization, but in the Middle East it is mostly associated with dictatorship. . . . The contradiction of secularists in many Muslim countries

34. Fontenay, "Un enseignement sur les religions," 45.
35. Jenkins, God's Continent, 4.
36. Barbier, "Pour une définition," 129.
37. Cesari, Islam and Democracy, 9–10.
38. Cesari, Islam and Democracy, 65.
39. Beresniak, La Laïcité, 7.
40. Machelon, La laïcité demain, 5.
41. Cesari, Islam and Democracy, 165.

is that they favour State control of religion and often ignore or even suppress traditional and popular expressions of it."[42]

From an evangelical perspective, the CNEF describes the tensions which exist in France as secularizing forces push religions into the private sphere and religions raise their claims to be heard in a democratic society. They understand that the balance is no longer between a dominant religion and an independent State, but in terms of equality between different religions in the midst of a laïque Republic which still bears the strong imprint of Catholicism.[43] Cabanel eloquently describes laïcité as a dying religion which once filled France with certitudes, where the emphasis on rights prevailed over duties, where the god of progress was dethroned in the crises of the twentieth century, among them the crisis of crimes against humanity. Other gods, secular and religious, have rushed to fill the vacant space. These new idols offer guaranteed rights for all differences, fulfillment for all sexual desires, and reparations for seemingly universal victimhood. As well, Islam has opposed laïcité and has provided the primary impetus for the renewed interest in laïcité beginning in 1989 with the first incident of the Islamic veil to 2004 and the law on religious symbols in public schools and has replaced Catholicism as the new adversary of laïcité.[44] In less than a quarter of a century after 1989 and the headscarf affair of Creil, France passed from the appeasement of an apparent secularization to the return of identity tensions motivated by affirmations as much religious as cultural. The principle of laïcité became more than ever of current importance.[45] Pena-Ruiz asserted that the essential debate was to know whether if a century after the law of 1905, the modification of the religious landscape, notably with the emergence of Islam as the second religion of France, called for a redefinition of its laïque principles.[46]

We discover that the Islamic headscarf incident (*l'affaire du foulard islamic*) in 1989 surfaces repeatedly as the singular event which triggered a reexamination of laïcité in modern, pluralistic France. We will return to that incident several times because of its prominence in the literature on laïcité. There are some who assert that the headscarf in the classroom represented a hindrance to the integration of many.[47] This event served notice to the French government of the necessity of integrating Islam into national life and

42. Roy, *Globalized Islam*, 3n2.

43. CNEF, *Laïcité française*, 18.

44. Cabanel, "La question religieuse," 177–79.

45. Rinnert, "Le principe de laïcité," 127.

46. Pena-Ruiz, *Qu'est-ce que la laïcité?*, 162.

47. Coq, *Laïcité et République*, 328.

of building bridges of communication. Some considered that the reaction of teachers and moderate Muslims against the false charges of discrimination leveled against the school's principal provided a warning to France about the global danger of Islamism.[48] Cesari contends that the headscarf controversy led to renewed debate about laïcité long considered settled:

> More important, perhaps, is that the headscarf controversy has brought to light the glaring disparity between the dominant sociocultural conception of secularism and its legal expression. In other words, the way in which most French citizens understand secularism is not at all the same as the law itself. The law merely provides for separation of Church and State—and therefore, religious neutrality in public institutions—and for the legal protection of all religious expressions.[49]

In 2010, further restrictions on religious expression were enacted with a law banning the full-face veil (*voile intégral/burqa*) in public. The law followed the logic of the ban on headscarves in 2004 in public schools. Although security concerns were invoked, many saw it as an attack on Islam; others as a reaffirmation of republican values and equality for women.[50] The law was overwhelmingly approved by the Senate and provided fines both for anyone wearing the veil and for anyone forcing a woman to wear the veil. The Conseil français du culte musulman (CFCM) mobilized imams to engage in theological dialogue with Muslim women to convince them that this particular type of veil was not essential to Islamic identity. Other currents of Islam resisted and challenged the law.[51]

These incidents have shaped divergent views on the capacity of Islam to adapt to Western society. French academic Jean-François Revel advances the idea that if Islam had not refused modern science, perhaps Islamic countries would not have suffered for the past three centuries from a negative cultural experience.[52] He also asserts and provides examples to show that Islamic tolerance goes in one direction regarding what they demand for themselves which they never extend to others.[53] In 2016, l'Institut Montaigne affirmed the possibility of French Islam: "*Un islam français est possible*."[54] The study reported that 28 percent of Muslims in France, and 50 percent of those

---

48. Finkielkraut and Lévy, *Le Livre et les livres*, 38.

49. Cesari, *Islam and Democracy*, 76.

50. Leclair, "La loi sur le voile."

51. Gabizon, "Le Parlement vote."

52. Revel, *L'obsession anti-américaine*, 200.

53. Revel, *L'obsession anti-américaine*, 125.

54. Karoui, *Un islam français*.

from 15 to 25 years old, had adopted values clearly opposed to those of the French Republic. At the same time, the study asserted that the majority of Muslims in France did not identify with radical Islam. While recognizing the necessity of the State to combat terrorism and to uphold the security of the nation, the report maintained that these measures would not be sufficient to preserve national cohesion and domestic peace. Several proposals were made to assist Islam in its integration into French society. One major proposal was the transformation of the relations of French Islam with those foreign powers which provide financial backing for various Islamic groups. A follow-up article in *Le Figaro* questioned the possibility of French Islam: "*L'islam peut-il être français?*"[55] Agreement is yet elusive and it remains to be seen what form of Islam can also be French.

Clearly, the emergence of Islam has provided the catalyst for the revival of interest in the meaning and the application of laïcité. This has led to an uneasy coexistence of Islam with French society for the last several decades. Cesari notes the widespread conflict expressed in language used by European political parties and concludes that the clash of civilizations is more evident in Europe than in the United States.[56] Baubérot adds that the emergence of the presence of Islam at a time of disenchantment with European secularization has generated tensions in all of Europe.[57] A study in 2013 entitled "*France 2013: les nouvelles fractures*" revealed the pessimism in France with one out of two French people believing the decline of France was inevitable. Three out of five perceived globalization as a threat for France and believed that France needed to protect itself from the world. Eighty-seven percent agreed with the statement that France needed a strong leader to bring order back to the nation. Concerning immigration and Islam, 70 percent believed there were too many foreigners in France and 74 percent found Islam intolerant and incompatible with French society.[58] Four years later, in March 2017, research showed similar findings. Sixty-five percent of French people considered that there were too many foreigners in France. In addition, 60 percent found Islam incompatible with the values of French society. The research revealed that the French were not indifferent to the challenges immigrants face, yet 61 percent believed that immigrants did not make enough effort to integrate French society and adopt the nation's values. Perhaps more surprising was that 60 percent of French no longer felt

55. Devecchio, "Hakim El Kouroi."
56. Cesari, *Islam and Democracy*, 32.
57. Baubérot, *Les laïcités*, 106.
58. Courtois, "Les crispations alarmantes."

like they were at home as before.[59] Douglas Murray, associate editor at the *Spectator*, describes the culture clash taking place in Europe where many immigrants do not share the values of host nations:

> Across some rather surprising learning moments—a terrorist attack here, an "honour" killing there, a few cartoons some-where else—the awareness grew that not everyone who had come to our societies shared our views. They did not share our views about equality between the sexes. They did not share our views on the primacy of reason over revelation. And they did not share our views on freedom and liberty.[60]

According to Aaron Petty, "Especially since the 2001 terrorist attacks in the United States and Madrid, and the London attacks in 2004 and 2005, the topic of religion in Europe has only grown more divisive."[61] Dalil Boubakeur (b. 1940), the rector of the Grand Mosque of Paris, considers that the date of September 11, 2001, marks the failed mission of certain magisterial theologians who did not know how, or were not able to protect the sacred enclosure of Islam, neither did they see its violent radicalization coming.[62]

Contrasts have been made with Islam in France and in the United States. According to Cesari, "These are the contrasting images of Islam on the two sides of the Atlantic: one, American, conciliatory even in the damaged environment of post-September 11; the other, European, more conflictual and hostile."[63] Different histories also account for the contrast since European Muslims came primarily from countries formerly colonized or under the influence of European nations.[64] Cesari notes that "despite the long-standing presence of Muslims in the United States, Islam's visibility in American society is a relatively recent phenomenon."[65] Although American attitudes toward Islam changed radically after September 11, 2001, in France, many have associated Islam with fanaticism since 1994.[66] As a further contrast, she asserts that "one must also take into account the prevailing idea of religion [in France] as a menace to public order—in contrast to the United States, where religion is seen as a unifying force."[67]

59. Paolini, "L'immigration et l'islam."
60. Murray, *Strange Death of Europe*, 261.
61. Petty, "Religion, Conscience, and Belief," 808.
62. Boubakeur, *L'Islam n'est pas une politique*, 39.
63. Cesari, *Islam and Democracy*, 2.
64. Cesari, *Islam and Democracy*, 12.
65. Cesari, *Islam and Democracy*, 17.
66. Cesari, *Islam and Democracy*, 36.
67. Cesari, *Islam and Democracy*, 70.

In past centuries, Europe had experienced an evolution in the process of secularization and the rejection of theological explanations of reality. As a result, religion became a private matter and was progressively banished from the public sphere. Joseph Yacoub argues that in Islam there has not been the equivalent of an analogous evolution, neither on the level of terminology nor on the level of thought and law.[68] After examining Arab constitutions, Yacoub concludes that in Islam the political, legal, and religious domains are intertwined.[69] Cesari asserts that "Islam appears as both a system of personal beliefs and as an ideology of resistance to Western oppression. Islam is the antidote to the decline/depravity of the Western world, and a weapon in the fight against an arrogant and meaningless culture."[70]

It is also necessary to recognize and examine the distinction some authors make between Islam and Islamism. Islamism is described as a political ideology founded specifically on the dream of unification, a dream which gnaws at Islamists with an anti-occidental ideology and leading to the clash of civilizations.[71] Aymeric Chauprade discusses reasons for this situation, the need to recognize the great diversity in the Islamic world, and multiple considerations to explain the present conflictual context. One perspective is to exclusively blame the West and its politics for the revival of Islamic aspirations, specifically support for the nation of Israel. Chauprade explains that this viewpoint, deviating from the usual accusations of Christianity's guilt, leads to a reversal of roles between victims and executioners. He argues that this guilt-ridden posture is not only dangerous for the West, it is contrary to the truth. He sees a genetic illness that runs through Islam, potentially contained in its own religious doctrine.[72] He adds that the States of the Muslim world collectively carry a part of the responsibility in the development of Islamism because they have tried to divert the radical energy of Islam from the critique of their own faults toward their Muslim or Occidental adversaries.[73] He also presents the viewpoint, however, that in some sense Islamism is the product of what Western powers have done in the Muslim world. Islam considers the United States unjust and Europe immoral, a Europe which no longer inspires respect or the desire of Muslims to assimilate. As a result, the resurgence of the headscarf can be interpreted, not only as a symptom of a geopolitical revival, but also as a symptom of

68. Yacoub, "Islam politique," 86.

69. Yacoub, "Islam politique," 87.

70. Cesari, *Islam and Democracy*, 105.

71. Chauprade, "Islam et islamisme," 95.

72. Chauprade, "Islam et islamisme," 97.

73. Chauprade, "Islam et islamisme," 98–99.

moral resistance.[74] Chauprade speaks ominously of the potential for un-
relenting terrorist attacks and the growing population disparities between
young Muslims and aging Europeans. He warns that in the next decades,
if France does not succeed with moderate Muslims to turn back political
Islam, far worse can be expected and the time will come where one can no
longer distinguish between Islam and Islamism.[75]

Does Islam have the capacity to adapt to a laïque society, to integrate
into another culture that does not give allegiance to the Quran or to any
other religious source of inspiration and authority? In Bernard Lewis's opinion, "Islam was never prepared, either in theory or in practice, to accord
full equality to those who held other beliefs and practiced other forms of
worship."[76] He echoes the importance of understanding the Islamic struggle
against "two enemies, secularism and modernism. The war against secularism is conscious and explicit, and there is by now a whole literature denouncing secularism as an evil neo-pagan force in the modern world and
attributing it variously to the Jews, the West, and the United States."[77]

The concept of the ummah (oumma/umma) in Islam represents what
some consider one of the major impediments to Islam's compatibility with
French republican values. The Constitution of Medina contains 47 articles
and aimed to organize the ummah.[78] Nadia Henni-Moulaï helps us understand the place and the complexity of the ummah in Islam, which she
considers a key concept in Islam and Islam's capacity for integration. She
maintains that if the idea of a Muslim community is widespread in public
opinion, the reality is more complex.[79] She questions whether the ummah
as a community of faith is seen in daily life. She argues that if there are
social, cultural or ethnic disparities in a mosque during prayer, in the reality of daily life French Muslims are like their fellow citizens: diverse and
distinct. To this she adds that there is the issue of religious movements
even inside the ummah.[80]

Olivier Roy has written extensively on globalized Islam which he defines as the way believers refer to the theological content of Islam in order
"to adapt and explain their behaviours in a context where religion has lost

74. Chauprade, "Islam et islamisme," 100.

75. Chauprade, "Islam et islamisme," 101.

76. Lewis, "Clash of Civilizations," 345.

77. Lewis, "Clash of Civilizations," 347.

78. Boubakeur, L'Islam n'est pas une politique, 19n5.

79. Henni-Moulaï, Portrait des musulmans, 7.

80. Henni-Moulaï, Portrait des musulmans, 27–29.

its social authority."[81] Global Muslims refer to "either Muslims who settled permanently in non-Muslim countries (mainly in the West), or Muslims who try to distance themselves from a given Muslim culture and stress their belonging to a universal *ummah*, whether in a purely quietist way or through political action."[82] Roy argues that since it appears that there is no possibility of a united Islamic State composed of the different movements, Islam has two choices. Islamist movements "could either opt for political normalisation within the framework of the modern nation-state" or for "a closed scripturalist and conservative view of Islam that rejects the nationalist and statist dimension in favour of the *ummah*, the universal community of all Muslims, based on sharia (Islamic law)."[83] Roy maintains that this latter framework has gained a sympathetic hearing "among rootless Muslim youth, particularly among second- and third-generation migrants in the West. . . . These Muslims do not identify with any given nation-state, and are more concerned with imposing Islamic norms among Muslim societies and minorities and fighting to reconstruct a universal Muslim community, or ummah."[84] One important feature of this perspective is "a new sectarian communitarian discourse, advocating multiculturalism as a means of rejecting integration into Western society."[85] He further speaks of the Islamic myth of "the unification of the religious and the political" and of post-Islamism where "both spheres are autonomous, despite the wishes of the actors concerned (the fundamentalists and the secularists)."[86]

The struggle between competing visions of Islam in non-Islamic nations such as France continues to unfold as Muslims either adapt to secular society or resist integration and embrace communitarianism. An important contribution comes from Dalil Boubakeur who maintains that the confusion between religion and politics has deformed Islam. A serene Islam is advocated which does not mix the domains of politics and religion, and which remains above partisan factions. Further, he proposes that Sharia must be revised in the light of human rights and modern values and that Islam cannot remain with an anachronistic, narrow vision of the Law.[87] He also asserts that Sharia, rightly understood, inspires all Muslims to practice that which is good, to love one's neighbor, to tolerance and to the sharing

81. Roy, *Globalized Islam*, ix.
82. Roy, *Globalized Islam*, ix.
83. Roy, *Globalized Islam*, 1.
84. Roy, *Globalized Islam*, 2.
85. Roy, *Globalized Islam*, 2.
86. Roy, *Globalized Islam*, 3.
87. Boubakeur, *L'Islam n'est pas une politique*, 22.

of values.[88] A vision of Islam is defended which contradicts views which present Islam as a religion incompatible with republican values, and he provides an example of the competing visions of Islam. He speaks of the historical formation of the ummah when Muhammed left Mecca to establish himself at Medina with the intention to transform society without political ambitions. It is argued that the Muslim Prophet never created a State in the classic sense of the term and did not give any indication of his succession. Reference is made to the Constitution of Medina, written during the Medinan Period (AD 622–630), which established an equal coexistence between Muslims, Jews, and Christians.[89] Boubakeur attempts to demonstrate that Islam does not seek to unite religion and politics. He disagrees with attempts to politicize Islam and expresses the conviction that history has shown that human manipulation of these two components without caution leads to dangers—violence, shedding of blood, intolerance.[90] The Prophet Muhammed serves as an example, according to Boubakeur, of someone who did not fight in order that Jews or Christians become Muslims, nor to bring the entire world into submission.[91]

The above-mentioned *l'affaire du foulard* in 1989 has become a major reference point for this clash of civilizations and the reexamination of laïcité in France. This incident was preceded in 1985 by an article in *Le Figaro* on immigration, "Will we still be French in 30 years?" Marianne, France's national symbol, was veiled. A dire prediction and bleak picture of France was presented with Islam portrayed as a threat to French national identity and republican values. When *l'affaire du foulard* took place four years later, many intellectuals described it as the Munich of the Republican school, possibly referring to the Munich Agreement in 1938 between Germany, Great Britain, France, and Italy which permitted German annexation of a portion of Czechoslovakia. In September 1991, a new image of a veiled Marianne graced the cover of *Le Figaro* to announce an interview in which a former president of the Republic compared immigration to an invasion. The relation between the principle of laïcité and the presence of Muslims in France would become the principal political debate of 2003.[92]

As religious-inspired confrontations multiplied, the French government acknowledged the necessity of Islamic integration and the creation of a French Islam. After a decade of debate, a significant step was taken by

88. Boubakeur, *L'Islam n'est pas une politique*, 24.

89. Boubakeur, *L'Islam n'est pas une politique*, 18–19.

90. Boubakeur, *L'Islam n'est pas une politique*, 27.

91. Boubakeur, *L'Islam n'est pas une politique*, 34.

92. Agulhon et al., *La République*, 59–60.

the French authorities in 2003 with the creation of the Conseil français du culte musulman (CFCM). The appearance of the CFCM, created as an association under the Law of Associations of 1901, signaled the institutional recognition of Islam. The CFCM became the official representation between Islam and the French government. Its creation was not without criticism, especially over the concern of the influence of fundamentalist streams of thought, and the question of whether the CFCM was truly representative of Muslims in France. Some doubted the wisdom of the French government in creating a privileged relationship with Islam. Since the creation of the CFCM, the debates continue on the place of Islam in French society and the government's relation with other religions.[93]

Another emerging area of concern and tension regarding Islam is the rise of anti-Semitism in France. This was highlighted in March 2018 by thousands of French marching in the streets of Paris following the brutal murder of an elderly Jewish woman.[94] Among those who marched were Muslim imams who confessed that Islamic anti-Semitism was the greatest threat that weighs on Islam in the twenty-first century. In turn, the imams were placed under police protection in fear of retaliation by extremists. A month later over 250 politicians, intellectuals, and artists signed a manifesto calling on Islam to denounce as obsolete those texts in the Quran calling for violence against Christians and Jews. Among the signatories were former president Nicholas Sarkozy, three former prime ministers, and a former mayor of Paris.[95] There are great concerns that the violence against Jews is revelatory of a worrisome ideological turning point in France which threatens French society, freedom, and the French Republic. As Lamin Sanneh observes, "The strategic question for Europe is whether radical Islam can in turn be domesticated and moderated before being launched to stem the tide of extremism in the Muslim heartlands."[96]

Laïcité and Republican Values

How should we understand the laïque model in a nation like France with republican values? A response to the question is complex due to the relationship between liberty and equality which occupies an important place in the discussions on laïcité. A contrast can be made between the United States' emphasis on the freedom of religion, conscience, education, and association,

93. Zeghal, "La constitution," 1–2.
94. "Mort de Mireille Knoll."
95. "Manifeste contre le nouvel antisémitisme."
96. Sanneh, "Europe," 125.

guaranteed by the State, and the republican laïcité in France where the school system and the State reinforce a strong idea of citizenship. The republican idea of citizenship has nothing do with ethnicity but is based on the values of liberty, equality, and fraternity, which ideally make the French nation accessible to all those who desire to integrate into such a project.[97]

In speaking of liberty and equality, Rognon and Weber argue that the sense one gives to laïcité probably depends on which of the two elements is privileged. They also maintain that the difficulty in agreeing on what the laïque ideal signifies, the difficulty one also meets in trying to translate this concept, to explain it abroad, is tied partly to this tension between liberty and equality which form this ideal.[98] They analyze and develop their thesis represented by two major philosophical traditions—the liberal tradition of John Locke and the social contract of Jean-Jacques Rousseau. The historical and etymological approaches to laïcité which support the two traditions are contrasted. The historical approach privileges the liberating aspect of laïcité where the State accepts, even guarantees the free expression of religions, as long as they do not trouble the public order. The autonomy of the State permits secularization, which translates into the acceptance of religious pluralism. If one privileges the etymological approach and its filiation with the Greek *laos*, however, one will insist more on the fact that laïcité requires equality where no one dominates nor is dominated. The priority then becomes the guarantee of this absolute equality for all members of a social body, legally, materially, and symbolically.[99]

The emphases of Locke and Rousseau function as contrasting lenses through which France might be viewed. The liberal tradition of Locke considers that the only function of the State is to preserve the natural rights of man in preventing wars. This function of conservation is not accompanied by the will to transform or to better society. In this tradition, the State essentially seems to be at the service of individual rights and neglects the public good. The State exists at the exterior of social life and intervenes only as the mediator of social conflicts. This stance corresponds to liberal democracies like Great Britain or the United States where private and professional life are central and public and political life are secondary. According to this analysis, there is little effort to redistribute riches, and the priority of the State is the protection of individual liberties rather than the struggle against inequities. This explains also why these governments have a conception of

97. Haarscher, *La laïcité*, 74

98. Rognon and Weber, *La laïcité*, 105–6.

99. Rognon and Weber, *La laïcité*, 106.

relations between the State and religions which is founded above all else on tolerance and the respect of religious pluralism.[100]

Lockean theory is contrasted with the more prevalent social contract of Jean-Jacques Rousseau developed in France which gives an absolute priority to the equality of citizens. In this theory, Rousseau critiques the State, which not only maintains economic inequities but supports political inequality. For that reason, he proposed another form of political organization which seeks to ensure the equality of citizens as the primary objective.[101] Since each citizen yields his individual rights to the community, the rights of the community prevail over individual rights. Although some have seen Rousseau as the theoretician of totalitarianism, France clearly disavows totalitarianism. Rognon and Weber assert that the liberty proposed by Rousseau, which the State allows, is not the "liberty of the fox in the chicken coop" or the law of the strongest.[102]

The different emphases of these two philosophical traditions helpfully shed light on the reasoning behind French laws which often perplex outsiders. The 2004 law banning conspicuous religious symbols in public schools illustrates the clash between liberty and equality. The earlier presenting issue was Islamic headscarves worn by Muslim schoolgirls in 1989. For some, the larger issue was what the headscarf represented and the suspicion that the headscarf was an attempt by Islamic fundamentalists (*intégristes*) to destabilize the laïque ideal.[103] The Conseil d'État initially ruled in 1989 that religious identifying symbols and dress were permitted as an expression of freedom of conscience. The Conseil's decision cited numerous international declarations, the French Constitution on equality, and the law of 1905 on freedom of conscience. Also cited were laws guaranteeing educational instruction with equal respect for all beliefs in public schools (December 31, 1959), the right to education in which the State respects the child's personality and the influence of families in the educational process (July 11, 1975), and laws against discrimination toward foreigners (August 2, 1989).[104]

The Conseil d'État was accused of vacillating in November 1989 in refusing to consider religious symbols contrary to laïcité and that political Islam, under the mask of religious freedom, was actually a struggle undertaken against the Republic.[105] The headscarf was described as a religious

---

100. Rognon and Weber, *La laïcité*, 107–8.

101. Rognon and Weber, *La laïcité*, 109–10.

102. Rognon and Weber, *La laïcité*, 111.

103. Coq, *Laïcité et République*, 267.

104. Conseil d'État, "Port par les élèves."

105. Coq, *Laïcité et République*, 266.

symbol, a sexist symbol contrary to the equality of the sexes and an attack on human rights.[106] Numerous cases would be considered and decided without satisfaction for the advocates of laïcité who saw in the headscarf affair a perfectly organized Islamist operation.[107] Others considered that a vocal Islamic minority, which refused laïcité and integration into French society, and which mixed politics and religion, would not be satisfied with compromises. The headscarf was seen as but one step leading to other demands. Coq summarizes a response to what he deemed the stubbornness of the Conseil d'État to act decisively:

> The French should be the last ones surprised [by the Conseil's decisions]. They are a people who elaborated with great pain a viable compromise between the Catholic majority and laïcité. It is inevitable that other conflicts appear at the time when the challenge of a new religion presents itself. Nevertheless, globally speaking, this is taking place more quickly with Islam.[108]

Over a period of fifteen years the mood in France changed with an increasingly visible and vocal Islamic presence. Between 1989 and 2004 there was a great deal of debate as to whether wearing the headscarf in public schools was contrary to republican values. The Conseil d'État ruling in 1989 permitting Islamic headscarves favored liberty of expression. The 2004 law reversed that decision in the name of equality. Under the banner of equality, restrictions were adopted by the law of March 15, 2004, which banned religious symbols in public schools which ostensibly manifested religious affiliation.[109] The Conseil Constitutionnel in November 2004 reaffirmed this decision and provided an interpretation of article one of the Constitution on the laïque character of the Republic. This was significant since it was the first time the Conseil made a pronouncement on the principle of laïcité based on the Constitution. In effect, it was determined that this article prevented anyone from taking advantage of religious beliefs to escape common rules governing relations between public establishments and individuals.[110]

France's closer alignment with Rousseau than Locke should not be misconstrued to diminish the French value of liberty. It is a question of emphasis. One needs only to look at the emblematic Marianne throughout French history. During tumultuous times the aspiration for liberty was preponderant, much more than the other components of the republican

106. Coq, *Laïcité et République*, 273.

107. Coq, *Laïcité et République*, 279.

108. Coq, *Laïcité et République*, 284.

109. Lefèvre, "Libertés de conscience," 145.

110. Barbier, "Pour une définition," 134.

ideal, equality or fraternity.[111] The sentiment appears to be that there is less discussion of liberty in a democratic society where liberty has largely been acquired. Today the issue of equality occupies much of the discussion on societal change. Rognon and Weber conclude that the French emphasis on equality undoubtedly explains why "laïcité à la française" appears at best incomprehensible, at worst authoritarian and totalitarian, to nations with a liberal culture.[112]

Current Perspectives on Laïcité

There are many perspectives on laïcité with books and articles too numerous to treat. The values of liberty and equality once again appear as competing emphases. For some, laïcité in France provides the possibility of placing all religions on the same level and allows a real dialogue which has no chance to exist if one of them has preeminence over the others.[113] For others, laïcité supported only by reason is able to develop humans in their liberty.[114] In reality, there are many nuances in the meaning and application of laïcité. The positions align on a continuum between *laïcité libérale (ouverte)* and *laïcité anticléricale (de combat)*. The divergent perspectives stem partly from the fact that laïcité has been constitutionally enshrined but not clearly juridically defined. We are reminded that the law of 1905 is referred to as the legal text for laïcité although the word itself is absent. The word appeared explicitly in 1946 in the Fourth Constitution and was repeated in the Fifth Constitution of 1958 presently in force. Yet, and this point requires emphasis, the word laïcité was not defined in the Constitutions. Laïcité is progressively defined in multiple legal texts in specific areas of application.[115]

Several of the most notable authors and their viewpoints deserve examination as representative of perspectives on the unsettled questions regarding laïcité in France. Barbier remarks that diverse conceptions have been proposed, sometimes leading to different or even opposite consequences. It seems that one freely interprets laïcité according to their situation, their needs, or their desires. This leads to divergences on the manner in which it applies in concrete situations. He admits that it is not easy to give a satisfying definition of laïcité, even if several exist. One speaks of *laïcité-séparation* and *laïcité-neutralité*, without knowing if these two

111. Agulhon et al., *La République*, 13–14.

112. Rognon and Weber, *La laïcité*, 111.

113. Korsia, "La laïcité," 83.

114. Billard, *De l'école à la République*, 195.

115. Robitzer, "Laïcité et réconciliation," para. 10.

definitions are identical or if one is better than the other. In any case, he
is of the opinion that these definitions have the merit of being simple and
clear and generally are acceptable.[116] He further makes a distinction between legislative laïcité established by the law of 1905 and constitutional
laïcité established in the 1946 and 1958 French constitutions. He considers
legislative laïcité well defined by the law of 1905 and its essence the non-
recognition and non-subsidization of any religion. Constitutional laïcité
lacks a formal definition but implies the absence of religion from the public sphere of the State. In his analysis, the juridical value of constitutional
laïcité is superior to legislative laïcité. He finds this fact regrettable since
laïcité is not defined in the Constitution.[117]

Henri Pena-Ruiz, winner of the Prix de la laïcité in 2014, has contributed to the study of laïcité with several important works. He views laïcité as a
unifying principle for people within the State which presumes a legal distinction between a person's private life as such and the public dimension as a citizen.[118] In his understanding, no spiritual conviction must enjoy recognition
or material advantages of which the corollary would be discrimination.[119]
He describes the political, laïque community as one in which the spiritual
option remains a private matter and which has for reference and foundation
that which is common to all apart from spiritual differentiations.[120] Contrary to clericalism, laïcité simultaneously gives sense to both democracy
and autonomous thinking. The ideal of laïcité, in eradicating all confessional
preference in the public domain, assures religions an even more stable liberty
and equality since none of them can hold the attributes of temporal domination.[121] Laïcité, when properly understood, frees the totality of the public
sphere from any grasp exercised in the name of a religion or of a particular
ideology and consequently excludes any public privilege attributed either
to religion or to atheism. The originality of laïcité resides in permitting everyone, believers or atheists, to live together without one or the other being
stigmatized because of their particular convictions.[122]

Jacques Robert distinguishes between "laïcité" and "laïcisme." Laïcisme seeks to deny or ignore religion in pushing it to the margins of society. It operates in the twenty-first century in refusing any public dimension

116. Barbier, "Pour une définition," 129–30.

117. Barbier, "Pour une définition," 133.

118. Pena-Ruiz, Qu'est-ce que la laïcité?, 11–12.

119. Pena-Ruiz, Qu'est-ce que la laïcité?, 21.

120. Pena-Ruiz, Qu'est-ce que la laïcité?, 27.

121. Pena-Ruiz, Qu'est-ce que la laïcité?, 35.

122. Pena-Ruiz, Qu'est-ce que la laïcité?, 71–73.

of religion in society. Laïcité, however, in a pluralistic society, becomes a place where diverse spiritual traditions communicate without privileging any tradition. Robert further describes two conceptions of laïcité: a radical concept of laïcité which guarantees the freedom to worship and which seeks a Catholic Church separated from Rome; and a moderate concept which insists on the freedom of worship and tolerance toward all religious traditions. He admits that France did not choose laïcité because it was perfect but because it was the best solution for the problem at that time given the dominance of the Catholic Church.[123]

Jean Baubérot has written extensively on the subject of laïcité and has co-authored books with others. In an important contribution written with Micheline Milot, four fundamental principles of laïcité are proposed and defended: (1) equality between religions; (2) liberty of conscience; (3) State neutrality; and (4) the separation of religions from the State. These principles are applied in changing social contexts. The first two principles are considered essential values, the last two are means to guarantee the outworking of laïcité.[124] Baubérot views laïcité essentially as non-discrimination. He argues for an enlarged sense of laïcité and liberty of conscience, far removed from the issues of 1905, which also concerns homosexuals who want to marry and citizens who want to die in dignity.[125]

Prisca Robitzer summarizes Baubérot and Milot's six portraits of laïcité which provide insight into different perspectives and support for varied arguments on the application of laïcité. The first portrait, the separation of Church and State, has often dominated the discussion. The law of 1905 which disestablished the Catholic Church in France serves to support an absolute separation between private and public spheres in society. The second portrait, authoritarian laïcité, places the surveillance of religions in the hands of the State as experienced under the Concordat. As a result, State interference in religious matters weakens State neutrality and undermines liberty of conscience. The third portrait, anticlerical laïcité, at first glance aims to prevent religious influence in political matters. In reality, this often leads to antireligious tendencies in imposing societal norms on religion while removing the latter's legitimacy. This portrait also rigidly observes a distinction between public and private space to confine religion to the private sphere. The fourth portrait, civic faith laïcité, requires allegiance toward common societal values. Religions are encouraged to moderate their differences as proof of loyalty to republican values. In its extreme forms,

123. Robert, "Fondements juridiques," 6–7.
124. Baubérot and Milot, *Laïcités sans frontières*, 75–77.
125. Baubérot, "La laïcité absolue n'existe pas," para. 1.

equality becomes conformity and the liberty of conscience is threatened. The fifth portrait, laïcité of acknowledgement, advocates social justice and the respect of individual choices. This perspective rests on the postulate of individual moral freedom in choices of behavior and worldview and argues that all choices are protected by the State if they do not contravene republican values. Yet tensions arise between State determination of the common good and the liberty of conscience. The sixth portrait, laïcité of collaboration, seeks to balance the State's independence from religious influence with the desire to collaborate with various religious and philosophical sensibilities. However, if ancient or majority religions are the ones privileged, as in Alsace-Moselle, the equality of religions and the neutrality of the State may be compromised.[126] These divergent, competing, and sometimes overlapping perspectives complicate any consensus on laïcité. When someone speaks about laïcité, it is indispensable to know out of which portrait they are operating in order to have meaningful discussion. Otherwise, the risk of confusion and misunderstanding is great.

From an evangelical viewpoint, the CNEF emphasizes more strictly the juridical nature of laïcité and the law of 1905. The CNEF opposes the vague, ideological assertions and additions drawn from the law by others. They recognize that this law, dating back over a century, existed before other fundamental texts and symbolically remains in France "the text of laïcité."[127] It remains no less true however that the law of 1905 is only one law of inferior value to other norms, and some articles of the law raise questions today. We are also reminded that the concept of laïcité has constitutional value and applies to all French territory while the law of 1905 does not apply because of the historical situation of Alsace-Moselle at the time. This leaves the application of laïcité open to diverse interpretations which are settled by the Conseil d'État.[128]

Professor Jacques Buchhold represents an evangelical or professing perspective on laïcité. He writes from the conviction that history teaches that the genetic heritage of laïcité includes a good part of Christian theology and presents what he calls a laïcité of Christian inspiration.[129] He contrasts that with laïcité of atheistic inspiration which rejects the Judeo-Christian ethic. According to him, atheistic laïcité absolutizes liberty and the interests of the individual.[130] He draws from Roger Williams whose theological reflection led

126. Robitzer, "Laïcité et réconciliation," para. 13–20.

127. CNEF, Laïcité française, 21.

128. CNEF, Laïcité française, 26–27.

129. Buchhold, "Le terreau théologique," 22.

130. Buchhold, "Église, islam et société," 27.

to the creation of the first State in the western world, more than a century before 1789, in which liberty of conscience and worship were guaranteed for all.[131] He claims that the great achievement and originality of Protestant theology in the sixteenth and seventeenth centuries consisted of a commitment to a theological militancy which included liberty of worship for all—heretics, Jews, Muslims and atheists.[132] For laïcité of Christian inspiration, the State must declare itself incompetent in religious matters; its responsibility under the first table of the Mosaic law is to guarantee the conditions for a right exercise of the freedom of conscience.[133] He adds that the State must enforce the second table of the law, the domain in which it is competent. Such a conception of laïcité will require the State to protect the unborn, the heterosexual character of marriage, and the rights of the poor.

Manuel Valls (b. 1962) writes from a unique, practical perspective as a French politician. Valls was mayor of Evry (Essonne) at the time of his writing on laïcité in 2005, and later served as Minister of the Interior (2012–2014) and Prime Minister (2014–2016). In his book he treats a wide range of laïcité-related topics which merit attention. As mayor, he observed the changes in his city as the mosque and pagoda were added to the religious landscape. Challenges appeared with the difficulty of reconciling the law of 1905 with the integration of other religions into French society. He emphasizes that there is no freedom without authority and without respect of republican values, and no equality without equality of opportunities. He recognizes in the twenty-first century that society is secularized and laicized, the Church has lost its former central role, and political power has been removed from its grasp.[134] He affirms that laïcité constitutes one of the means to moderate social and human relations. Valls asserts that French society is not threatened by religion in itself but by the tribalizations underway, or that which he calls the hardening of identities.[135] He expresses concern that elements of Islam seek political influence in France and that one of the principal unresolved dilemmas is how to live together with this new religion which did not participate historically in the construction of French national identity.[136]

In reference to the law of 1905, Valls considers religious belief and citizenship compatible. However, he questions the necessity to create a formal,

---

131. Buchhold, "Le terreau théologique," 20.

132. Buchhold, "Le terreau théologique," 23.

133. Buchhold, "Le terreau théologique," 31.

134. Valls, *La laïcité en face*, 16.

135. Valls, *La laïcité en face*, 24.

136. Valls, *La laïcité en face*, 28.

governmental document specifically for Islam which demonstrates an issue specific to Islam tied to the question of social integration and democracy. The document, *Principes et fondements juridiques régissant les rapports entre les pouvoirs publics et le culte musulman en France*, was approved and signed in the presence of Minister of the Interior Jean-Pierre Chevènement on January 28, 2000. Among other provisions, the text stipulated that Muslim associations would adhere to legal principles contained in the text, that they were attached to fundamental principles of the French Republic, and that they specifically subscribed to Articles 10 and 11 of the *Déclaration des droits de l'homme et du citoyen* relating to the freedom of the press and religious freedom. Muslim associations would recognize the first article of the French Constitution affirming the laïque character of the Republic and would also respect the dispositions of the law of 1905 concerning the separation of Church and the State. However, Valls expressed concern that in many countries from which Muslims have entered France, the two dimensions of religion and politics are mingled. One major objection to the document was that the *Principes et fondements* did not explicitly address the right to change one's religion.[137]

French sociologist Jean-Paul Willaime has written at length on contemporary issues relating to religion and laïcité. An article written in 2014 provides a thoughtful analysis of the place of religions in the twenty-first century and helpful reflections on a way forward in the debate on laïcité. He asks whether laïcité in France is threatened now that religions have emerged from the private sphere and have become a problem for society and for political authorities. He elaborates four factors which explain the return of religions as a problem and subject of intense debates: religious pluralism in the religious landscape particularly with the presence of Islam and the advances of Protestant evangelicalism; the internal complexity of religious confessions; the nature of questions on the political agenda regarding, among others, same-sex marriage, artificial insemination, abortion, and euthanasia; and European multiculturalization of religious expression, both Islamic and Christian. These four factors contribute to the increased visibility and presence of religious dimensions, even if globally, the proportion of "no religion" increased in France (50 percent in 2008 versus 27 percent in 1981), as in other European countries.[138] In this context, Willaime does not believe that laïcité itself has been called into question. Rather laïcité is questioned in the manner in which it is understood and applied and the ways in which the place and the role

137. Valls, *La laïcité en face*, 35–36.

138. Willaime, "L'expression des religions," 5–6.

of religions are conceived in democracies founded on the separation of Church and State, as well as on the respect of the liberty of conscience, of thought, and of religion. He recognizes the importance of religion in society in providing answers to significant questions of life and death, in orienting behavior according to ethical norms, and in ways of expressing emotions individually and collectively. He believes that religions provide the infrastructure through which humans seek to control their existence and understand their place in time and space. He argues that religion as a social and cultural phenomenon, however, requires a *laïcité d'intelligence* to integrate the dimensions of human existence. In the case of religious excesses leading to intolerance or violence, laïcité is also protection against religions when they want to impose their normativity by constraint. While recognizing the risks of religious isolation, fanaticism, and intolerance, Willaime asserts that the risks are low in France. He argues that in democratic countries, rather than exercise resistance by a defensive conception of laïcité which aims to protect society from religions, one can more easily welcome a proactive and inclusive conception of laïcité which, sufficiently assured of itself, positively takes into consideration the contributions of religious components of society.[139] He concludes by affirming that there is a place for a civic and laïque recognition of religions in the public sphere. If democratic humanism has often developed in opposition to religions, these religions, in a secular, disenchanted world, might become valuable guarantors for democracy.[140]

Finally, there are militant atheists who see laïcité as a step toward the complete eradication of religion from society. Fetouh states that certain militant atheists desire that the neutrality of public employees be equally imposed on citizens in public space. This confuses laïcité, which is the separation of the State and religion, and secularization which is the natural and progressive detachment of society from religiosity.[141] An atheistic agenda shares the skepticism of all-encompassing narratives consistent with postmodern thought. Jean-François Lyotard defined postmodernism as incredulity toward metanarratives (*l'incrédulité à l'égard des métarécits*), where the narrative function loses the great hero, the great perils, the great voyages, and the great goal.[142] Lyotard argued that postmodernism is "characterized by no grand totalizing master narrative but by smaller and multiple narratives which do not seek (or obtain) any universalizing stabilization

139. Willaime, "L'expression des religions," 7–9.
140. Willaime, "L'expression des religions," 14.
141. Fetouh, "La laïcité," 48.
142. Lyotard, *La condition postmoderne*, 7–8.

or legitimation."[143] Philosophy professor Michel Onfray serves as an able representative of French atheistic, postmodern philosophy which criticizes tradition, religion and rationality of Western modernity. In this vein, Onfray rejects the Old Testament and Gospel narratives, and maintains that the Christian Bible is the result of "ideological fabrication."[144] He follows the pragmatism of scientific knowledge which "questions the validity of narrative statements" and "classifies them according to another mentality: savage, primitive, underdeveloped, backward, foreign, based on opinions, on customs, on authority, on prejudices, on ignorance, on ideologies."[145] He speaks for atheists who reject "the existence of God as a fiction devised by men desperate to keep on living in spite of the inevitability of death."[146] He asserts that "religion is a fabric woven with fictions and metaphysical placebos."[147] Further, religion is "anchored in tradition and cashes in on nostalgia. Philosophy looks to the future."[148] Onfray does not believe that dechristianization has sufficiently progressed in France and proposes that "another push is needed before we can call ourselves truly republican."[149] For him, the "negation of God is not an end in itself, but a means of working toward a post-Christian society."[150] He objects to the Apostle Paul who was a "stickler for the licit/illicit rule in the sexual domain."[151] In that, he heartily follows the postmodern revolution against morality.[152] Onfray concludes that "we must fight for a post-Christian secularism, that is to say atheistic, militant, and radically opposed to choosing between Western Judeo-Christianity and its Islamic adversary—neither Bible nor Koran."[153] Onfray's writings have been analyzed by Protestant writers and critiqued for their lack of substantive argumentation in the defense of philosophical atheism. In fact, according to Philippe Serradji, rather than defend or support atheism, Onfray merely attacks religion in general with a special disdain for

---

143. Hutcheon, "Incredulity Toward Metanarrative," 39.

144. Onfray, *Atheist Manifesto*, 117.

145. Lyotard, *La condition postmoderne*, 48.

146. Onfray, *Atheist Manifesto*, 15.

147. Onfray, *Atheist Manifesto*, 37–38.

148. Onfray, *Atheist Manifesto*, 39.

149. Onfray, *Atheist Manifesto*, 51.

150. Onfray, *Atheist Manifesto*, 56.

151. Onfray, *Atheist Manifesto*, 71.

152. Zarka, "Le pouvoir sur le savoir," 4.

153. Onfray, *Atheist Manifesto*, 219.

Christianity. He accompanies his attacks with a unilateral reading of history filled with distortions and omissions.[154]

From this typology of laïcité, we better understand the difficulty of agreement among those holding different perspectives. Pena-Ruiz writes that there are many who admit the principle of laïcité with the condition that they redefine the sense.[155] Or, according to Poulat, "The word laïcité among us is a convenience of language, like Noah's hammer which often hides much ignorance and error."[156] From a Christian perspective, in the midst of ambiguity and divergence, Robitzer believes that churches seek and initiate the process of reconciliation, not from a disembodied existential affirmation of liberty of conscience or equality of citizens, but from the incarnate biblical revelation of love for one's neighbor.[157]

Return to Laïcité of Combat and State Neutrality

Cabanel views France entering a fifth secular model beginning in the 1980s and continuing to this day in relations between the State and religions.[158] The first four secular models, at intervals of approximately 100 years, correspond to the Edict of Nantes (1598), the Revocation of the Edict of Nantes (1685), the French Revolution (1789), and the Law of Separation (1905).

Laïcité re-emerged in the last few decades with some extolling open laïcité (*laïcité ouverte*) and others advocating militant laïcité (*laïcité de combat*). There was a change in understanding laïcité from an outdated, accessory mainstay of republican speeches to a major political issue, feverously debated in the most diverse social spaces, and exalted either as an essential principle for living together or denounced as a factor of intolerance.[159] An interesting contrast has been presented between Catholicism a century ago and Islam today. Islam has appeared as a major religion at the end of the twentieth century making claims similar to Catholicism at the beginning of the twentieth century. Due to the confrontation between Islam and a laïque Republic, *laïcité-combat* might reappear. France finds itself facing a religion whose ideological position, in the minds of some, corresponds to that of Catholicism under the

---

154. Serradji, "La montée de l'athéisme."

155. Pena-Ruiz, *Qu'est-ce que la laïcité?*, 17.

156. Poulat, "Culture laïque," 61.

157. Robitzer, "Laïcité et réconciliation," para. 30.

158. Cabanel, "La question religieuse," 172.

159. Monod, *Sécularisation et laïcité*, 7.

Third Republic where the imam is similar to the priest of the past with a message which might contradict republican ideals.[160]

According to Rémond, the irruption of Islam has relaunched anticlericalism.[161] Beresniak goes further in affirming that the three monotheistic religions and innumerable sects, form a holy alliance—Islamic veil, cross, and kippa—but have the same combat. He makes the accusation that churches fight today in the name of tolerance, in the name of democracy, in the name of pluralism, notions that they rejected until yesterday. In his opinion, it is necessary to clearly determine the limits of tolerance and liberty.[162] Rognon and Weber likewise express their concern that the rise of religious fundamentalisms has strengthened the resolve of religious groups to refuse the gains achieved by laïcité. Their conviction has been reinforced that laïcité represents the only guarantee against obscurantism and against a return to conservative traditions. Islamic fundamentalism is the one most often invoked although all the monotheistic religions, Christian, Muslim, and Jewish, in their view, share the same vision for relations between women and men.[163]

In his writings, political scientist Laurent Bouvet has entered the arena to contest Islamic influence and to criticize the Left for complicity in their incoherent support of Islamic inroads in French society. One prominent incident concerned the female leader of a left-leaning university student union who appeared in a television interview with an Islamic headscarf. Bouvet clearly supported the young women's right to have religious convictions and to dress accordingly. He found it incomprehensible, however, that the political Left, which militates for personal liberties, would have as representative someone who showcases a radical, political expression of Islam in which women are devalued. He believes Islam seeks to exercise its influence by any means possible and advocates the necessity to serenely, firmly, and with determination combat Islamic ideology in the same way the deadly ideologies of the twentieth century were combatted.[164]

The institutional separation of Church and State accomplished in 1905 required State neutrality in religious matters. This affirmation of neutrality is widely accepted, but the nature and extent of neutrality is now being debated. In one sense, the State does not officially recognize any religion. In another sense, it recognizes their equality in guaranteeing their full liberty.

160. Viguier, "La laïcité," 84–85.

161. Rémond, L'anticléricalisme, 374.

162. Beresniak, La Laïcité, 7–9.

163. Rognon and Weber, La laïcité, 99.

164. Sugy, "Polémique."

The law of 1905 intended to prevent the Church from interfering in matters of State. The law respects religion, but religion cannot trample the law.[165] The law stipulated that the State would guarantee the free exercise of religion while neither recognizing nor subsidizing any religion. According to Robert, this posture of neutrality has both negative and positive aspects. It is negative in the sense that the State recognizes the right of all confessions without embracing any. It is positive in that the State engages itself to protect the free exercise of religion and to provide the means for its free exercise. Positive neutrality includes providing chaplains for hospitals, prisons, and some boarding schools so that those with limited movement or freedom may exercise their right to practice religion. It has also included providing regulations for the slaughter of animals for religious purposes.[166]

There is considerable discussion today on the relationship between the law of 1905 and the present-day 1958 Constitution in the application of laïcité and the neutrality of the State. The first article of the 1958 Constitution guarantees equality before the law for all citizens without distinction as to origin, race, or religion, and respect for all beliefs. Although the principle of State neutrality is well established, there is no expectation that the State remain a spectator of social life.[167] Some are of the opinion that to understand laïcité as a principle of constitutional value one must return to the law of 1905 and the notions of laïque tolerance and cultural pluralism.[168] The law of 1905, however, had religious pluralism in view, not cultural pluralism, and neutrality cannot be separated from liberty and tolerance. No liberty is absolute, and tolerance has its limits. So how neutral is the State in religious matters? Does respect for all beliefs extend to all religious practices? Baubérot and Milot affirm that absolute neutrality does not exist. Political authority, however, must show itself impartial regarding different convictions.[169]

The application of neutrality presents interesting, practical challenges. Pena-Ruiz asserts that the laïque State's confessional neutrality does not signify that the State must be indifferent to all values and principles.[170] There are times the State must intervene along with the expectation that communities or churches must exist in a democracy without deconstructing

165. Soppelsa, "De la laïcité," 3.

166. Robert, "Fondements juridiques," 8–9.

167. Beresniak, La Laïcité, 60.

168. Beresniak, La Laïcité, 7.

169. Baubérot and Milot, Laïcités sans frontières, 79.

170. Pena-Ruiz, Qu'est-ce que la laïcité?, 24.

it.[171] Coq warns that reducing the idea of laïcité to an absolute principle of neutrality, of freedom without limits for religions or for religious currents, makes the universal principle of religious freedom an abstract and deconstructing principle for society.[172] One difficulty confronting French society and testing the concept of neutrality is the emergence of religious cults (*sectes*) disconnected from mainstream religious currents. A cult or sect is understood as a counter-society which inserts itself into public society yet seeks to withdraw its members from society's common values. The sect is led by a spiritual guru who requires absolute obedience and extends his authority over the social and personal life of its followers. The result is another society in the interior of public society.[173]

Koubi asserts that laïcité cannot be reduced simply to the neutrality of public institutions.[174] There is likewise the affirmation that there are forms of religious community which are not acceptable in a democratic society.[175] Questions are being asked as new religious issues arise in a multi-confessional, pluralistic society. Does the State have the right to intervene on the behalf of children in need of a transfusion whose parents are Jehovah's Witnesses? Does the State need to recognize bigamy as practiced by some religions? Can the State oppose female genital excision practiced for religious purposes? In short, how far can the State exercise control or forbid customs and traditions which are deemed essential by religions yet antithetical to republican values?[176]

In answer to those questions, Pena-Ruiz recognizes that it is not necessary for the State to define what characterizes a true religion as distinguished from a sect. According to him, sects are not defined and judged by their beliefs but by their actions which are contrary to republican values and constitute crimes, whether abuse of people in distress, false advertising, the illegal practice of medicine, or manipulation.[177] Coq asserts that it is the responsibility of democratic society to undertake the dismantling of sectarian reasoning. He does not view this as contrary to the principle of the liberty of conscience or the right of religions to organize. On the contrary, he affirms that by their very existence sectarian groups are a serious violation to the public order established in a lawful State. The liberty

171. Coq, *Laïcité et République*, 255.
172. Coq, *Laïcité et République*, 327.
173. Coq, *Laïcité et République*, 256–57.
174. Koubi, "La laïcité," 55.
175. Coq, *Laïcité et République*, 255.
176. Beresniak, *La Laïcité*, 29.
177. Pena-Ruiz, *Qu'est-ce que la laïcité?*, 94–95.

of conscience is an individual right and the liberty of worship does not authorize any group to undermine hard-won freedoms or to subvert the social and republican order.[178]

In the past, the State granted religious rights to French citizens of minority religions to place them on equal ground with the majority religion. Today, the State seeks to integrate a larger number of religions from diverse backgrounds into the Republic with its values. Beresniak writes that laïcité is an ideology which recognizes diversity and seeks peace by the means of mutual respect. Difficulties arise when one deals with minorities who demand liberty in the name of France's principles and who refuse others liberty in the name of their own beliefs.[179] In other words, if the State limits itself to a passive neutrality, all religions and all sects have absolute liberty to teach their principles, even to the disdain of others. Religions can freely impose total submission on their faithful and, as independent communities, religions and sects establish their own schools and their own rules for living. As a result, the State under the guise of neutrality limits its role to observation so that churches trouble each other the least possible. In Beresniak's opinion, this principle of non-intervention leads to committing the offence of non-assistance to a person in danger.[180]

France faces the challenge of remaining neutral toward religion when religions refuse to accept the values of the Republic—liberty, equality, fraternity. The question of tolerance arises, and it must be asked if tolerance which tolerates intolerance abandons all ground to it and contributes to the birth of a totalitarian order.[181]

Laïcité, Politics, and Concordataire Status of Alsace-Moselle

There have been renewed calls in the twenty-first century to alter or revoke the concordataire status of Alsace-Moselle. This region of France, under German control at the time of the law of 1905, retained its privileged status granted by the 1801 Concordat. Four religious confessions—Catholicism, Reformed Protestantism, Lutheranism, Judaism—to this day continue to benefit from State subsidies. Other confessions—Evangelical Protestantism, Buddhism, Islam—are not accorded the same status. There have been attempts to assist other religions, but nothing has been done either to undermine advantages

178. Coq, Laïcité et République, 257–58.

179. Beresniak, La Laïcité, 61.

180. Beresniak, La Laïcité, 89–90.

181. Beresniak, La Laïcité, 62.

accorded to the concordataire confessions or to extend full benefits to non-concordataire confessions. For example, in 1996, there was a proposal for an Islamic school of theology alongside Protestant and Catholic schools. The project was not realized, but the proposal affirmed that the concordataire enclave Alsace-Moselle, long considered an anomaly and somewhat archaic, could become the laboratory for the integration of Islam in the midst of the closed club of ancient recognized religions.[182]

In 2012, then-president François Hollande (b. 1954) was asked in an interview if he would work for a change in status in Alsace-Moselle. In response, he affirmed his commitment to maintaining the region's concordataire status due to the historical situation of the region which was attached to Germany between 1871 and 1918. He viewed the distinction of this region from the rest of the country as an essential component of its identity and further believed that the region could maintain its distinction of limitations placed on stores opening on Sunday even if the rest of the country changed.[183]

In 2013, the Constitutional Council rejected a motion from an organization promoting laïcité (L'APPEL) which demanded the application of the law of 1905 in Alsace-Moselle. The stated goal of this organization is to have the law of 1905 enforced throughout France and to emphasize the respect of republican values (Liberté, Egalité, Fraternité, Laïcité). The Constitutional Council (les Sages) maintained that the concordataire status in these departments (Haut-Rhin, Bas-Rhin, Moselle) was a republican tradition observed by all French governments since 1919 and that laïcité had constitutional value in France except in these three departments. Reference was made to the 1958 Constitution of the Fifth Republic which had not questioned or altered the status quo. It was determined that Parliament could not override the law of 1905 without censure from the Constitutional Council. During his campaign, President Hollande promised to place the law of 1905 in the Constitution with an exception for Alsace-Moselle.[184]

Evangelicals have joined the call for the law of 1905 to be applied in Alsace-Moselle and for the elimination of subsidies to the concordataire religious confessions. Several articles with opposing viewpoints appeared in the Protestant weekly Réforme in March 2018. The first article, written by historian Sébastien Fath, raised the issue concerning the inequalities in Alsace-Moselle where Lutheran and Reformed churches are subsidized by the State, and where Evangelicals, Muslims, and Buddhists face discrimination.

182. Cabanel, Les mots de la laïcité, 6–7.

183. Hollande, "Le régime concordataire."

184. "L'Alsace-Moselle garde le concordat."

Fath referred to the above-mentioned 2013 ruling by the Constitutional Council which maintained the status quo in Alsace-Moselle in keeping with history and tradition. Yet he considers that ending this discriminatory practice would be in keeping with laïcité.[185] The article provoked an uproar. A rejoinder swiftly followed from Christian Albecker, president of l'Union des Églises protestantes d'Alsace et de Lorraine (UEPAL). Albecker scolded Fath for his apparent ignorance of the regional context. He reminded readers that the Constitutional Council had determined that the legal and histori-cal status of Alsace-Moselle was compatible with the French Constitution, and also that there was no possibility of extending those benefits to other religious confessions. He protested that Protestants did not consider their privilege as a right to defend at all costs but as a possible model of relations with the State.[186] Fath responded to clarify that the title attributed to his ar-ticle, chosen by *Réforme*, might have led some to believe that he was seeking an extension of public financing for all religions. He made clear that his point was to remove the discriminatory State funding. This change would allow the State to use those funds for other purposes including the promotion of laïcité. He also reiterated that evangelicals do not seek State funding for their churches and consider State subsidies contrary to the principle of separation. He recognized that surrendering State financing would be painful for the re-cipients and exhorted them to have the courage to take that step and become self-financing as are the non-concordataire religions.[187]

During the French presidential campaign in 2017, the topic of laïcité received unprecedented attention. Five candidates were routinely questioned on their understanding of laïcité. The responses and exchanges are informa-tive in revealing the divergences on several contemporary issues, including the maintenance of the Concordat in Alsace-Moselle, the burkini, and cur-rent religious questions in society.[188] The importance of understanding these issues should not be underestimated. Disagreements among the candidates revealed the divisions in French society. As one example, the burkini inci-dents divided the political left torn between the issues of antiracism and femi-nism.[189] Some viewed the burkini and the burqa as part of a political struggle against religious manipulation and inequality. For them, the issue revealed a totalitarian and extremist conception of Islam, with sexual, moral, legal, and civil overtones. It was viewed as a violation of the law adopted in 2010

185. Fath, "Alsace-Moselle: Quels droits."
186. Albecker, "Alsace-Moselle: Un modèle."
187. Fath, "Vers la fin de la discrimination concordataire," para.5.
188. "Ce que proposent les cinq principaux candidats."
189. "Le burkini interdit."

banning facial dissimulation in public.[190] Others saw the issue in terms of the principles of laïcité which guarantee religious freedom, to believe or not believe, and the expression of religious convictions.[191] The balance between liberty and equality once again was front and center.

Emmanuel Macron (*En Marche!*), later elected president, supported the maintenance of the Concordat in Alsace-Moselle and opposed banning the burkini on beaches or prohibiting the headscarf in institutions of higher learning or public spaces. He proposed training in French for Muslim religious leaders on republican values. He stated that the problem was not laïcité but Islam, although not Islam in itself but in certain areas of conduct. He also suggested specific teaching on religious realities in schools. He expressed his wish that French Muslims become prouder of being French than being Muslim. For Macron, the Republic is not multicultural. It is diverse, indivisible, and pluralistic.

Benoît Hamon, the socialist candidate (*Parti socialiste*), supported the enlargement of the Concordat in Alsace-Moselle to benefit Islam. There was no mention in the article on extending benefits to other non-concordataire confessions. He proposed a tax on halal food products to finance Islam and the creation of a special phone number (*numéro vert*) to alert authorities of all violations related to laïcité. He opposed a ban on the veil in institutions of higher learning and in public. He proposed the closure of places of worship that promote hatred or violence. He considered the law of 1905 as one of the most beautiful laws of the Republic and promised to fight against the imposition of the veil and other forms of female submission.

Jean-Luc Mélenchon (*La France insoumise*) campaigned with the promise to end the Concordat in Alsace-Moselle and to extend the application of the law of 1905 to all French territory, including overseas possessions. He stated that laïcité is the condition for the liberty of conscience for everyone, of the equality and fraternity of all citizens. He admitted that he was personally opposed to the burkini and the veil, but equally opposed to laws banning them. He wanted to ban elected and appointed government leaders from attending religious ceremonies in the exercise of their office. He opposed public funds for constructing places of worship and for subsidizing religious activities. He quoted Victor Hugo to show that Church and State each have their own place in society. He considered laïcité threatened and used in public debate to hide other goals.[192]

190. Audouin, "Burqa, voile."

191. "Interdire le 'burkini' au nom de la laïcité?"

192. Hullot-Guiot, "Mélenchon veut abolir le Concordat."

Marine Le Pen (*Front national*) supported the maintenance of the Concordat in Alsace-Moselle and expressed the desire to reinstate laïcité everywhere. She proposed the banning of all conspicuous religious signs in public places, including the burkini, and supported the modification of the Labor Code to forbid religious symbols. She stated that the provision of childcare services in public places with a Christian preference was justified by the millenary history of Christianity in France. She expressed her intention to establish the respect of laïcité and neutrality in sport clubs and opposed foreign countries funding religion in France. She viewed laïcité as the ultimate protection against communitarianism which in her opinion threatened the nation's unity.

In 2018, under President Emmanuel Macron, the French government issued what many considered a landmark document on laïcité. Gilles Clavreul, the governmental representative, travelled for four months, primarily in urban areas of France, before establishing the report. During his travels he was alarmed by observations of communities contesting the principles of laïcité. According to the report, the manifestations and the perturbations they entailed were the result in most cases of an unbending, radical Islam, but also involved fundamentalist Catholics, evangelicals, and orthodox Jews in areas of educational, cultural, and recreational activities. Examples included veil-wearing Muslim women providing home childcare services and refusing to return children to their fathers at the end of the day, proselytism by assistants working in public schools, community prayer organized by Muslims and Christians, and halal and kosher meals offered in schools in violation of laïque principles.[193]

The document stated that its purpose was to examine issues related to laïcité and republican values. These issues concerned the respect of principles of laïcité in relation to religious confessions in the areas of education, extracurricular activities, and cultural practices. Cultural practices included prayers in public spaces, religious meeting places, ritual slaughter of animals, and the administration of cemeteries and burial practices. Other issues indirectly related to laïcité were also addressed. These issues arose from religious practices or convictions not considered violations of laïcité as such but possibly jeopardizing certain principles which govern living together in a laïque society. Among the concerns were equality between men and women, and the respect of others with differences in deeply-held beliefs and in sexual orientation.[194] The terrorist attacks in Paris and Montrouge in January 2015 were singled out as a dividing point in calling for renewed efforts to reinforce

193. Clavreul, *Laïcité: Valeurs de la République*, 5.
194. Clavreul, *Laïcité: Valeurs de la République*, 3.

republican values and promote laïcité, a subject on which the document admitted there had never been consensus. Concerning laïcité and its history, the document summarized the issue in a remarkable way:

> Laïcité has been the subject of inflammatory debates and this is not the place to recall its long history. Laïcité crystalizes fierce, opposing viewpoints, viewpoints which have been sharpened and changed in nature over the last thirty years as Islam has claimed its rightful place in French society. There have been certain events, designated generally by the terms of Islamism or radical Islam, which have jeopardized in various degrees, and in some cases openly challenged, principles consecrated by the Republic.[195]

The document explicitly recognized that although laïcité and religion were not the only sensitive issues in French society, they were perhaps the ones where the position of the State appeared less stable to onlookers. There was also this startling admission:

> It is clear that there is no consensus on the definition of laïcité or its reach and that the dynamic of these last few years has been more centrifugal than centripetal. . . . The difficulty in producing a consensus on the very definition of laïcité has been felt well beyond the polemic between political leaders and debates between those who are knowledgeable. . . . This instability is the source of uncertainties, of incomprehension, and at times even of conflicts.[196]

Le Figaro published an article which summarized the main points of the report and proposed measures: (1) Subsidies from the State for employment and cultural events conditioned on the respect of laïcité or obligatory training sessions on laïcité; (2) Training all government workers on the subject of laïcité by the year 2020; (3) Incorporation of the study of laïcité in training students for leadership roles; (4) Establishment of a mapping system to determine problem areas and incidents of non-observance of republican values; (5) Transformation of organizations against racism and anti-Semitism into departmental organizations to promote laïcité and republican values.[197]

At the time of writing, the proposals of this important document are under consideration. Their application and resulting consequences for

195. Clavreul, *Laïcité: Valeurs de la République*, 4.

196. Clavreul, *Laïcité: Valeurs de la République*, 4.

197. Berdah et al., "Laïcité."

religions and religious rights in French society remain to be seen. The French government seeks the integration of Islam. The question persists, however, as to whether Islam, or which form of Islam, will adapt to a laïque society and respect the values of the Republic. The issue of laïcité endures at the forefront of politics and its meaning and application continue to be contested.

President Emmanuel Macron has followed his predecessors of the past twenty years in invoking the need to set boundaries for the organization of French Islam. Former presidents have had little success in resolving the tensions, and many of the issues remain the same. Macron recognizes the need for the creation of truly representative bodies for a religion known for its divisions, regulation of the finances for places of worship and more accountability for funds, training of imams to replace both those from other countries and self-proclaimed imams, and the independence of French imams from foreign powers.[198] He presented his wishes for 2018 to representatives of the Orthodox, Jewish, Catholic, Islam, Buddhist, and Protestant faiths. Laïcité was mentioned several times with references to the law of 1905. He expressed his desire for a balance between religion and the State, the freedom to believe in God, and respect for the values of the Republic. In his speech he carefully presented his perspective on French history and laïcité:

> The history of the French Republic is not the same for all religions which are represented here, which is our strength, but we must also speak the truth, that each of your religions have not built the same rapport with the political powers in our history, and the history of our country is not the same with each of your religions. It is the fruit of this history which led to the law of 1905, by the anticlericalism of that time, that we have been able to transcend. . . . This law of 1905 is part of a treasure which is ours, [but it] had not taken into consideration the religious reality with and by Islam, because Islam was not present in our society as it is today.[199]

Macron believes that the present organizational structures of Islam in France have weaknesses. First, the Fondation pour l'Islam de France, created by the French government in 2016, is limited in its action since it deals almost exclusively with socio-cultural projects and not with religious matters. Second, only 10 percent of Muslims in France feel that they are represented by the CFCM. During his campaign for the presidency, Macron supported the creation of a national federation of French Islam to gather all the local Muslim associations created within the framework of the law

198. Chihizola, "Le défi."

199. Macron, "Transcription du discours."

of 1905. He referenced Tunisia as a model where Islam is compatible with democracy. The president wants more clarity on the financing of Islam and the training of imams and wants all imams to receive training on the subject of laïcité.[200] Political scientist Stéphane Rozès considers that through events connected with radical Islam, Macron is confronted by the most dramatic moment of his career in articulating his vision for national unity. Rozès sees the need for the nation to know how Macron will enforce laïcité when some consider laïcité Islamophobic.[201]

President Macron addressed the Conférence des évêques de France in April 2018. In his speech, he pleaded for an historical reconciliation between the Republic and the Catholic Church. Preempting any criticism of violating laïcité, he justified his presence by stating that if he did not recognize the place of Catholicism, he would condemn himself to an incomplete view of France in misunderstanding the nation, its history, and its citizens. To a standing ovation, he concluded by speaking of the most indestructible attachments between the French nation and Catholicism and proclaimed that France had been strengthened by the involvement of Catholics.[202] One prominent evangelical blogger extolled the brilliant speech on laïcité and the relations between the State and religions. He applauded this encounter and previous gatherings where the president expressed himself from a pattern of thought in conformity to the founding fathers of the law of 1905. Macron was further praised because he dared affirm with serenity that religions, when they are in their role (respecting the laïque Republic and the principle of separation, without hegemonic desire), can also do good works which includes their spiritual contribution.[203] Others defended the speech against critics and insisted that the president had not questioned laïcité but rather had expressed his preference and vision for a laïcité of dialogue rather than a laïcité of combat and exclusion. The president's presence was viewed as a corrective for an injustice since past presidents had participated in important events organized by Judaism and Islam.[204]

His speech was not unanimously praised. Former presidential candidate Jean-Luc Mélenchon tweeted that the link with the Catholic Church, which the president wanted to repair, in fact had not been damaged by the law of 1905 but that the link had been broken. According to Mélenchon, for the president to question the separation of churches and State

200. "Quelle organisation pour l'Islam."

201. Cuénod, "Macron devra trouver les mots."

202. Guénois, "Emmanuel Macron."

203. Fath, "Grand discours d'Emmanuel Macron."

204. Tincq, "Non, Emmanuel Macron."

was irresponsible and would open the door for fundamentalists of all religions.[205] Former Minister of Education and unsuccessful presidential candidate Benoît Hamon tweeted that the encouraging words of the president on the Catholic Church's protection of life repeated the words of antiabortionists and adversaries of euthanasia.[206] Olivier Faure, new first secretary of the Socialist Party, tweeted that according to the law of 1905 there was no link to be restored between the Catholic Church and the State.[207] Within a few days, the philosopher Henri Pena-Ruiz denounced the president's speech. He accused the president of inventing an imaginary history and mistaking himself for a monarch seeking to reestablish the connection between the altar and the throne. Pena-Ruiz characterized the speech as closer to a concordataire, neo-Gallican posture than a laïque approach. He recognized the right of the president to privately prefer Catholicism, but insisted that he could not show a preference in the exercise of his functions. To do so, according to Pena-Ruiz, is antilaïque and in contradiction to the obligation of neutrality of the State.[208] This incident was followed by another in May 2018 when the president was criticized by the Masons who largely supported him in seeking the presidency. According to Le Figaro, the Masons espouse a strict view of laïcité and expressed their concern that the president was advancing initiatives favorable toward religions. They asserted that the law of 1905 concerning the separation of Church and State was threatened. Philippe Foussier, the current grand master of the Grand Orient de France, was roundly applauded in his appeal for laïcité, nothing but laïcité. For him, religious questions must not invade social and civic life.[209]

European Union and Laïcité

The political divide remains on the topic of laïcité and every presidential remark on laïcité is scrutinized by defenders of diverse visions of the place of religion in French society. The emergence of the European Union (EU) has opened new challenges and avenues of debate concerning laïcité à la française. The Charter of Fundamental Rights of the European Union was first proposed in December 2000. This was an undertaking to articulate common principles of life in society and the contours of democracy as the EU opened up toward Eastern Europe nations. The search for commonality

205. Mélenchon, "Monsieur le président."
206. Hamon, "Qd @EmmanuelMacron."
207. Faure, "Mais de quoi nous parle-t-on?"
208. Pena-Ruiz, "Un discours."
209. Nouzille, "Macron et les francs-maçons."

among nations with different political structures and religious systems presented enormous challenges. These were national contexts with differences in traditions and in their constitutional texts. The pursuit of a common identity with common values was undertaken even if the question of religious identity remained a controversial point of divergence. There was recognition that the nations of the European Union entered into a process of convergence, not only in areas of technology and economics, but also in the area of fundamental values.[210]

In preliminary discussions, Pope John Paul II argued for the inclusion of the mention of Europe's Christian roots in the Charter's final text. Italy and Poland supported this reference to Europe's religious past. According to reports, the German delegation requested a mention of religion since their own constitution refers to God. In the Vatican's opinion, the principal opposition to any consideration of this came from the French government, prisoner of a laïciste ideology.[211] It was reported that then-French Prime Minister Lionel Jospin requested the removal of the words "religious heritage" in one version of the preamble which did not respect the context of laïcité à la française. A subsequent version replaced "religious" with "spiritual." The root of the issue stemmed from different forms of laïcité and the relationships between churches and the State in Germany and France. Changes in the text were made through pressure on the leadership and without debate in the convention meetings. The removal of religious references was also justified since the Charter with its fundamental rights was oriented toward the future and not the past. There was recognition of the need for a laïque model in Europe compatible with national models.[212]

The EU claims to promote a *laïcité de médiation*. Those who desire special recognition for historical churches may not be completely satisfied with this form of laïcité which is exercised without official recognition yet with informal relations.[213] The EU considers churches part of civil society and not simply as religions operating in the private sphere. Rognon and Weber write, "Whatever the churches may say themselves, European institutions treat them as lobbies, lobbies considered positively and rather well treated, lobbies somewhat special, but without special status."[214] For the EU, churches have an important connection to civil society, essential for many in their identification and life in community. The *laïcité de médiation* is

210. Charentenay, "La Charte européenne," 154–55.

211. Latala and Rime, *Liberté religieuse*, 53.

212. Rognon and Weber, *La laïcité*, 156.

213. Rognon and Weber, *La laïcité*, 163.

214. Rognon and Weber, *La laïcité*, 162.

presented as more open than a *laïcité de séparation*, more flexible and more respectful than a *laïcité of intégration*.[215]

The EU position led inevitably to clashes with member nations, principally France. In 2003, President Jacques Chirac established an independent commission presided by Bernard Stasi to study the constitutional principle of laïcité.[216] There were some who sensed antireligious tendencies in the hearings. During the deliberations, commission members were made aware that Muslims in France often perceived laïcité as an alibi to oppose their projects.[217] The results of the commission's study seemed to confirm these suspicions in the minds of many, particularly Muslims. The government voted the law in March 2004, previously mentioned, which prohibited the wearing of religious symbols or clothing in public primary, middle, and high schools which ostensibly manifest religious identification. Article 10 of the European Charter was invoked against this law.[218] With the adoption of the Treaty of Lisbon in December 2007, the Charter acquired legal status which presented challenges to French laïcité and legal decisions enacted by France. The French government contended that the 2004 law reaffirmed the principle of laïcité and is not opposed to religions. In this instance, the claim was made that the constraint for wearing the veil translates also into the desire to refuse to women, in the name of Islam, the equality to which they aspire.[219] According to this interpretation, the law simply allows the State to contest manifestations of affiliations which are in opposition to individual liberties.[220]

The tension between the EU and France stems partly from France's social and historical context which we have seen in previous chapters. Jeantet argues that initially the right to wear the headscarf in 1989 was defended under the banner of a more open *nouvelle laïcité* in the name of the liberty of expression and human rights in France.[221] In the following decade, for many, the headscarf came to symbolize oppression and discrimination against women by fundamentalist factions in Muslim countries.[222] The headscarf controversy highlighted historical tensions in France on women's rights. Women did not receive the right to vote until

---

215. Rognon and Weber, *La laïcité*, 164.

216. Commission Stasi, "Commission de réflexion."

217. Lalmy, "Les collectivités," 44.

218. Rognon and Weber, *La laïcité*, 80.

219. Rognon and Weber, *La laïcité*, 100–101.

220. Jeantet, "L'école et la laïcité," 35.

221. Jeantet, "L'école et la laïcité," 36.

222. Haarscher, *La laïcité*, 77.

1944, almost forty years after the law of 1905 which had been proclaimed as a law of emancipation of all citizens.[223] For many French women, wearing an Islamic headscarf became more than simply a religious symbol. The headscarf was viewed as a marker of submission and inequality between men and women and indicative of other inequalities in French society in education, politics, and employment. Cesari asserts that "the moral and cultural code of the Muslim woman is constantly seen as the antithesis of that of the Western woman, an opposition also claimed by Western-born female converts to Islam."[224] Seen in this light, l'affaire du foulard fiercely rekindled a debate and a new reading of the law of 1905.[225]

The balance between liberty and equality discussed earlier remains part of the ongoing debate on laïcité and the conflict between individual rights and group identity. This one example shows the difficulties of the application of laïcité in a laïque Republic which is now part of a larger international community, a community with different relationships between religion and the State. There is tension between immigrants and their values and the values of the new community of which they have become part. Cesari opines that "Islam will only cease to be alien once Muslims living in the West are able to express their criticisms of the democratic process, without being accused of disloyalty or being seen as a danger to society."[226]

Christian Pluralism, Muslim Immigration, and Practical Issues

A Christian response to Islam has recently been written and deserves attention. Matthew Kaemingk writes from the context of the policy of failed multiculturalism in the Netherlands with application particularly for North America. He critiques two major responses to Islam which he describes as "the antagonism of right-wing nationalism or the romanticism of left-wing multiculturalism."[227] There are numerous similarities between the Netherlands and the situation in France which make the proposals and practical application relevant to French Christians facing a growing Islamic presence.

In both the Netherlands and France religion was banished to the private sphere and marginalized. Islam and other religions were deprived of a voice in public space. As an immigrant religion, Islam's marginalization

223. Mamet-Soppelsa, "Les femmes et la laïcité," 40.

224. Cesari, Islam and Democracy, 157.

225. Mamet-Soppelsa, "Les femmes et la laïcité," 42.

226. Cesari, Islam and Democracy, 158.

227. Kaemingk, Christian Hospitality, 2.

led to isolation and communities of Muslims disconnected from public life which contributed to extremism and terrorism. Kaemingk asserts that "the growing numbers, visibility, and strength of Islam in what was thought to be secular Europe has been deeply unsettling for Europeans who believed the old secularization thesis."[228] He holds that early Christian pluralists saw "the French Revolution as a destructive force of ideological violence and hegemony in Europe."[229] In referring to the headscarf affair, he explains that in the name of public secularity, "schoolgirls in France, for example, have been banned from wearing the hijab in government-run schools."[230]

Kaemingk's goal in addressing the Islamic challenge is to provide Christians "an outside perspective, a fresh approach, a different angle—one that actually emerges out of their own Christian conviction."[231] Kaemingk reaches back to Abraham Kuyper (1837–1920) to define the forms of human freedom as they operate within Kuyper's view of Christian pluralism and to address and alleviate the fear and suspicion in encounters with Muslim immigrants. He clarifies that he is not using the word pluralism theologically as found in soteriological debates which concern ultimate destinies. He explores the question, "How should Muslims be treated while they are still alive?"[232] In attempting to answer that question, he maintains "an uncompromising commitment to the exclusive lordship of Jesus Christ" and "an uncompromising commitment to love those who reject that lordship."[233] His proposal for the North American context involves Christians working together for the common good in order to gain a hearing for the gospel.

Kaemingk contrasts Christian pluralism with four other responses—assimilation, moderation, retreat, and retribution. He affirms that "early Christian pluralists argued for the formation of a state and society in which all worldviews could publically flourish and advocate for their own unique visions for the common good."[234] He believes that the goal of a Christian response to Muslim immigration is not integration or assimilation. In this vision of Christian pluralism, Muslims practice their faith in the public sphere of life alongside other religions. According to Kaemingk,

> Drawing on Abraham Kuyper's Trinitarian pluralism, contemporary Christians will be better equipped to resist today's

228. Kaemingk, *Christian Hospitality*, 4–5.

229. Kaemingk, *Christian Hospitality*, 83.

230. Kaemingk, *Christian Hospitality*, 165.

231. Kaemingk, *Christian Hospitality*, 4.

232. Kaemingk, *Christian Hospitality*, 15.

233. Kaemingk, *Christian Hospitality*, 16.

234. Kaemingk, *Christian Hospitality*, 82.

xenophobic cries for Islamic assimilation. They will know that
God the Son is sovereign over the history, culture, and politics
of their nation. . . . Demanding that their Muslim neighbors
alter their clothing, practices, or institutions will be seen as
tantamount to denying the good cultural gifts that the Holy
Spirit gave them.[235]

Kuyper's Christian pluralism anticipated the return of Christ in glory accompanied by coercion when every knee would bow to his sovereignty.
Yet his "pluralist movement needed to respect Christ's exclusive rights to
temporal sovereignty by engaging their diverse neighbors with 'persuasion
to the exclusion of all coercion.'"[236] In the end, he calls Christians to action
in seeing Muslims as created in the image of God and serving them for the
sake of Christ without abandoning their theological convictions. In fact,
Kaemingk boldly advocates that "Christian disciples must make hospitality,
not justice, the primary frame through which they understand their public
and political obligations toward Islam."[237] Lest anyone misunderstand his
call for hospitality as utopian, he affirms that "the hospitality of the cross is
neither soft nor permissive. It does not appease, it is not naïve about worldly
violence, nor is it incapable of defending itself. . . . Terrorism must be pun-
ished and justice must be executed if hospitality endures."[238]

In reflecting on Kaemingk's salutary proposals, it should be remembered that "a radicalized perception of Islam is not as common in the United
States as it is in Europe, and hostility in the United States is less the result
of competing national identities and more something that stems from the
constant redefinition of and shifting balance between ethnic groups."[239]
Also, as Cesari observes, "American Islamophobia tends to focus more on
the religious aspects of Islam, in contrast to European Islamophobia before
September 11, which was largely focused on cultural issues."[240] The contexts are also vastly different between Europe and North American because
of the difference between the immigrants themselves in these places. In
the United States, Islam remains a minority religion. In France, Muslims
outnumber evangelical Protestants. Kaemingk writes, "Muslims living in
America today are significantly more privileged and powerful than those
in Europe. It is therefore important to note that the differences in the

235. Kaemingk, *Christian Hospitality*, 156.

236. Kaemingk, *Christian Hospitality*, 125.

237. Kaemingk, *Christian Hospitality*, 186.

238. Kaemingk, *Christian Hospitality*, 187.

239. Cesari, *Islam and Democracy*, 32.

240. Cesari, *Islam and Democracy*, 40.

debates over Islam and in Europe and North America are thanks, in part, to the significant differences of socioeconomic power and privilege possessed by European versus American Muslims."[241] In the United States, Muslim immigrants were largely educated professionals whose employment and Islamic organizations allowed them to function in a foreign culture and determined their degree of assimilation. Another significant difference is that whereas "most European countries have drawn Muslim immigrants from two or three specific countries (often their old colonies), the United States has drawn from a wide diversity of Muslims from every Islamic country."[242] Regardless of these differences, the principles enunciated by Kaemingk on hospitality and Christian pluralism should resonate with French Christians as they address the Islamic question. And as Cesari recognizes, since September 11, 2001, "the gap between American and European experiences in matters of Islam, it would seem, is shrinking."[243]

Finally, we should consider some of the recurring issues in France largely related to Islam and connected with the application of laïcité where there is no consensus. There are those who regret that the law in 2004 was limited to religious concerns which appeared to target Muslims and was silent on other issues relating to laïcité. These thorny and unresolved problems occur regularly in education, school meals, and sports. The issues include special meals for different religions, students wearing clothing with designer names and images, and professors solicited by businesses to use certain teaching materials. For some, the educational system has become a tool of social reproduction when it should be a crucible of common values and the emancipation of the individual.[244] For example, in 2003, the mayor of Sarcelles in suburban Paris, decided that meatless meals would be offered to children in primary schools at the request of the Jewish community. This decision followed one made several years earlier when meals were offered without pork to accommodate Muslims. The mayor highlighted that the schools were adapting themselves to the changing tastes of children. Many advocates of laïcité viewed the mayor's decisions as voiding the meaning of laïcité and, even if legal, inconsistent with the law forbidding religious symbols in public schools which passed the following year in 2004. Opponents of religious concessions stressed that the mayor's decisions risked creating multiple communities in the heart of public, laïque education.[245]

241. Kaemingk, *Christian Hospitality*, 267.
242. Kaemingk, *Christian Hospitality*, 268.
243. Cesari, *Islam and Democracy*, 32.
244. Jeantet, "L'école et la laïcité," 37.
245. Lalmy, "Les collectivités," 44.

Public pools have also been an object of debate and divergent opinions. Muslim and Jewish communities have requested and received special accommodation for slots allotted where there is no mixed swimming between sexes. Defenders of laïcité do not represent the issue as denying the right of Muslims and Jews to freely engage in practices which respect their religious convictions. They do contest whether these religions should be accorded special treatment in public places. Preferential treatment is viewed as denial of public space to others. Strict views on laïcité regard public spaces as mixed spaces and challenge reserving public spaces to accommodate selective religious practices. The situation is complex and not yet resolved to everyone's satisfaction.[246]

Legal expert Nancy Lefèvre describes one relatively recent challenge to the application of laïcité illustrated in what came to be known as l'affaire Baby Loup. The incident in 2014 involved a female Muslim employee of a private nursery school who contested her termination for wearing an Islamic veil. The school justified its decision to terminate employment based on internal regulations which imposed laïcité and neutrality on all employees of the association. The Court of Cassation ruled that the affair was outside the field of application of laïcité since laïcité did not apply to private organizations. The court clearly halted attempts to extend the principle of laïcité to private structures providing childcare. Arguments continue over what constitutes public and private space and the application of laïcité in these domains. Lefèvre believes l'affaire Baby Loup demonstrates several current challenges regarding laïcité. These challenges include the debate surrounding the difficulty of applying the principle of laïcité, the general public's misunderstanding of the principle, and the necessity of court intervention to bring clarity in seeking to balance liberty of conscience and the neutrality of the State.[247]

These examples of the struggle for religious freedom and expression reveal that the debate on laïcité in France continues. Many of the challenges to laïcité and their resolution are being decided case-by-case in the legal system. If history is any guide in these matters, there should be little expectation that opposing perspectives will arrive at a consensus. Lacking consensus, there is the hope that common ground might be found to uphold State neutrality and the freedom of religious expression.

246. Lalmy, "Les collectivités," 44.
247. Lefèvre, "Libertés de conscience," 147.

7

Conclusion and Implications for Gospel Ministry

At the outset, this study sought to understand the historical origins and evolution of the concept and meaning of laïcité in France and the possible contribution of laïcité to the decline of institutional religion in the twentieth and twenty-first centuries following the enactment of the Law of Separation in 1905. State neutrality and the disestablishment of the Catholic Church in 1905 led to freedom of conscience and religious expression which benefited non-concordataire churches. The growing presence and influence of Islam at the end of the twentieth century reopened the debate on laïcité and on the place of religion in French society.

We have seen that the Protestant Reformation in the sixteenth century introduced revolutionary ideas which contradicted the teaching of the established Church. These teachings undermined and threatened the Church's authority and contributed to the wars of religion. The Edict of Nantes in 1598 under Henry IV sowed the seed for the freedom of conscience for Reformed believers and introduced the concepts of religious pluralism and incipient laïcité.[1] In the following centuries, the Revocation of the Edict of Nantes in 1685 under Louis XIV and persecution of the Huguenots, the Enlightenment, the French Revolution in 1789, the Napoleonic Concordat in 1801, the disastrous Franco-Prussian War in 1870, the rise of anticlericalism in the late nineteenth century and the Dreyfus Affair all conspired to create a religion-weary nation. The French Revolution produced a break with organized and obligatory religion in article 10 of the *Déclaration des droits de l'homme et du citoyen*. The radical idea was declared that no one should be troubled for religious opinions. Yet not until 1905 and the legal separation of Church and State was there a positive proclamation of the freedom of conscience, the free exercise of religion, and the neutrality of the

---

1. Monod, *Sécularisation et laïcité*, 47.

State. Today, France is a laïque nation, juridically established in 1905 and enshrined constitutionally in 1946 and 1958.

Toward the end of the twentieth century, major challenges surfaced to confront the well-established principle of laïcité and republican values. The Islamic headscarf affair in 1989 became a major point of reference and led to protracted legal challenges. Initially, the Conseil d'État ruled that headscarves worn by female Muslim students and other religious symbols were permitted and that individual public schools could handle the issue with dialogue and reasonable accommodations. Terrorist attacks and a sense of insecurity led to debate and restrictions on religious expression. In 2004, a law was passed which overturned the 1989 Conseil d'État decision. Islamic headscarves were banned in public schools along with religious symbols from both Judaism and Christianity. Eventually, the full-face Islamic veil was banned in public in 2010.[2] The Baby Loup incident captured national attention in 2014 in the distinction between private and public establishments. Contention over the burkini riveted the public eye on French beaches in 2016 following terrorist attacks in Nice. Presidential candidates sparred over laïcité-related issues leading up to the 2017 elections, including the concordataire status of Alsace-Moselle. President Emmanuel Macron has promised to address the issues relating to laïcité and Islam. His perspective and remarks have been both applauded and denounced.

The Conseil d'État maintains that the twenty-first century faces new expressions of laïcité (*nouvelle, plurielle, ouverte, aménagée, revisitée*) to meet recent current and pressing challenges. The advent of religious pluralism and the presence of Islam, Buddhism, and other religions, virtually unknown in France a century earlier when the law of 1905 was enacted, have arisen to challenge and unsettle the status quo. A major question is the place occupied by Islam and more generally a return to religion. Thus, the Conseil d'État has determined that the concept of laïcité is in fact an evolving concept, as evidenced by the application in the time of the law of 1905 and the texts that followed. However, the concept is not susceptible to just any interpretation.[3]

The year 2018 opened with an announcement that the government wanted to slightly modify the law of 1905 and ended with the CNEF announcing that they were waiting for the government's project concerning the announced modification of the law of 1905.[4] At this time of writing, the reopened "laïcité question" remains unsettled. The struggle for the

2. Kovacs, "Niqab: la France sermonnée."

3. Conseil d'État, "Un siècle de laïcité," 247.

4. Sauvaget, "Associations cultuelles."

meaning and application of laïcité in France continues to this day, five hundred years after the principle was first introduced in the sixteenth century, over one hundred years after the law of 1905, and over fifty years after the declaration of laïcité first appeared in the French Constitution. The failure of twentieth-century ideologies and the rise of Islam have contributed to renewed interest in the study of laïcité and in the relation of Church and State in a pluralistic, multicultural society.

Sociologists have brought precise analysis on the cultural changes of believers in a democratic and laïque society. When we understand the history of religion in France, it should be unsurprising to discover that many French people harbor resentment, hatred, indifference or opposition toward religion. Coq reminds us that it is undeniable that religious memory is full of wounds and that images from the past continue to present obstacles to a good understanding of the gospel. Even more, these negative images feed prejudices against religion today.[5] It can be argued from this survey of French laïque history that religion as experienced in France needed to be removed from its place in the political sphere. As a consequence, religion in general declined and became a private affair, and twentieth-century ideologies rushed in to fill the void. These ideologies lacked the power to sustain and satisfy, and some led to untold suffering and loss of life.[6] Yet recent studies demonstrate that if religion is in decline, it has not died. According to the Pew Research Center's 2018 survey of religious identity and meaning, "Western Europe, where Protestantism originated and Catholicism has been based for most of its history, has become one of the world's most secularized regions."[7] The largest share of the population, in spite of recent immigration trends, is non-practicing Christians who identify as Christians, but rarely attend church services. Of those surveyed in France, 18 percent identified as church-attending Christians, 46 percent as non-practicing Christians, 28 percent as religiously unaffiliated, and 8 percent as other religion or unable to determine. Religion has disenchanted. Religion has not disappeared.

Preparation for Ministry in Laïque France

Secular society, even disillusioned, seems more favorable to the discovery of the good news than a religious society which constrains consciences.[8] If

---

5. Coq, *Laïcité et République*, 305.
6. Coq, *Laïcité et République*, 310.
7. Pew Research Center, "Being Christian in Western Europe."
8. Coq, *Laïcité et République*, 308.

there is a favorable reception for the good news in secular society, how does that provide direction for engagement in mission in this context? The nature of the mission task leads to the challenges and complexity of cross-cultural ministry in the twenty-first century which compel serious preparation for gospel ministry. This preparation should take into consideration the target nation's religious history and the nature of relations between Church and State. Thus, there are important practical questions which arise from this study of laïcité in French history, particularly for those who minister or desire to minister in France in a cultural context shaped by laïcité. What does the history and religious climate in France mean for ministry in France? What do cross-cultural workers need to understand in order to build relationships or to even initiate gospel encounters? How does one prepare for ministry in a complex nation like France? This writer draws from his experience in France and from the experience and observations of others.

This author has written elsewhere on preparation for cross-cultural ministry more generally.[9] The following proposals specifically address challenges American evangelical missionaries face in France. These observations are merely suggestive and are no guarantee of fruitful ministry for those who sense a call to ministry in France. Neither do they provide assurance that those who follow these recommendations will succeed in acclimating to life in another culture. Americans leave a nation saturated by religion and with a massive evangelical population for a nation where religion is marginalized and Protestants of all stripes lag behind Muslims in number. Chapter 5 presented some of Allen Koop's research findings concerning the American evangelical effort in France after World War II. His observations are relevant and should be taken to heart by anyone considering ministry in France. Koop described the difference between laïque France and the United States which "still left plenty of room for religion. Twentieth-century France, however, threatened Christianity with a harsh climate."[10] This harsh climate took its toll on eager but unprepared missionaries who were viewed by the French "as part of the new American invasion."[11] The difficulty of engaging in ministry was complicated by the backgrounds and unpreparedness of the missionaries. Many of these "missionaries, often young and inexperienced, arrived with visionary goals of evangelizing France, only to find how poorly prepared they were for living in a new culture where even ordinary activities like taking the metro to

9. Davis, *Crossing Cultures.*

10. Koop, *Evangelical Missionaries*, 5.

11. Koop, *Evangelical Missionaries*, 10.

language study could be trying experiences."[12] The complexity of life and ministry in France requires deep consideration of history, culture and language. Without a sufficient mastery of the French language, without the expansion of a speaker's linguistic and cognitive competency, cross-cultural workers will not be able to understand or engage in complex discussions of issues which concern French people. These discussions concern religious questions and center on history, on current events and challenges to laïcité in the twenty-first century, on the suspicions of a society fearful of immigration, and on religious perceptions formed through centuries of chaotic relations between Church and State. French people must be met where they are before they can be pointed to the hope of the gospel.

France has proved itself less welcoming than many other fields of service. There are French writers like Yves Lacoste who believe that evangelical churches should be considered as agents of geopolitical influence under the authority of American leaders.[13] Others are more guarded. Michael Mallèvre elaborates the commonalities in doctrine and values between Catholics and evangelicals which might lead to a "co-belligerence against pervasive relativism."[14]

At this juncture, it might be helpful to outline specific considerations for those who sense a calling to minister in secular France with the particularities of French culture, the place of religion, and with differences in thinking, behavior, and attitudes. First, along with language, culture, and history studies required in cross-cultural settings, one must understand the challenges of ministry in a society which has taken great pains to separate religion from the public sphere. One American missionary who spent years in France states, "In France, generations of religious and ideological conflicts led to what some have labeled 'utter secularity,' devoted to the destruction and replacement of Christianity" and that "we must not allow the cultural sophistication, education and advanced technology of the French to hide their enormous spiritual needs."[15] Someone coming from the United States, where Congress opens its sessions with prayer, will be bewildered by the virtual absence of any religious language in political discourse. This requires an understanding of secularization as a process which inevitably occurs once the sacred no longer dominates and determines a society's orientation. One European writes that secularization results in "the marginalization of the church, repression of the Christian narrative,

---

12. Koop, *Evangelical Missionaries*, 12.
13. Lacoste, "Les évangéliques," 6.
14. Mallèvre, *Les évangéliques*, 108.
15. Bjork, *Unfamiliar Paths*, 51.

an increasing alienation of our culture from its Christian past, and a great deal of timidity within the church."[16] These results are more pronounced in Europe than in the United States due to the history of state churches. In addition, cross-cultural workers must confront the darkness and superstition of the occult which occupies a significant place in France and has grown into a multi-billion-dollar business. Each year fifteen million people consult the more than one hundred thousand mediums practicing in France. Sociological research has shown that people no longer have a spiritual compass which religions had provided. In times of crisis, they are looking for certitudes they cannot find in politics or rationality. This reality presents both a challenge and an opportunity for cross-cultural workers. The combat against dark forces cannot be entered without prayer and the power of the Holy Spirit to break the bonds of evil.[17]

Second, in France the process of secularization, which we have seen as the natural and progressive detachment of society from religiosity, must be understood alongside laïcité, the legal imposition of separation between the Church and the State. Our study has shown the complexity of the idea, the evolution of the meaning, and the case-by-case application of laïcité as new issues arise. The twenty-first century has reopened the debate on the place of religion in society which had been settled for most of the twentieth century. There are almost daily references to laïcité in newspapers, on Twitter, and in symposiums. The government is presently in consultation with representatives from major religions with one of the main objectives identified as the reduction of foreign influences. The current president envisages a reform of the law of 1905 on the separation of Church and State in order to adapt it to the surge of Islam. He has been asked to clarify his understanding of laïcité and has stressed that laïcité is not a struggle against religion.[18]

Third, cross-cultural workers should be prepared for the kind of welcome they will receive. This aspect was touched on earlier but needs repeating. Missiologists agree that "evangelical Christianity is seen as an Anglo-Saxon imposition on France together with the cultural, linguistic and economic 'imperialisms' perceived to be eroding the French way of life."[19] Many French people view evangelicals in the same vein as cults. When this writer lived in Laon, France in the late 1980s and early 1990s, the Church of Jesus Christ of the Latter-Day Saints (Mormons) rented a property near our house. In the minds of many French people, the only things that distinguished us from

16. Paas, "Church Planting," para.1.

17. Cohen and Galtier, "Quand ils n'ont pas de réponse."

18. "Macron: La laïcité."

19. Johnstone and Mandryk, *Operation World*, 256.

Mormons were the white shirts of the young missionaries and some of their taboos. What linked us was our nationality, our accent, and our non-affiliation with the Catholic Church.

In order to gain a measure of legitimacy, cross-cultural workers would do well to partner with French nationals to help them understand the context in which they plan to serve. The CNEF, which represents the majority of evangelicals in France, has written extensively on laïcité although many of their writings require a knowledge of the French language. Concerning the law of 1905, evangelicals consider themselves "the principal beneficiaries of this legal structure, commend the balance and pacification which result from it, and affirm their attachment to article one concerning the freedom of conscience and the free exercise of religions."[20] The application of the law concerning religious questions—including Jewish kippahs, Islamic veils, Christian crosses—continues to be decided in the courts. Gaining insight into French history and culture will not be accomplished overnight. Yet it cannot be ignored and is necessary in order to have effective ministry in a laïque nation.

Church Planting and Muslim Evangelization

The growth of evangelicalism in France has been well documented. Alfred Dittgen provides statistics which show that the overall number of Protestants in France, about one million, remained practically unchanged between 1980 and 2005. What changed was the reduction in the number of Protestants in historic confessions and the increase of evangelical Protestants. This leads Dittgen to declare that "Protestantism was 'saved' by the evangelicals."[21] Fath wrote in 2005 that the number of evangelicals had multiplied sevenfold in the past sixty years.[22] André Pownall examines the second half of the twentieth century with a focus on Paris and its suburbs. He describes the region transformed from a desert to a well-watered garden as evangelical churches took root.[23] He surveys the religious history of Paris along with the development of the city and the construction of new urban centers to meet the population growth. The Paris agglomeration (*petite couronne*) grew to ten million inhabitants by the beginning of the twenty-first century.[24] The CNEF claims that since 1970, more than 1,750 Protestant evangelical churches

20. CNEF, "La #Loi1905."

21. Dittgen, "Religions et démographies," 16.

22. Fath, *Du Ghetto au réseau*, 325.

23. Pownall, "Un demi-siècle d'implantation," 47.

24. Pownall, "Un demi-siècle d'implantation," 51–52.

have been planted in France with a total of 2,521 evangelical churches now in France, a church for every 29,000 inhabitants.[25]

An important question looms large for French Christians as they engage in mission in their own nation. What is their attitude toward the presence and growth of Islam, the second largest religion after Catholicism, and how do they view the evangelization of Muslims? Muslim evangelism remains difficult owing to the fact that Islam becomes the primary identifying marker in a country of immigration and as a result there are often more Muslim fundamentalists in France than in Muslim countries.[26] As a convert from Islam to Christianity, Father Paul-Élie Cheknoun recounts that his efforts at street evangelism are met by criticism of his apostasy. Yet he has recently observed more and more Muslim converts to Christianity who have joined evangelical churches. Although there are reports worldwide of a massive number of Muslim conversions, little has been found to document and substantiate that in France.[27] An interview with Virginie Larousse, chief editor of Monde des Religions highlighted that Islam and evangelical churches are the most attractive religions in France in numbers of conversions. Although precise statistics are unavailable, these two religions appear to draw the same number of new followers, each with an estimated four thousand conversions each year. At the same time the Catholic Church is experiencing the most loss.[28]

Part of the difficulty in the evangelization of Muslims is found in a 2018 report by the Pew Research Center which analyzes the opinions of practicing Christians, non-practicing Christians, and those without religious affiliation. The study revealed that practicing Christians are more critical of Muslims and immigration than the other two groups, were more likely to believe that Muslims want to impose their religious law on everyone, and consider Islam incompatible with the culture and values of France.[29] One evangelical French pastor expressed his perspective and concerns on the presence of Islam and the ambivalence among Christians. He had planted a multiethnic church in Saint-Denis, a suburb of Paris which has a large Muslim population, but where little Muslim evangelization took place. He wrote,

> People we could not reach a few years ago are at our doorstep.
> If we don't reach them for Christ, Islam will dominate France.

25. Liechti, Églises protestantes évangéliques.

26. Rivallain, "La conversion des musulmans."

27. Goepp, "Millions des musulmans se convertissent."

28. Larousse, "Et la religion."

29. Kloeckner, "Les chrétiens plus critiques."

As a French person, I would feel they are a threat. As a Christian, I see them as an opportunity. They are probably easier to talk to about the Lord than the French. One difference between the Gospel and Islam is that we are pressed for time because we want the salvation of individuals. Islam has time because they are working at controlling geographical areas. Procreation is the major way Islam spreads. It needs to place people in a country. Then it is just a matter of time.[30]

Richard Kronk has extensively researched Muslim conversion in France. He provides examples of the challenges faced by Muslim converts to Christianity. His research primarily deals with Christians of Maghrebi background (CMB) from Algeria, Morocco, and Tunisia. He analyzes possible causes for the failure of CMBs to integrate into French evangelical Protestant churches (FEPC) and provides examples of the common experience of unsuccessful integration into these churches. Kronk discovered numerous obstacles to integration including the "differing political, social, cultural and religious roots of the two communities."[31] In particular, he cites the colonial history and French-Algerian war (1954–1962) which led to independence. Another major obstacle is "the question of anonymity [which] becomes a high priority due to the stigma in the Maghrebi community associated with conversion to a rival faith."[32] He considers Muslim conversions to Christianity "equally on-going and unquantifiable," and recognizes that "there exists no central registration for keeping track of new adherents to the Christian faith."[33] Other obstacles for new Muslim converts include French evangelical customs of drinking wine, greeting the opposite sex with a kiss (bise), and eating pork. These practices are often insurmountable for someone "who has lived his whole life understanding that abstinence from alcohol and refraining from touching a non-family member of the opposite sex was illustrative of a wise and holy person."[34] Muslims who converted to Christianity "cited relationships with Christians, contact with a FEPC and access to the Bible as key factors in conversion."[35] According to Kronk, "it is telling that 100% of the respondents indicated that having a personal relationship with someone in the church was a key element

---

30. Personal email with the author, September 22, 2018.
31. Kronk, "Christians of Maghrebi Background," 16–17.
32. Kronk, "Christians of Maghrebi Background," 24.
33. Kronk, "Christians of Maghrebi Background," 29.
34. Kronk, "Christians of Maghrebi Background," 83.
35. Kronk, "Christians of Maghrebi Background," 129.

in their initial affiliation."[36] He asserts that "relationships with advocates are the single most important factor in enabling the person of Maghrebi background to negotiate the tradition transition from Islam (whether as a nominal or practicing adherent) to Christianity."[37] A final issue of interest for church planters "is the on-going debate over whether to establish churches of CMB or integrate believers into existing French Churches. This question continues to polarize both missionaries and CMB alike."[38] Kronk maintains that "all of the French mission organizations seek integration of the CMB into the existing French Churches as a primary goal, whereas, the non-French mission organizations are generally those seeking to establish CMB Churches."[39] Finally, he claims that "the current climate of religious pluralism and global instability seems to be contributing to a general receptivity on the part of Muslims to the gospel in France" and contends that "the future of sustained ministry to Muslims in France is in the hands of the growing number of Christians of Maghrebi background."[40]

French believers recognize that recent efforts of evangelization demonstrate that the best method of sustainable development is probably planting new churches. It is by the presence of born-again believers, functioning locally as a body of Christ, that the gospel usually becomes visible and understandable.[41] Secular media has also taken notice of the surge in church planting. According to Daniel Liechti, president of the commission for church planting in the CNEF, the French employ the strategy of multiplying churches accessible to people rather than growing existing churches. New churches take from seven to twelve years to reach the first threshold of stability. These churches also promote small groups in homes where people more easily talk about life and ask questions.[42]

Church planting in France has considerable obstacles to overcome. Past church planting efforts were largely spearheaded by foreigners after which nationals were expected to take over and provide direction and support for the churches. Liechti believes this separation of responsibilities is a considerable psychological hindrance for church multiplication.[43] He believes it would be wiser to have teams composed of French and foreign

36. Kronk, "Christians of Maghrebi Background," 147.
37. Kronk, "Christians of Maghrebi Background," 149.
38. Kronk, "Christians of Maghrebi Background," 270.
39. Kronk, "Christians of Maghrebi Background," 270.
40. Kronk, "Egalité, Fraternité, and Cous-cous," 56.
41. CNEF, "Une église," para 1.
42. "L'implantation d'Églises."
43. Liechti, "Bâtir des Églises majeures," 24.

co-laborers according to their gifting and not based on national origin or financial support. There is likewise the observation that it seems difficult for a church to penetrate areas with the gospel where there are more than ten thousand inhabitants and the church risks losing its visibility.[44] Liechti provides statistics which show that the greatest concentration of evangelical churches is in Alsace and in regions where the Huguenots were prominent. These disparities lead him to propose the "necessary strategic planting of a great number of new churches."[45] He sees a major hindrance to church planting with too many full-time workers maintaining existing churches to the detriment of the need of creating new churches. He asserts that "priorities must be rebalanced to free up as soon as possible hundreds of workers with the support of their church, totally or partially, for developing the process of creating daughter churches."[46] In 2017, the Faculté Libre de Théologie Évangélique (FLTE) added a concentration on Evangelization and Church Planting to meet the need to prepare students for church planting in France.[47] French Christians should be encouraged to continue the work they have begun. They will normally be the best evangelists and church planters. There should be the formation of genuine partnership between them and their foreign colleagues.

Laïcité in France continues to evolve in meaning and application as new challenges are presented. We have seen some of those changes since the enactment of the law of 1905. The disestablishment of the Catholic Church took place in a homogeneous society where the majority of citizens were at least nominal Catholics. The Church adapted to its changed status with continuing influence but without political power. During the twentieth century the Muslim presence increased through immigration and Islam became the second largest religion in France. Early immigrants from former French colonies experienced difficulties in integration but religion was mostly a private matter without political demands.

While the nation remains nominally Roman Catholic, many French have rejected the institutionalized Church. French resistance to religion and to perceived foreign expressions of religion (i.e., evangelical faith) makes perfect sense when viewed from their standpoint. Anthropological research and experience show "that systems of belief are eminently reasonable when viewed from within or . . . when we participate in the lives of people who

44. Liechti, "Bâtir des Églises majeures," 27.
45. Liechti, "Bâtir des Églises majeures," 27.
46. Liechti, "Bâtir des Églises majeures," 30.
47. FLTE, "Parcours évangélisation."

hold those beliefs."[48] The battle for different visions of laïcité continues to occupy an important place in French society. It is too soon to predict which vision will triumph. What is certain is that the advance of the gospel must continue regardless of political forces at work to marginalize religion, that cross-cultural workers must be prepared for the challenges of ministry in a secular nation, and that in the end the gospel will triumph and even the gates of hell will not prevail against Christ's church.

48. Robbins, *Cultural Anthropology*, 15.

Bibliography

Abdennour, Bidar. *Les rencontres de la laïcité: Laïcité et religion dans la France d'aujourd'hui*. Toulouse: Éditions Privat, 2016.

Abel, Olivier. "Que veut dire la laïcité?" *CEMOTI* 10 (1990) 3–14. Online. http://www. persee.fr/doc/ cemot_0764-9878_1990_num_10_1_935.

Adeney, Bernard T. *Strange Virtues: Ethics in a Multicultural World*. Downers Grove, IL: InterVarsity, 1995.

Agulhon, Maurice, et al. *République en représentations: Autour de l'œuvre de Maurice Agulhon*. Paris: Publications de la Sorbonne, 2006.

Albecker, Christian. "Alsace-Moselle: Un modèle des relations des Églises avec l'État." *Réforme*, March 26, 2018. Online. https://www.reforme.net/religion/ protestantisme/2018/03/26/alsace-moselle-un-modele-des-relations-des-eglises- avec-letat-par-christian-albecker/.

Alberigo, Giuseppe. "Facteurs de 'laïcité' au Concile Vatican II." *Revue des Sciences Religieuses* 74 (2000) 211–25. Online. https://www.persee.fr/doc/ rscir_0035-2217_2000_num_74_2_3531.

Allier, Raoul. "A propos de la Séparation." *Le Siècle*, November 6, 1904. Online. http:// gallica.bnf.fr/ark:/12148/bpt6k745970z/f1.item.

———. "La Séparation au Sénat." *Cahiers de la Quinzaine* 4 (1905) 111–17. Online. https://archive.org/stream/s7cahiersdelaquinz01pg#page/110/mode/2up/search/ allier.

Amson, Daniel. *La querelle religieuse: Quinze siècles d'incompréhensions*. Paris: Éditions Odile Jacob, 2004.

Anns, Lucy Rebecca. "Multiculturalism in France and the Policy of Laïcité: The Source of Potential Contradictions?" PhD diss., Loughborough University, 2010. Online. https://socratichive.wordpress.com/politics-and-religion/dissertation-on-france.

"Après la loi de séparation." *Le Journal*, December 7, 1905. Online. http://gallica.bnf. fr/ark:/12148/bpt6k7627824r/f1.item.r=discussion%20th%C3%A9orique%20 application%20pratiqua.

"Au jour le jour." *Le Constitutionnel*, December 10, 1905. Online. http://gallica.bnf.fr/ ark:/12148/bpt6k689282r/f1.item.

Audouin, Corinne. "Burqa, voile . . . ce qui est interdit et où." *France Inter*, August 26, 2016. Online. https://www.franceinter.fr/justice/burkini-ce-que-dit-la-loi.

Augustin, Jacques. *Laïcité ou danser avec le diable*. Paris: Les Éditions du Panthéon, 2017.

Aulard, Alphonse. *Polémique et Histoire*. Paris: Édouard Cornély, 1904. Online. http://classiques.uqac.ca/classiques/aulard_alphonse/polemique_et_histoire/ polemique_et_histoire.html.

Bacot, Jean-Pierre. *Une Europe sans religion dans un monde religieux.* Paris: Éditions du Cerf, 2013.

Bacquet, Sylvie. "Religious Freedom in a Secular Society: An Analysis of the French Approach to Manifestation of Beliefs in the Public Sphere." In *Religion, Rights and Secular Society: European Perspectives,* edited by Peter Cumper et al., 251–70. Cheltenham, UK: Edward Elgar, 2012.

Barbara, Augustin. "Sous le foulard la laïcité." *Hommes et Migrations* 1129–30 (1990) 87–90. Online. http://www.persee.fr/doc/homig_1142-852x_1990_num_1129_1_1431.

Barbier, Maurice. "Esquisse d'une théorie de la laïcité." *Le Débat* 77 (1993) 64–76.

———. *La Laïcité.* Paris: Éditions L'Harmattan, 1998.

———. "Pour une définition de la laïcité française." *Le Débat* 134 (2005) 129–41. Online. https://www.diplomatie.gouv.fr/IMG/pdf/0205-Barbier-FR-5.pdf.

Barrett, Michael, ed. *Reformation Theology.* Wheaton, IL: Crossway, 2017.

Barzun, Jacques. *From Dawn to Decadence (1500 to the Present): 500 Years of Western Cultural Life.* New York: Harper Collins, 2000.

Bastière, Jean-Marie. "14–18: La grande illusion de la fraternité." *Le Figaro,* November 27, 2013. Online. http://www.lefigaro.fr/livres/2013/11/27/03005-20131127ARTFIG00341-14-18-la-grande-illusion-de-la-fraternite.ph.

Baty, Claude. "Les Églises évangéliques libres de France: Leur histoire à travers la genèse et l'évolution de leurs principes jusqu'en 1951." MA thesis, Faculté Libre de Théologie Evangélique de Vaux-sur-Seine, 1981.

Baubérot, Jean. "1905–2005: La laïcité française et les minorités religieuses." *Études théologiques et religieuses* 82 (2007) 67–80. Online. https://www.cairn.info/revue-etudes-theologiques-et-religieuses-2007-1-page-67.htm.

———. "Enjeux passés et présents de la laïcité." *Autres Temps. Les cahiers du christianisme social* 30 (1991) 26–45. Online. http://www.persee.fr/doc/chris_0753-2776_1991_num_30_1_1452.

———. *Histoire de la laïcité en France.* Paris: Presses Universitaires de France, 2017.

———. "La laïcité à la française et la minorité protestante." *Autres Temps. Les cahiers du christianisme social* 10 (1986) 5–14. Online. http://www.persee.fr/doc/chris_0753-2776_1986_num_10_1_1079.

———. "La laïcité absolue n'existe pas, c'est un idéal à atteindre." *l'Humanité,* February 28, 2014. Online. https://www.humanite.fr/debats/jean-bauberot-la-laicite-absolue-n-existe-pas-c-es-560090.

———. *La laïcité falsifiée.* Paris: La Découverte, 2014.

———. "La laïcité française et ses mutations." *Social Compass* 45 (1998) 175–87.

———. *La laïcité, quel héritage: De 1798 à nos jours.* Geneva: Labor et Fides, 1990.

———. "L'affaire des foulards et la laïcité à la française." *L'Homme et la société* 120 (1996) 9–16. Online. http://www.persee.fr/doc/homso_0018-4306_1996_num_120_2_2836.

———. *Les laïcités dans le monde.* 4th ed. Paris: Presses Universitaires de France, 2016.

———. *Les sept laïcités françaises: Le modèle français de laïcité n'existe pas.* Paris: Maison des Sciences de l'Homme, 2015.

———. *Petite histoire du christianisme.* Paris: Éditions Librio, 2008.

———. *Vers un nouveau pacte laïque?* Paris: Éditions du Seuil, 1990.

Baubérot, Jean, and Marianne Carbonnier-Burkard. *Histoire des Protestants: Une minorité en France (XVIe–XXIe siècle).* Paris: Éditions Ellipses, 2016.

Baubérot, Jean, and Michel Wieviorka. *De la séparation des Églises et de l'État à l'avenir de la laïcité*. Paris: Éditions de l'Aube, 2005.

Baubérot, Jean, and Micheline Milot. *Laïcités sans frontières*. Paris: Éditions du Seuil, 2011.

Baudouin, Jean, and Philippe Portier, eds. *La Laïcité, une valeur d'aujourd'hui? Contestations et renégociations du modelé français*. Rennes: Presses Universitaires de Rennes, 2015.

Baziou, Jean-Yves. "Le cadre de la laïcité française." *Mélange de Science Religieuse 72* (2015) 35–46.

Begley, Louis. *Why the Dreyfus Affair Matters*. New Haven: Yale University Press, 2009.

Bellah, Robert N. "La Religion Civile en Amérique." *Archives de sciences sociales de religions* 35 (1973) 7–22.

Bélorgey, Jean-Michel. "Terroirs de la laïcité." *Revue Politique et Parlementaire* 1038 (2006) 52–59.

Bencheikh, Ghaleb. "L'Islam au risque de la laïcité." In *La laïcité: Des combats fondateurs aux enjeux d'aujourd'hui*, edited by Jean-Michel Ducomte et al., 87–97. Toulouse: Éditions Privat, 2016.

Benedetti, Guy. "2004: Année de la laïcité dans le XXe à Paris." *Hommes et Migrations* 1259 (2006) 87–92. Online. https://www.persee.fr/doc/homig_1142-852x_2006_num_1259_1_4423.

Benedict, Philip. "The Wars of Religion, 1562–1598." In *Renaissance and Reformation France, 1500–1648*, edited by Mack P. Holt, 147–75. New York: Oxford University Press, 2002.

Benedict, Philip, and Virginia Reinburg. "Religion and the Sacred." In *Renaissance and Reformation France, 1500–1648*, edited by Mack P. Holt, 119–46. New York: Oxford University Press, 2002.

Berdah, Arthur, et al. "Laïcité: Les 5 propositions choc du rapport Clavreul remis au gouvernement." *Le Figaro*, March 3, 2018. Online. http://www.lefigaro.fr/politique/2018/02/22/01002-20180222ARTFIG00155-laicite-les-5-propositions-choc-du-rapport-clavreul-remis-au-gouvernement.php.

Beresniak, Daniel. *La Laïcité*. Paris: Jacques Grancher, 1990.

Bergeron, Jacques. *Le droit d'être un chrétien moyen*. Paris: Éditions du Cerf, 2004.

Berthoud, Pierre. "La faculté libre de théologie reformée—Rétrospective et prospective." *La Revue reformée* 208 (2000). Online. https://larevuereformee.net/articlerr/n208/la-faculte-libre-de-theologie-reformee-retrospective-et-prospective.

Billard, Jacques. *De l'école à la République: Guizot et Victor Cousin*. Paris: Presses Universitaires de France, 1998.

Bire, Anatole. *La séparation des Églises et de l'État: Commentaire de la Loi du Décembre 9, 1905*. Paris: Arthur Rousseau, 1905.

Birnbaum, Jean, and Frédéric Viguier, eds. *La Laïcité, une question au présent*. Nantes: Éditions Cécile Defaut, 2006.

Bjork, David E. "The Future of Christianity in Western Europe: The End of a World." *Missiology* 34 (2006) 309–24.

———. *Unfamiliar Paths: The Challenge of Recognizing the Work of Christ in Strange Clothing: A Case Study from France*. 2nd ed. Pasadena, CA: William Carey, 2014.

Bloch, Jonathan. *La Réforme Protestante, de Luther à Calvin: La réponse aux abus de la religion catholique*. Namur, Belgium: Lemaitre, 2015.

Blough, Neal. "Église de professants en recherche de racines: Réforme radicale." *Fac-Réflexion* 19 (1992) 19–33.

Bobineau, Olivier, and Stéphane Lathion. *Les musulmans, une menace pour la République?* Paris: Éditions Desclée de Brouwer, 2012.

Bock, Jonathan. "Europe: Christendom Graveyard or Christian Laboratory?" *International Bulletin of Missiological Research* 31.3 (2007) 113–14.

Bossy, John. *Christianity in the West, 1400–1700.* Oxford: Oxford University Press, 1985.

Boubakeur, Dalil. *Non! L'Islam n'est pas une politique.* Paris: Desclée de Brouwer, 2003.

Boucher, François. "Open Secularism and the New Religious Pluralism." PhD diss., Queen's University, 2012.

Boussinesq, Jean. *La laïcité française: Mémento juridique.* Paris: Éditions du Seuil, 1994.

Bowen, John R. *Why the French Don't Like Headscarves: Islam, the State, and Public Space.* Princeton, NJ: Princeton University Press, 2007.

Boyer, Alain. *La loi de 1905: Hier, aujourd'hui, demain.* Lyon: Éditions Olivetan, 2005.

———. "La place et l'organisation du culte musulman en France." *Études* 395 (2001) 619–29. Online. https://www.cairn.info/revue-etudes-2001-12-page-619.htm.

Bray, Gerald. "Late-Medieval Theology." In *Reformation Theology,* edited by Michael Barrett, 67–110. Wheaton, IL: Crossway, 2017.

Briand, Aristide. *La Séparation: Application du régime nouveau.* Paris: Bibliothèque-Charpentier, 1909.

———. *La Séparation: Rapport fait au nom de la Commission de la Chambre des Députés, suivi des pièces annexes.* Paris: Édouard Cornély, 1905.

Brown, Frederick. *For the Soul of France: Culture Wars in the Age of Dreyfus.* New York: Knopf, 2010.

Bruley, Yves, ed. *1905, la séparation des Églises et de l'État: Les textes fondateurs.* Paris: Éditions Perrin, 2004.

———. *La laïcité française.* Paris: Éditions du Cerf, 2016.

Buchhold, Jacques. "Église, islam et société." *Revue théologie évangélique* 5 (2006) 19–30.

———, ed. *Laïcités: Enjeux théologiques et pratique.* Charols: Éditions Excelsis, 2002.

———. "Le terreau théologique: L'héritage professant de la laïcité." In *Libre de le dire: Fondements et enjeux de la liberté de conscience et d'expression en France,* edited by Louis Schweitzer et al., 19–33. Marpent, France: BLF Éditions, 2015.

Cabanel, Patrick. *Entre religions et laïcité: La voie française, XIXe–XXIe siècles.* Toulouse: Éditions Privat, 2007.

———. "La 'question religieuse' et les solutions en France (XVI–XXI siècle)." In *La Laïcité, une question au présent,* edited by Jean Birnbaum et al., 165–84. Nantes: Éditions Cécile Defaut, 2006.

———. *Le Dieu de la République: Aux sources protestantes de la laïcité (1860–1900).* Rennes: Presses Universitaires de Rennes, 2003.

———. *Les mots de la laïcité.* Toulouse: Presses Universitaires du Mirail, 2004.

Cahm, Eric. *The Dreyfus Affair in French Society and Politics.* New York: Longman, 1996.

Cameron, Euan. *The European Reformation.* 2nd ed. Oxford: Oxford University Press, 1991.

Camilleri, Carmel. "Différences culturelles et laïcité." *Hommes et Migrations* 1129–1130 (1990) 37–40. Online. https://www.persee.fr/doc/homig_1142-852x_1990_num_1129_1_1413.

Canivez, Patrice, and Dominique Desvignes. "Ecole—Citoyenneté—Laïcité." *Spirale: Revue de recherches en éducation* 7 (1992) 103–16. Online. https://www.persee.fr/doc/spira_0994-3722_1992_num_7_1_1863.

Capéran, Louis. *Histoire de la laïcité républicaine: La laïcité en marche.* Paris: Nouvelles Éditions Latines, 2008.

Carbonnier-Burkard, Marianne. *La révolte des Camisards.* Rennes: Éditions Ouest-France, 2012.

Carenco, Jean-François. *L'Édit de Nantes: Sûreté et Education,* edited by Marie-José Lacava and Robert Guicharnaud. Montauban: Société Montalbanaise d'Étude de Recherche sur le Protestantisme, 1999.

Carluer, Jean-Yves. "Liberté de dire, liberté de croire: Deux siècles de défi évangélique, 1815–2015." In *Libre de le dire: Fondements et enjeux de la liberté de conscience et d'expression en France,* edited by Louis Schweitzer et al., 35–73. Marpent, France: BLF Éditions, 2015.

"Ce que proposent les cinq principaux candidats sur la laïcité." *Le Républicain Lorraine,* March 31, 2017. Online. https://www.republicain-lorrain.fr/actualite/2017/03/31/francois-fillon-(les-republicains).

Cerf, Martine, and Marc Horwitz. *Dictionnaire de la laïcité.* 2nd ed. Paris: Armand Colin, 2016.

Cesari, Jocelyne. *When Islam and Democracy Meet: Muslims in Europe and in the United States.* New York: Palgrave Macmillan, 2004.

Champion, Françoise. "La laïcité n'est plus ce qu'elle était." *Archives de sciences sociales des religions* 116 (2001) 41–52. Online. https://journals.openedition.org/assr/2775?lang=en.

Chamson, André. *Suite Camisarde.* Paris: Éditions Omnibus, 2002.

Charentenay, Pierre de. "La Charte européenne et la laïcité." *Études* 395 (2001) 153–64.

Charriaut, Henri. *Après la Séparation.* Paris: Félix Alcan, 1905.

Chassaigne, Philippe. "Laïcité: Les Îles Britanniques." In *La Laïcité, une question au présent,* edited by Jean Birnbaum et al., 185–96. Nantes: Éditions Cécile Defaut, 2006.

Chaunu, Pierre, and Eric Mension-Rigau. *Baptême de Clovis, baptême de la France: De la religion d' État à la laïcite d'État.* Paris: Éditions Balland, 1996.

Chauprade, Aymeric. "Islam et islamisme." *Revue Politique et Parlementaire* 1038 (2006) 95–101.

Chihizola, Jean. "Le défi de l'organisation de l'islam de France." *Le Figaro,* February 12, 2018. Online. http://www.lefigaro.fr/politique/2018/02/11/01002-20180211 ARTFIG00166-le-defi-de-l-organisation-de-l-islam-de-france.php.

Cholvy, Gérard. *Être chrétien en France au XIXe siècle: 1790–1914.* Paris: Éditions du Seuil, 1997.

Clavreul, Gilles. *Laïcité: Valeurs de la République et exigences minimales de la vie en société: Des principes à l'action.* Paris: Ministère de l'Intérieur, 2018. Online. http://www.laicite-republique.org/IMG/pdf/rapport_lai_cite_clavreul.pdf.

Clemenceau, George. "Discours pour la liberté." *Cahiers de la Quinzaine* 5 (1903) 5–56. Online. https://archive.org/stream/s5cahiersdelaquinz01pg#page/n574/mode/1up/search/clemenceau.

———. "La guerre du Pape." *L'Aurore,* May 18, 1904. Online. http://gallica.bnf.fr/ark:/12148/bpt6k729098h.item.

Conseil National des Évangéliques de France (CNEF). *La Laïcité française: Entre l'idée, l'Histoire, et le droit positif.* Marpent, France: Éditions BLF, 2013.

———. "La #Loi1905 de séparation des églises et de l'État date du 9 décembre 1905. Les évangéliques, principaux utilisateurs de cette structure juridique, saluent l'équilibre et l'apaisement qui en découlent, et affirment leur attachement à l'article 1 concernant la liberté de conscience et le libre exercice des cultes." Twitter (@comcnef), December 10, 2018, 2:15 p.m. https://twitter.com/comcnef/status/1072208187053494273.

———. "Une église pour 10,000 habitants: Le projet." 2011. Online. http://www.1pour10000.fr/le-projet/presentation.

Cohen, Florence, and Ludovic Galtier. "Quand ils n'ont pas de réponse, les gens vont voir des médiums." *RTL*, February 13, 2016. Online. https://www.rtl.fr/actu/debats-societe/quand-ils-n-ont-pas-de-reponse-les-gens-vont-voir-des-mediums-explique-le-voyant-claude-alexis-7781865894.

Cohen, Martine. "Religions et laïcité en Europe." *Sociétés contemporaines* 37 (2000) 5–10. Online. http://www.persee.fr/doc/socco_1150-1944_2000_num_37_1_1717.

Combarieu, Abel. *Sept ans à l'Élysée avec le président Émile Loubet: De l'affaire Dreyfus à la conférence d'Algésiras, 1899–1906.* Paris: Librairie Hachette, 1932.

Combes, Émile. "La Politique du Ministère." *L'Humanité*, September 5, 1904. Online. http://gallica.bnf.fr/ark:/12148/bpt6k250326g.item.

———. *Une campagne laïque (1902–1903).* 2nd ed. Paris: Simonis Empis, 1904.

Commission Stasi. "Commission de réflexion sur l'application du principe de laïcité dans la République." *Le Monde*, December 12, 2003. Online. https://www.lemonde.fr/archives/article/2003/12/12/le-rapport-de-la-commission-stasi-sur-la-laicite_4288804_1819218.html.

Conseil d'État. "Port par les élèves de signes d'appartenance à une communauté religieuse: Avis rendus par l'assemblée générale du Conseil d'État." *Direction des Affaires Juridiques*, November 27, 1989. Online. http://affairesjuridiques.aphp.fr/textes/avis-n-346-893-du-conseil-detat-27111989-port-du-foulard-islamique.

———. "Un siècle de laïcité." In *Études et documents du Conseil d'État*, edited by Olivier Schrameck, 241–402. Paris: La Documentation française, 2004.

Cook, Malcolm, and Grace Davie, eds. *Modern France: Society in Transition.* London: Routledge, 1999.

Coq, Guy. "Christianisme et laïcité." *Hommes et Migrations* 1218 (1999) 5–13. Online. http://www.persee.fr/doc/homig_1142-852x_1999_num_1218_1_3289.

———. *Laïcité et République: Le lien nécessaire.* Paris: Éditions du Félin, 2003.

———. "Un principe universel." *Hommes et Migrations* 1258 (2005) 6–11. Online. http://www.persee.fr/doc/homig_1142-852x_2005_num_1258_1_4388.

Cornette, Joël. *Histoire de la France: L'affirmation de l'État absolu, 1492–1652.* Paris: Hachette Supérieur, 2009.

Costa-Lascoux, Jacqueline. *Les trois âges de la laïcité: Débat avec Joseph Sitruk, Grand Rabbin de France.* Paris: Hachette, 1996.

Courtois, Gerard. "Les crispations alarmantes de la société française." *Le Monde*, January 25, 2013. Online. https://www.lemonde.fr/politique/article/2013/01/24/les-crispations-alarmantes-de-la-societe-francaise_1821655_823448.html.

Coutel, Charles, and Jean-Pierre Dubois. *Vous avez dit laïcité?* Paris: Éditions du Cerf, 2016.

Cuénod, Jean-Noël. "Macron devra trouver les mots pour faire face à l'islam politique." *Tribune de Genève*, March 28, 2018. Online. https://www.tdg.ch/monde/europe/macron-devra-trouver-mots-face-islam-politique/story/16001895.

Damien, André. *État et religion*. Paris: Presses Universitaires de France, 2005.

Dansette, Adrien. *Histoire religieuse de la France contemporaine sous la Troisième République*. Paris: Éditions Flammarion, 1951.

Daucourt, Gérard, and Marcel Manoël. *Églises et laïcité en France: Études et propositions*. Paris: Éditions du Cerf, 1998.

Davie, Grace. "Is Europe an Exceptional Case?" *International Review of Missions* 95 (2006) 247–58.

———. "Understanding Religion in Europe: A Continually Evolving Mosaic." In *Religion, Rights, and Secular Society: European Perspectives*, edited by Peter Cumper et al., 251–70. Cheltenham, UK: Edward Elgar, 2012.

Davies, Norman. *Europe: A History*. Oxford: Oxford University Press, 1996.

Davis, Stephen M. *Crossing Cultures: Preparing Strangers for Ministry in Strange Places*. Eugene, OR: Wipf & Stock, 2019.

Davis, William Stearns. *A History of France: From the Earliest Times to the Treaty of Versailles*. New York: Houghton Mifflin, 1919.

Debray, Régis. *Ce que nous voile le voile: La République et le sacré*. Paris: Éditions Gallimard, 2004.

———. "Rapport à Monsieur le Ministre de l'Éducation Nationale: L'enseignement du fait religieux dans l'École laïque." February 2002. Online. https://www.education.gouv.fr/sites/default/files/2020-02/5914-pdf-43979.pdf.

———. *Un mythe contemporain: Le dialogue des civilisations*. Paris: CNRS, 2007.

Debray, Régis, and Didier Leschi. *La laïcité au quotidien: Guide pratique*. Paris: Éditions Gallimard, 2016.

Debré, Jean-Louis. *La laïcité à l'école: Un principe républicain à réaffirmer*. Paris: Éditions Odile Jacob, 1997.

Delahaye, Jean-Paul, and Jean-Pierre Obin. "Faut-il changer la laïcité?" *Hommes et Migrations* 1258 (2005) 12–27. Online. http://www.persee.fr/doc/homig_1142-852x_2005_num_1258_1_4389.

Delfau, Gérard. *Éloge de la laïcité*. Paris: Éditeur Vendémiaire, 2012.

Déloye, Yves. "La laïcité française au prisme de son histoire." In *La Laïcité, une question au présent*, edited by Jean Birnbaum et al., 23–36. Nantes: Éditions Cécile Defaut, 2006.

Delsol, Chantal. *Les pierres d'angle: A quoi tenons-nous?* Paris: Éditions du Cerf, 2014.

Delumeau, Jean. *Le christianisme va-t-il mourir?* Paris: Hachette Édition, 1977.

Delumeau, Jean, and Monique Cottret. *Le catholicism entre Luther and Voltaire*. Paris: Presses Universitaires de France, 2010.

Demers, Bruno, and Yvan Lamonde. *Quelle laïcité?* Montreal: Éditions Médiaspaul, 2014.

Devecchio, Alexandre. "Hakim El Kouroi/Xavier Lemoine: 'L'islam peut-il être français?'" *Le Figaro*, January 26, 2018. Online. http://www.lefigaro.fr/vox/religion/2018/01/26/31004-20180126ARTFIG00070-hakim-el-karouixavier-lemoine-8220l-islam-peut-il-etre-francais8221.php.

Dittgen, Alfred. "Religions et démographie en France: Des évolutions contrastées." *Population & Avenir* 684 (2007) 14–18.

Ducomte, Jean-Michel. *La Laïcité*. Toulouse: Milan Presse, 2001.

Dusseau, Joëlle. "L'histoire de la Séparation: Entre permanences et ruptures." *Revue Politique et Parlementaire* 1038 (2006) 13–22.

"Enfin." *La Lanterne*, December 8, 1905. Online. http://gallica.bnf.fr/ark:/12148/bpt6k7509725n/f1.item.r=bas%20eglise%20vive%20republique.

Esteve-Bellebeau, Brigitte, and Mathieu Touzeil-Divina, eds. *Laï-cité(s) et discrimination(s)*. Paris: Éditions L'Harmattan, 2017.

Evans, G. R. *The Roots of the Reformation: Tradition, Emergence, and Rupture*. Downers Grove, IL: IVP Academic, 2012.

Faculté Libre de Théologie Évangélique (FLTE). "Parcours évangélisation et implantation d'Églises." Online. http://flte.fr/se-former/formations/residentiellelmd/parcours-evangelisation-et-implantation-degliscs.

Faltin, Lucia, and Melanie J. Wright, eds. *The Religious Roots of Contemporary European Identity*. London: Continuum International, 2007.

Fath, Sébastien. "Alsace-Moselle: Quels droits pour les pasteurs évangéliques?" *Réforme*, March 21, 2018. Online. https://www.reforme.net/religions/protestantismes/alsace-moselle-quels-droits-pour-les-pasteurs-evangeliques.

———. "De la non-reconnaissance à une demande de légitimation? Le cas du Protestantisme évangélique." *Archives de sciences sociales des religions* 50 (2005) 151–62. Online. http://www.jstor.org/stable/30128895.

———. *Du Ghetto au réseau: Le protestantisme évangélique en France, 1800–2005*. Geneva: Labor et Fides, 2005.

———. "Grand discours d'Emmanuel Macron aux Bernardins: Le texte." *Blog de Sébastien Fath* (blog) April 4, 2018. Online. http://blogdesebastienfath.hautetfort.com/archive/2018/04/11/l-integralite-du-discours-d-emmanuel-macron-aux-bernardins-6042692.html.

———, ed. *La diversité évangélique*. Charols: Éditions Excelsis, 2003.

———. "Les protestants évangéliques français: La corde raide d'un militantisme sans frontière." *Études* 403 (2005) 351–61.

———. *Une autre manière d'être chrétien en France: Socio-histoire de l'implantation baptiste (1810–1950)*. Geneva: Éditions Labor et Fides, 2001.

———. "Vers la fin de la discrimination concordataire: Le débat continue." *Blog de Sébastien Fath* (blog), March 29, 2018. Online. http://blogdesebastienfath.hautetfort.com/archive/2018/03/28/vers-la-fin-de-la-discrimination-concordataire-le-debat-continue.html.

Faure, Olivier. "Mais de quoi nous parle-t-on? L'église catholique n'a jamais été bannie du débat public. Quel lien restaurer avec l'Etat? En République laïque aucune foi ne saurait s'imposer à la loi. Toute la loi de 1905. Rien que la loi." Twitter (@faureolivier), April 9, 2018, 3:42 p.m. https://twitter.com/faureolivier/status/983430055526354946.

Fer, Yannick, and Gwendoline Malogne-Fer, eds. *Le protestantisme évangélique à l'épreuve des cultures*. Paris: Éditions L'Harmattan, 2013.

Ferjani, Mohamed-Cherif. *Islamisme, laïcité, et droits de l'homme: Un siècle de débat sans cesse reporté au sein de la pensée arabe contemporaine*. Paris: Éditions L'Harmattan, 2000.

Ferry, Luc, et al. *Le Nouvel Antisémitisme en France: Retour sur l'affaire Sarah Halimi*. Paris: Éditions Albin Michel, 2018.

———. *L'homme-Dieu ou le Sens de la vie*. Paris: Éditions Grasset, 1996.

Fetouh, Marik. "La laïcité: D'un principe cohésif à une légitimation du rejet." In *Laï-cité(s) et discrimination(s)*, edited by Brigitte Esteve-Bellebeau et al., 45–57. Paris: Éditions L'Harmattan, 2017.

Fiala, Pierre. "Les termes de la laïcité. Différenciation morphologique et conflits sémantiques." *Mots* 27 (1991) 41–57. Online. http://www.persee.fr/doc/mots_0243 -6450_1991_ num_27_1_1606.

Finkielkraut, Alain. "La laïcité à l'épreuve du siècle." *Pouvoirs* 75 (1995) 53–60.

Finkielkraut, Alain, and Benny Lévy. *Le Livre et les livres: Entretiens sur la laïcité*. Paris: Éditions Verdier, 2006.

Fix, Andrew C. *Prophecy and Reason: The Dutch Collegiants in the Early Enlightenment*. Princeton, NJ: Princeton University Press, 1991.

Fleurons, Émile. *Les associations cultuelles: L'application pratique*. Paris: Imprimerie Paul Dupont, 1906. Online. https://archive.org/details/sc_0000926071_0000000 1367362.

Fontenay, Élisabeth de. "Un enseignement sur les religions à l'école." In *La Laïcité, une question au présent*, edited by Jean Birnbaum et al., 37–45. Nantes: Éditions Cécile Defaut, 2006.

Fourest, Caroline. *Génie de la laïcité*. Paris: Grasset et Fasquelle, 2016.

France, Anatole. *L'Église et la République*. Paris: Éditions Édouard Pelletan, 1905. Online. https://fr.wikisource.org/wiki/Livre:Anatole_France_-_L'Église_et_la_ République .djvu.

Furet, François. *La Révolution: De Turgot à Jules Ferry: 1770–1880*. Paris: Hachette Livre, 1988.

———. *Penser la Révolution française*. Paris: Éditions Gallimard, 1978.

Gabizon, Cecilia. "Le Parlement vote l'interdiction du voile intégral." *Le Figaro*, September 14, 2010. Online. http://www.lefigaro.fr/actualite-france/2010/09/13/01016-20100913ARTFIG00662-burqa-les-integristes-prets-a-defier-la-loi.php.

Gaillard, Jean-Michel. "L'invention de la laïcité (1598–1905)." In *1905, la séparation des Églises et de l'État: Les textes fondateurs*, edited by Yves Bruley, 19–36. Paris: Éditions Perrin, 2004.

Gastaldi, Nadine. "Le Concordat de 1801." *Histoire par l'image*, November 2004. Online. http://www.histoire-image.org/etudes/concordat-1801.

Gauchet, Marcel. *La religion dans la démocratie: Parcours de la laïcité*. Paris: Éditions Gallimard, 1998.

Gaudelet, Bruno, and Antigone Mouchtouris. *Laïcité et religions: À L'aube du vingt-et-unième siècle*. Perpignan: Presses Universitaires de Perpignan, 2010.

Gildea, Robert. *The Past in French History*. New Haven: Yale University Press, 1994.

Goepp, Isabelle. "Des millions des musulmans se convertissent au christianisme chaque année." *Journal Chrétien*, June 27, 2017. Online. https://www.chretiens.info/39881/ des-millions-de-musulmans-se-convertissent-au-christianisme-chaque-annee.

Gordner, Matthew J. "Challenging the French Exception: 'Islam' and Laïcité." *In-Spire Journal of Law, Politics and Societies* 3 (2008) 72–87.

Greely, Andrew M. *Religion in Europe at the End of the Second Millennium: A Sociological Profile*. New Brunswick, NJ: Transaction, 2003.

Grévy, Jérôme. *Le Cléricalisme? Voilà l'ennemi! Un siècle de guerre de religion en France*. Paris: Armand Colin, 2005.

Guéant, Claude. "Une laïcité respectée pour renforcer la cohésion nationale." *Portail du Gouvernement*, April 19, 2011. Online. http://archives.gouvernement.fr/fillon_version2/gouvernement/claude-gueant-une-laicite-respectee-pour-renforcer-la-cohesion-nationale.html.

Guénois, Jean-Marie. "Emmanuel Macron tend la main aux catholiques." *Le Figaro*, April 10, 2018. Online. http://www.lefigaro.fr/actualite-france/2018/04/09/01016-20180409ARTFIG00353-emmanuel-macron-tend-la-main-aux-catholiques.php.

Haarscher, Guy. *La laïcité*. 2nd ed. Paris: Presses Universitaires de France, 1998.

Habermas, Jürgen, et al. *An Awareness of What is Missing: Faith and Reason in a Post-secular Age*. Cambridge: Polity, 2010.

Habermas, Jürgen, and Joseph Ratzinger. *The Dialectics of Secularization: On Reason and Religion*. San Francisco: Ignatius, 2007.

Hall, Douglas John. *The End of Christendom and the Future of Christianity*. Harrisburg, PA: Trinity, 1995.

Hamon, Benoît. "Qd @EmmanuelMacron salue dans son discours le devoir de l'Eglise 'de protéger la vie' . . . 'la vie de l'enfant à naitre, celle de l'être parvenu au seuil de la mort' et indique que 'cette cohérence s'impose à tous,' il reprend les mots des anti-IVG et des opposants à l'euthanasie." Twitter (@benoithamon), April 10, 2018, 6:38 a.m. https://twitter.com/benoithamon/status/983655333930430464.

Harzoune, Mustapha. "Les nouveaux hussards de la laïcité." *Hommes et Migrations* 1259 (2006) 119–28. Online. http://www.persee.fr/doc/homig_1142-852x_2006_num_1259_1_4430.

Hassine, Khadija Ksouri Ben. *La laïcité: Que peut nous en apprendre l'histoire?* Paris: Éditions L'Harmattan, 2009.

Heath, Richard. *The Reformation in France: From the Revocation of the Edict of Nantes to the Incorporation of the Reformed Churches Into the State*. 1888. Reprint, London: Forgotten Books, 2015.

Henni-Moulaï, Nadia. *Portrait des musulmans de France: Une communauté plurielle*. Paris: Fondation pour l'innovation politique, 2016.

Hiebert, Paul G. *Transforming Worldviews: An Anthropological Understanding of How People Change*. Grand Rapids: Baker Academic, 2008.

Hollande, François. "Le régime concordataire." *20 Minutes*, April 23, 2012. Online. http://www.20minutes.fr/strasbourg/922105-20120423-je-remettrai-cause-regime-concordataire-dit-francois-hollande.

Holt, Mack P., ed. *Renaissance and Reformation France, 1500–1648*. New York: Oxford University Press, 2002.

Hooft, Visser't W. A. "Evangelism Among Europe's Neo-Pagans." *International Review of Mission* 66 (1977) 349–60.

Hullot-Guiot, Kim. "Mélenchon veut abolir le Concordat d'Alsace-Moselle." *Libération*, February 15, 2017. Online. https://www.liberation.fr/politiques/2017/02/15/melenchon-veut-abolir-le-concordat-d-alsace-moselle_1548582.fr.

Hutcheon, Linda. "Incredulity Toward Metanarrative: Negotiating Postmodernism and Feminisms." In *Collaboration in the Feminine: Writings on Women and Culture from Tessera*, edited by Barbara Godard, 186–92. Toronto: Second Story, 1994. Online. https://tspace.library.utoronto.ca/bitstream/1807/10250/1/Hutcheon1994Incredulity.pdf.

Hutchison, William R. "Innocence Abroad: The 'American Religion' in Europe." In *Church History* 51 (March 1982) 71–84.

Ibrahim, Amr H. "La laïcité spécifique de l'Islam." *Autres Temps. Les cahiers du christianisme social* 10 (1986) 21–30. https://www.persee.fr/doc/chris_0753-2776 _1986_num_10_1_1081.

"Interdire le 'burkini' au nom de la laïcité?" *Le Monde*, August 31, 2016. Online. http://www.lemonde.fr/idees/article/2016/08/31/interdire-le-burkini-au-nom-de-la-laicite_4990237_3232.html.

Jaurès, Jean. "La Provocation." *L'Humanité*, May 17, 1904. Online. https://gallica.bnf.fr/ark:/12148/bpt6k250215f/f1.item.

———. "L'enseignement laïque." *L'Humanité*, August 18, 1904. Online. https://www.humanite.fr/node/340288.

Jeanlet, Thierry. "L'école et la laïcité." *Revue Politique et Parlementaire* 1038 (2006) 29–38.

Jenkins, Philip. *God's Continent: Christianity, Islam, and Europe's Religious Crisis*. New York: Oxford University Press, 2007.

Johnstone, Patrick, and Jason Mandryk. *Operation World: Twenty-First-Century Edition*. 6th ed. Pasadena, CA: WEC, 2001.

Juvin, Philippe. "Crèche de Noël: le témoignage du maire de La Garenne Colombes." *Le Figaro*, December 19, 2014. Online. http://www.lefigaro.fr/vox/societe/2014/12/19/31003-20141219ARTFIG00402-creche-de-noel-le-temoignage-du-maire-de-la-garenne-colombes.php.

Kaemingk, Matthew. *Christian Hospitality and Muslim Immigration in an Age of Fear*. Grand Rapids: Eerdmans, 2018.

Kahn, Pierre. *La Laïcité*. Paris: Le Cavalier Bleu, 2005.

———. "La laïcité est-elle une valeur?" *Spirale: Revue de recherches en éducation* 39 (2007) 29–37. Online. http://www.persee.fr/doc/spira_0994-3722_2007_num _39_1_1251.

Kärkkäinen, Veli-Matti. *An Introduction to the Theology of Religions: Biblical, Historical, and Contemporary Perspectives*. Downers Grove, IL: InterVarsity, 2003.

Karoui, Hakim El. *Un islam français est possible*. Paris: Institut Montaigne, 2016. Online. https://www.institutmontaigne.org/ressources/pdfs/publications/rapport-un-islam-francais-est_-possible.pdf.

Keiger, J. F. V. *Raymond Poincaré*. Cambridge: Cambridge University Press, 2002.

Kelley, Donald R. *The Beginning of Ideology: Consciousness and Society in the French Reformation*. Cambridge: Cambridge University Press, 1981.

Kepel, Gilles. *La Revanche de Dieu: Chrétiens, juifs et musulmans à la reconquête du monde*. Paris: Éditions du Seuil, 1991.

Kessel, Patrick, et al. "Ni plurielle, ni de combat: La laïcité." *Hommes et Migrations* 1218 (1999) 64–75. Online. https://www.persee.fr/doc/homig_1142-852X_1999_num_1218_1_3297.

Khiari, Saad. *L'Islam et les valeurs de la République*. Paris: Fondation pour l'innovation politique, 2015.

Kintzler, Catherine. *Penser la laïcité*. Paris: Minerve, 2014.

———. *Qu'est-ce que la laïcité?* Paris: Librairie Philosophique J. Vrin, 2007.

Kloeckner, Joséphine. "En Europe, les chrétiens plus critiques que les autres envers les musulmans." *La Croix*, May 30, 2018. Online. https://www.la-croix.com/Religion/Catholicisme/Monde/En-Europe-chretiens-critiques-autres-envers-musulmans-2018-05-30-1200943091.

Koop, Allen V. *American Evangelical Missionaries in France, 1945–1975*. Lanham, MD: University Press of America, 1986.

Korsia, Haïm. "La laïcité: Valeur du judaïsme français." *Revue Politique et Parlementaire* 1038 (2006) 80–84.

Koubi, Geneviève. "La laïcité: Un principe sans résonance religieuse." In *La Laïcité, une question au présent*, edited by Jean Birnbaum et al., 47–57. Nantes: Éditions Cécile Defaut, 2006.

Kovacs, Stéphane. "Niqab: La France sermonnée par des experts de l'ONU." *Le Figaro*, October 23, 2018. Online. http://www.lefigaro.fr/actualite-france/2018/10/23/01016-20181023ARTFIG00142-l-onu-condamne-l-interdiction-francaise-de-la-burqa.php.

Kronk, Richard. "Christians of Maghrebi Background and French Evangelical Protestant Churches: The Role of Social, Cultural, and Religious Values in Conversion and Affiliation." PhD diss., Evangelische Theologische Faculteit, 2016.

———. "Egalité, Fraternité, and Cous-cous." In *Margins of Islam: Ministry in Diverse Muslim Contexts*, edited by Gene Daniels et al., 47–58. Pasadena, CA: William Carey, 2018.

"La Loi de Séparation." *La Justice*, December 9, 1905. Online. http://gallica.bnf.fr/ark:/12148/bpt6k8269377/f4.item.

"La Protestation du Pape." *L'Humanité*, May 17, 1904. Online. https://gallica.bnf.fr/ark:/12148/bpt6k250215f/f1.item.

"La Séparation votée." *Le Petit Parisien*, December 7, 1905. Online. http://gallica.bnf.fr/ark:/12148/bpt6k561992c/f1.item.r=mod%C3%A9ration.

"La Séparation votée." *Le Siècle*, December 8, 1905. Online. https://gallica.bnf.fr/ark:/12148/bpt6k7463635/f1.item.zoom.

Lacava, Marie-Jose, and Robert Guicharnaud, eds. *L'Édit de Nantes: Sûreté et Education*. Montauban, France: Société Montalbanaise d'Étude de Recherche sur le Protestantisme, 1999.

Lacorne, Denis. *Les frontières de la tolérance*. Paris: Éditions Gallimard, 2016.

Lacoste, Yves. "Les évangéliques à l'assaut du monde." *Hérodote: Revue de géographie et de géopolitique* 119 (2005) 5–8.

"L'affaire des évêques." *L'Humanité*, July 17, 1904. Online. http://gallica.bnf.fr/ark:/12148/bpt6k250276w.langFR.

Lalmy, Pascal-Eric. "Les collectivités locales et la laïcité." *Revue Politique et Parlementaire* 1038 (2006) 43–47.

Lalouette, Jacqueline. *La République anticléricale (XIXe–XXe siècle)*. Paris: Éditions du Seuil, 2002.

———. *La séparation des Églises et de l'État: Genèse et développement d'une idée, 1789–1905*. Paris: Éditions du Seuil, 2005.

"L'Alsace-Moselle garde le concordat." *Le Figaro*, April 2, 2013. Online. http://www.lefigaro.fr/politique/2013/02/21/01002-20130221ARTFIG00751-l-alsace-moselle-garde-le-concordat.php.

Lambert, Jean. "Laïcité et religions sans frontières." *Autres Temps. Les cahiers du christianisme social* 33 (1992) 41–53. Online. http://www.persee.fr/doc/chris_0753-2776_1992_num_33_1_1503.

Larousse, Virginie. "Et la religion à laquelle les Français se convertissent le plus est . . . " *Atlantico*, November 21, 2014. Online. http://www.atlantico.fr/decryptage/et-religion-laquelle-francais-se-convertissent-plus-est-virginie-larousse-1867240.html.

Lassieur, Pierre. *La laïcité est-elle la neutralité? Histoire du débat, depuis 1850 jusqu'aux manuels de philosophie d'aujourd'hui.* Paris: Éditions François-Xavier de Guibert, 1996.

Latala, Renata, and Jacques Rime, eds. *Liberté religieuse et Église catholique: Héritage et développements récents.* Fribourg, Switzerland: Academic, 2009.

Laurence, Jonathan, and Justin Vaïsse. *Integrating Islam: Political and Religious Challenges in Contemporary France.* Washington, DC: Brookings, 2006.

"Le burkini interdit dans une quinzaine de communes." *Libération,* August 19, 2016. Online. http://www.liberation.fr/france/2016/08/19/le-burkini-interdit-dans-une-quinzaine-de-communes_1473469.

Le Goff, Jacques, and René Rémond. *Histoire de la France religieuse: Du Roi très chrétien à la laïcité républicaine (XVIIIe–XIXe siècle).* Vol. 3. Paris: Éditions du Seuil, 2001.

Leclair, Agnès. "La loi sur le voile intégral promulguée." *Le Figaro,* October 20, 2010. Online. http://www.lefigaro.fr/actualite-france/2010/10/12/01016-20101012ARTFIG 00820-la-loi-sur-le-voile-integral-promulguee.php.

Lecourt, Dominique. "Grammaire d'un mot: Laïcité." *Hommes et Migrations* 1146 (1991) 38–40. Online. http://www.persee.fr/doc/homig_1142-852x_1991_num_ 1146_1_1713.

Lefebvre, Solange. "Origines et actualité de la laïcité: Lecture socio-théologique." *Théologiques* 61 (1998) 63–79. Online. https://www.erudit.org/fr/revues/ theologi/1998-v6-n1-theologi1870/024956ar.

Lefèvre, Nancy. "Libertés de conscience et d'expression: D'une haute reconnaissance juridique à des fragiles équilibres." In *Libre de le dire: Fondements et enjeux de la liberté de conscience et d'expression en France,* edited by Louis Schweitzer et al., 127–54. Marpent, France: BLF Éditions, 2015.

Lemaire, Jacques. *La Laïcité en Amérique du Nord.* Bruxelles: Éditions de l'Université de Bruxelles, 1990.

Leustean, Lucian N., and John T. S. Madeley. *Religion, Politics, and Law in the European Union.* Abingdon, UK: Routledge, 2010.

Lewis, Bernard. "The Clash of Civilizations." In *The Middle East and Islamic World Reader,* edited by Marvin E. Gettleman et al., 345–48. New York: Grove, 2003.

Liechti, Daniel. "Bâtir des Églises majeures: Un défi à relever." *Fac-Réflexion* 45 (1998) 18–32.

———. *Les Églises protestantes évangéliques en France: Situation 2017.* Paris: CNEF, 2017. Online. http://lecnef.org/cartes-et-chiffres/livret-cartographique-2017.

Lignerolles, Philippe de. *Tolérance et laïcité à l'occasion du IVe centenaire de l'édit de Nantes.* Nantes: Éditions Siloë, 2005.

Lillback, Peter A. "The Relationship of Church and State." In *Reformation Theology,* edited by Michael Barrett, 675–719. Wheaton, IL: Crossway, 2017.

"L'implantation d'Églises: Le pari évangélique pour essaimer." *Le Point,* March 10, 2018. Online. http://www.lepoint.fr/societe/l-implantation-d-eglises-le-pari-evangelique-pour-essaimer-10-03-2018-2201315_23.php.

Lindberg, Carter. *The European Reformation.* Oxford: Blackwell, 1996.

Liogier, Raphaël. "Laïcité on the Edge in France: Between the Theory of Church-State Separation and the Praxis of State-Church Confusion." *Macquarie Law Journal* 9 (2009) 25–45.

Lorcerie, Françoise. "Laïcité 1996: La République à l'école de l'immigration?" *Revue française de pédagogie* 117 (1996) 53–85. Online. http://www.persee.fr/doc/rfp_0556-7807_1996_num_117_1_1185.

Lyotard, Jean-François. *La condition postmoderne: Rapport sur le savoir.* Paris: Les Éditions de Minuit, 1979.

Machelon, Jean-Pierre. *La laïcité demain: Exclure ou Rassembler?* Paris: CNRS Éditions, 2012.

Maclure, Jocelyn, and Charles Taylor. *Laïcité et liberté de conscience.* Montréal: Éditions du Boréal, 2010.

Macron, Emmanuel. "Transcription du discours des vœux du Président de la République aux autorités religieuses." Speech delivered January 4, 2018. Online. http://www.elysee.fr/declarations/article/transcription-du-discours-des-v-ux-du-president-de-la-republique-aux-autorites-religieuses.

"Macron: La laïcité n'est pas la lutte contre la religion." *Le Figaro,* June 26, 2018. Online. http://www.lefigaro.fr/flash-actu/2018/06/26/97001-20180626FILWWW00342-macron-la-laicite-n-est-pas-la-lutte-contre-la-religion.php.

Magnan, André. "Lire Voltaire pour être libre." *France Culture,* September 9, 2018. Online. https://www.franceculture.fr/conferences/universite-de-nantes/lire-voltaire-pour-etre-libre.

Magraw, Roger. *France 1800–1914: A Social History.* Abingdon, UK: Routledge, 2002.

Magstadt, Thomas A. *Understanding Politics: Ideas, Institutions, and Issues.* 12th ed. Boston: Cengage, 2017.

Mallèvre, Michel. *Les évangéliques: Un nouveau visage du christianisme?* Paris: Éditions jésuites, 2015.

Mamet-Soppelsa, Patricia. "Les femmes et la laïcité." *Revue Politique et Parlementaire* 1038 (2006) 39–42.

"Manifeste contre le nouvel antisémitisme." *Le Parisien,* April 21, 2018. Online. http://www.leparisien.fr/societe/manifeste-contre-le-nouvel-antisemitisme-21-04-2018-7676787.php.

Mariot, Nicolas. *Tous unis dans la tranchée? 1914–1918: Les intellectuels rencontrent le peuple.* Paris: Éditions Seuil, 2013.

Maslowski, Michel. "Les chrétiens avec ou sans Dieu et l'État laïque en Pologne." In *La Laïcité, une question au présent,* edited by Jean Birnbaum et al., 197–217. Nantes: Éditions Cécile Defaut, 2006.

Maurois, André. *Histoire de la France.* Paris: La Librairie Vuibert, 2017.

Mayeur, Jean-Marie. *La question laïque: XIXe–XXe siècle.* Paris: Fayard, 1997.

———. *La Séparation des Églises et de l'État.* Ivry-Sur-Seine: Les Éditions de l'Atelier, 2005.

McCaffrey, Edna. *The Return of Religion in France: From Democratisation to Postmetaphysics.* New York: Palgrave Macmillan, 2009.

McCrea, Ronan. *Religion and the Public Order of the European Union.* New York: Oxford University Press, 2010.

McGrath, Alister E. *Luther's Theology of the Cross.* Oxford: Wiley-Blackwell, 2011.

McManners, John. *Church and State in France, 1870–1914.* London: SPCK, 1972.

Mehl, Roger. "Pouvoir, religion et laïcité." *Autres Temps. Les cahiers du christianisme social* 1 (1984) 56–64. Online. http://www.persee.fr/doc/chris_0753-2776_1984_num_1_1_924.

Meiers, Heather. "Difference and Laïcité: France's Headscarf Debates and the Banning of Religious Symbols in French Public Schools." MA Thesis, University of Kansas, 2007.

Méjan, L. V. *La Séparation des Églises et de l'État*. Paris: Presses Universitaires de France, 1959.

Mélenchon, Jean-Luc. "Monsieur le président, le lien avec les églises n'a pas été abimé ! Il a été rompu en 1905! Remettre en cause la séparation des églises et de l'État, c'est ouvrir la porte de la politique aux fondamentalistes de toutes les religions. C'est irresponsable." Twitter (@JLMelenchon), April 10, 2018, 4:05 a.m. https://twitter. com/JLMelenchon/status/983615797389086721.

Merriman, John. *A History of Modern Europe*. 3rd ed. New York: Norton. 2010.

Miaille, Michel. *La laïcité: Solutions d'hier, problèmes d'aujourd'hui*. 3rd ed. Paris: Éditions Dalloz, 2016.

Micheline, Milot. *La laïcité*. Montréal: Éditions Novalis, 2008.

Monod, Jean-Claude. *Sécularisation et laïcité*. Paris: Presses Universitaires de France, 2007.

Montclos, Xavier de. *Histoire religieuse de la France*. Paris: Presses Universitaires de France, 1988.

Monteil, Pierre-Olivier. "Laïcité, religion, école." *Autres Temps. Les cahiers du christianisme social* 30 (1991) 3–4. Online. http://www.persee.fr/doc/chris _0753-2776_1991_ num_30_1_2544.

———. "Les exigences de la laïcité." *Autres Temps. Cahiers d'éthique sociale et politique* 69 (2001) 3–5. Online. http://www.persee.fr/doc/chris_0753-2776_2001_num_ 69_1_2251.

"Mort de Mireille Knoll: 'L'antisémitisme est un signe inquiétant de l'affaiblissement de la démocratie.'" *Le Monde*, March 29, 2018. Online. http://www.lemonde.fr/ societe/article/2018/03/29/mort-de-mireille-knoll-l-antisemitisme-est-un-signe-inquietant-de-l-affaiblissement-de-la-democratie_5278257_3224.html.

Moulaye, Hassane. "La question de la laïcité en Islam." *Autres Temps. Les cahiers du christianisme social* 13 (1987) 70–76. Online. http://www.persee.fr/doc/ chris_0753-2776_1987_num_13_1_1143.

Moyères, Luc. *Laïcité, Islam . . . quelques repères: Essai pour comprendre la laïcité, pour une coexistence enfin apaisée avec les religions, et en particulier l'Islam*. Middletown, DE: n.p., 2017.

Mun, Albert de. *Contre la séparation*. Paris: Librairie Vve Ch. Poussielgue, 1905. https:// archive.org/stream/contrelasparatoomuna#page/n3/mode/2up.

———. "La guerre religieuse." *Le Figaro*, February 4, 1906. Online. http://gallica.bnf.fr/ ark:/12148/bpt6k287247w/f1.item#.

———. "La lettre aux évêques." *La Croix*, March 28, 1906. Online. https://gallica.bnf. fr/ark:/12148/bpt6k256409w/f1.item.

———. "La séparation de l'Église et de l'État." *Le Figaro*, September 23, 1904. Online. https://gallica.bnf.fr/ark:/12148/bpt6k75045k.pdf.

Münster, Arno. *Jean Jaurès: Un combat pour la laïcité, la République, la justice sociale et la paix: Quelques réflexions en marge d'une commémoration*. Paris: Éditions L'Harmattan, 2015.

Murray, Douglas. *The Strange Death of Europe: Immigration, Identity, Islam*. London: Bloomsbury, 2017.

Newbigin, Lesslie. *The Gospel in a Pluralistic Society*. Grand Rapids: Eerdmans, 1989.

Noll, Mark A. *The New Shape of World Christianity: How American Experience Reflects Global Faith*. Downers Grove, IL: IVP Academic, 2009.

Nouzille, Vincent. "Macron et les francs-maçons: Le bras de fer." *Le Figaro*, June 8, 2018. Online. http://www.lefigaro.fr/politique/2018/06/08/01002-20180608ARTFIG 00036-macron-et-les-francs-macons-le-bras-de-fer.php.

Onfray, Michel. *Atheist Manifesto: The Case Against Christianity, Judaism, and Islam.* Translated by Jeremy Leggatt. Paris: Éditions Grasset & Fasquelle, 2005; New York: Arcade, 2007.

Orange,Valérie. "Laïcités dans le monde et approches plurielles des discriminations." In *Laï-cité(s) et discrimination(s),* edited by Brigitte Esteve-Bellebeau et al., 29–43. Paris: Éditions L'Harmattan, 2017.

Paas, Stefan. "Church Planting and Church Renewal." *Journal of Missional Practice* 1 (2012). Online. http://journalofmissionalpractice.com/church-planting-church-renewal.

Pagnol, Marcel. *Le Château de ma mère.* Paris: Éditions de Fallon, 1988.

Paillard, Christophe. "Voltaire entre tolérance et laïcité." *Histoire, monde et cultures religieuses* 43 (2017) 35–50.

Palmer, Susan. *The New Heretics of France: Minority Religions, La République, and the Government-Sponsored "War on Sects."* Oxford: Oxford University Press, 2011.

Paolini, Esther. "L'immigration et l'islam crispent de plus en plus les Français." *Le Figaro,* July 7, 2017. Online. http://www.lefigaro.fr/actualite-france/2017/07/03/01016-20170703ARTFIG00256-l-immigration-et-l-islam-crispent-de-plus-en-plus-les-francais.php.

Pédérzet, J. *Cinquante ans de souvenirs religieux et ecclésiastiques.* Paris: Librairie Fischbacher, 1896. Online. https://archive.org/stream/eglisesreformeesoopede#page/n7/mode/2up.

Péguy, Charles. "Notre patrie." *Cahiers de la Quinzaine* 3 (1905) 7–87. Online. https://archive.org/stream/s7cahiersdelaquinzo1pg#page/n165/mode/2up/search/notre+patrie.

———. "Waldeck-Rouseau: Premier discours au sénat." *Cahiers de la Quinzaine* 6 (1904) 69–87. Online. https://archive.org/details/s6cahiersdelaquinzo4pg.

Pelletier, Denis. "L'Europe des religions aujourd'hui." *Vingtième Siècle, Revue d'histoire* 66 (2000) 5–12. Online. http://www.persee.fr/doc/xxs_0294-1759_2000_num_66_1_4558.

Pena-Ruiz, Henri. "Culture, cultures, et laïcité." *Hommes et Migrations* 1259 (2006) 6–16. Online. http://www.persee.fr/doc/homig_1142-852x_2006_num_1259_1_4414.

———. *Dieu et Marianne: Philosophie de la laïcité.* Paris: Presses Universitaires de France, 2005.

———. *Qu'est-ce que la laïcité?* Paris: Éditions Gallimard, 2003.

———. "Un discours d'une confusion significative." *Marianne,* April 13, 2018. Online. http://www.laicite-republique.org/IMG/pdf/180413mariannepenaruiz.pdf.

Petty, Aaron R. "Religion, Conscience, and Belief in the European Court of Human Rights." *The George Washington International Law Review* 48 (2016) 807–51.

Pew Research Center. "Being Christian in Western Europe." *Pew Forum,* May 29, 2018. Online. http://www.pewforum.org/2018/05/29/being-christian-in-western-europe.

———. "Secular Europe and Religious America: Implications for Transatlantic Relations." *Pew Forum,* April 21, 2005. Online. http://www.pewforum.org/2005/04/21/secular-europe-and-religious-america-implications-for-transatlantic-relations.

Peyrat, Napoléon. *Histoire des Pasteurs du Désert: Depuis la Révocation de l'Édit de Nantes jusqu'à la Révolution Française (1685–1789).* 1842. Reprint, Paris: Mon Autre Librairie, 2017.

Pius X. "Une fois encore." Encyclical delivered January 6, 1907. Online. http://w2.vatican.va/content/pius-x/fr/encyclicals/documents/hf_p-x_enc_06011907_une-fois-encore.html.

———. *"Vehmenter Nos."* Encylical delivered February 11, 1906. Online. http://w2.vatican.va/content/pius-x/fr/encyclicals/documents/hf_p-x_enc_11021906_vehementer-nos.html.

Portier, Philippe. *L'État et les religions en France: Une sociologie historique de la laïcité.* Rennes: Presses Universitaires de Rennes, 2016.

Poulat, Émile. *Église contre bourgeoise: Introduction au devenir du catholicisme actuel.* Paris: Berg, 2006.

———. *Notre laïcité ou les religions dans l'espace public.* Paris: Éditions Desclée de Brouwer, 2014.

———. *"Pour une véritable culture laïque."* In *La Laïcité, une question au présent,* edited by Jean Birnbaum et al., 59–74. Nantes: Éditions Cécile Defaut, 2006.

Pownall, André. "Un demi-siècle d'implantation d'Églises évangéliques en région parisienne, (1950–2000)." *Théologie Évangélique* 4 (2005) 47–79.

Prêtre, Isabelle. *Laïcité chérie . . . : Jusqu'où vas-tu nous conduire?* Saint-Maurice, Switzerland: Éditions Saint-Augustin, 2016.

Prévotat, Jacques. *Être chrétien en France au XXe siècle: De 1914 à nos jours.* Paris: Éditions du Seuil, 1998.

"Quelle organisation pour l'Islam dans la République française." *En Marche,* February 10, 2018. Online. https://en-marche.fr/articles/actualites/quelle-organisation-pour-l-islam-dans-la-republique-francaise.

Queyranne, Jean-Jacques. "Ouverture des rencontres." In *La Laïcité, une question au présent,* edited by Jean Birnbaum et al., 7–13. Nantes: Éditions Cécile Defaut, 2006.

Ragi, Tariq. "Islam et laïcité." *Agora débats/jeunesses* 30 (2002) 4–13. Online. https://www.persee.fr/doc/agora_1268-5666_2002_num_30_1_2037.

Ratzinger, Joseph Cardinal. *Europe Today and Tomorrow: Addressing Fundamental Issues.* San Francisco: Ignatius, 2007.

Rémond, René. *L'anticléricalisme en France: De 1815 à nos jours.* Paris: Fayard, 1999.

———. *L'invention de la laïcité: De 1789 à demain.* Paris: Bayard, 2005.

Renan, Ernest. *Questions contemporaines.* Paris: Michel Lévy, 1868. Online. https://gallica.bnf.fr/ark:/12148/bpt6k2558887/f2.image.

Réveillard, Eugène. *La séparation des Églises et de l'État: Précis historique discours et documents.* Paris: Librairie Fischbacher, 1907.

Revel, Jean-François. *L'obsession anti-américaine: Son fonctionnement, ses causes, ses inconséquences.* Paris: Éditions Plon, 2002.

Rinnert, Anne. "Le principe de laïcité est plus que jamais d'actualité." In *Laï-cité(s) et discrimination(s),* edited by Brigitte Esteve-Bellebeau et al., 127–33. Paris: Éditions L'Harmattan, 2017.

Rivallain, Youna. "La conversion des musulmans au christianisme est trop peu évoquée." *Le Monde,* March 3, 2018. Online. http://www.lemondedesreligions.fr/une/la-conversion-des-musulmans-au-christianisme-est-trop-peu-evoquee-19-03-2018-7095_115.php.

Robbins, Richard H. *Cultural Anthropology: A Problem-Based Approach.* 2nd ed. Itasca, IL: Peacock, 1997.

Robert, Jacques. "Les fondements juridiques de la laïcité." *Revue Politique et Parlementaire* 1038 (2006) 7–12.

Robert, Paul, et al. *Le Nouveau Petit Robert de la Langue Française.* Paris: Le Robert, 2007.

Robespierre, Maximilien. *Œuvres de Maximilien Robespierre (July 27, 1793–July 27, 1794).* Paris: Presses Universitaires de France, 1967. Online. https://archive.org/stream/oeuvrescomplte10robe#page/n5/mode/2up.

Robitzer, Prisca. "La construction mentale de la laïcité: Étude de représentation et mise en évidence de mécanismes cognitifs constitutifs de l'idéologie." PhD diss., École pratique des hautes études, 2008.

———. "Laïcité et réconciliation: Enjeux et limites." *La Revue reformée* 264 (2012). Online.   http://larevuereformee.net/articlerr/n264/laicite-et-reconciliation-enjeux-et-limites.

Rognon, Évelyne, and Louis Weber. *La laïcité, un siècle après:1905–2005*. Paris: Éditions Nouveaux Regards, 2005.

Rorty, Richard. "Anticlericalism and Atheism." In *The Future of Religion*, edited by Richard Rorty et al., 29–42. New York: Columbia University Press, 2007.

Rosanvallon, Pierre. *Le Modèle politique français: La société civile contre le jacobinisme de 1789 à nos jours*. Paris: Éditions du Seuil, 2004.

Roure, Henri. *Sauvons notre laïcité! Essai sur la crise musulmane en France*. Vendres, France: Éditions Auteurs d'Aujourd'hui, 2016.

Roy, Olivier. *Globalized Islam: The Search for a New Ummah*. New York: Columbia University Press, 2004.

———. *La laïcité face à l'islam*. Paris: Éditions Stock, 2005.

Sabatier, Paul. À *propos de la séparation des Églises et de l'État*. Paris: Librairie Fischbacher, 1906. Online. https://archive.org/details/proposdelaseparaoosaba.

Sadi, Hocine. "La laïcité à l'épreuve de l'intégration." *Hommes et Migrations* 1259 (2006) 64–69. Online. http://www.persee.fr/doc/homig_1142-852x_2006_num_1259_1_4419.

Sanneh, Lamin. "Can Europe Be Saved? A Review Essay." *International Bulletin of Missiological Research* 31 (2007) 121–25.

Sarkozy, Nicholas. *La République, les religions, l'espérance*. Paris: Éditions du Cerf, 2004.

Sauvaget, Bernadette, et al. "Associations cultuelles: Le gouvernement veut retoucher discrètement la loi de 1905." *La Libération*, January 11, 2018. Online. https://www.liberation.fr/france/2018/01/11/associations-cultuelles-le-gouvernement-veut-retoucher-discretement-la-loi-de-1905_1621800.

Savart, Claude. "De la laïcité." *Revue d'histoire de l'Église de France* 78 (1992) 137–49. Online. http://www.persee.fr/doc/rhef_0300-9505_1992_num_78_200_1065.

Schweitzer, Louis, et al. *Libre de le dire: Fondements et enjeux de la liberté de conscience et d'expression en France*. Marpent, France: BLF Éditions, 2015.

Séguy, Jean. *Les sectes protestantes dans la France contemporaine*. Paris: Éditions Beauchesne, 1956.

Serradji, Philippe. "La montée de l'athéisme contemporain." *La Revue reformée* 259 (2011). Online. http://larevuereformee.net/articlerr/n259/la-montee-de-l%E2%80%99atheisme-contemporain-2.

Sévillia, Jean. *Quand les catholiques étaient hors la loi*. Paris: Éditions Perrin, 2006.

Sfeir, Antoine, and René Andrau. *Liberté, égalité, islam: La République face au communautarisme*. Paris: Éditions Tallandier, 2005.

Simon, Hippolyte. *Vers une France païenne?* Paris: Éditions Cana, 1999.

Simon-Nahum, Perrine. "Le scandale de la *Vie de Jésus* de Renan. Du succès littéraire comme mode d'échec de la science." *Mil neuf cent. Revue d'histoire intellectuelle* 25 (2007) 61–74. Online. http://www.cairn.info.

Smiles, Samuel. *The Huguenots in France*. 1873. Reprint, London: Forgotten Books, 2018.

"Sondage: La laïcité à l'école, c'est pas gagné!" *Le Parisien*, September 23, 2015. Online. http://www.leparisien.fr/espace-premium/actu/la-laicite-a-l-ecole-c-est-pas-gagne-23-09-2015-5117683.php.

Soppelsa, Jacques. "De la laïcité." *Revue Politique et Parlementaire* 1038 (2006) 2–5.
————. "États-Unis: God Bless America." *Revue Politique et Parlementaire* 1038 (2006) 48–51.

Speelman, Ge, et al. *Muslims and Christians in Europe: Breaking New Ground. Essays in Honour of Jan Slomp.* Kampen, Netherlands: Kok, 1993.

Stumpf, Samuel Enoch. *From Socrates to Sartre: A History of Philosophy.* 5th ed. New York: McGraw-Hill, 1993.

Sugy, Paul. "Polémique sur la militante voilée de l'UNEF: La réponse de Laurent Bouvet." *Le Figaro,* May 15, 2018. Online. http://www.lefigaro.fr/vox/politique/2018/05/15/31001-20180515ARTFIG00148-polemique-sur-la-militante-voilee-de-l-unef-la-reponse-de-laurent-bouvet.php.

Tavoillot, Pierre-Henri. "Les deux laïcités." *Blog de Pierre-Henri Tavoillot* (blog), January 30, 2016. Online. http://pagepersodephtavoillot.blogspot.com/2016/01/les-deux-laicites.html.

Taylor, Charles. *A Secular Age.* Cambridge: Harvard University Press, 2007.

Temperman, Jeroen. *State-Religion Relationships and Human Rights Law: Towards a Right to Religiously Neutral Governance.* Leiden: Martinus Nijhoff, 2010.

Tennant, Agnieszka. "The French Reconnection." *Christianity Today,* February 25, 2005. Online. http://www.christianitytoday.com/ct/2005/march/20.28.html.

Tincq, Henry. "Non, Emmanuel Macron n'a pas remis en cause la laïcité en appelant les religions à s'engager dans le débat public." *Slate,* April 10, 2018. Online. http://www.slate.fr/story/160219/religion-laicite-discours-bernardins-conference-eveques-de-france-emmanuel-macron-separation-eglise-etat.

Tribalat, Michèle. *Assimilation: La fin du modèle français.* Paris: Éditions du Toucan, 2013.

Tripier, Yves. *La Laïcité: Ses prémices et son évolution depuis 1905.* Paris: Éditions L'Harmattan, 2003.

Trueman, Carl R., and Eunjin Kim. "The Reformers and Their Reformation." In *Reformation Theology,* edited by Michael Barrett, 111–41. Wheaton, IL: Crossway, 2017.

Tulard, Jean. "Contre-Révolution." *Encylclopaedia Universalis.* Online. http://www.universalis.fr/encyclopedie/contre-revolution.

"Une Date." *Le Radical,* December 7, 1905. Online. https://gallica.bnf.fr/ark:/12148/bpt6k76095130.item.

Valls, Manuel. *La laïcité en face: Entretiens avec Virginie Malabard.* Paris: Desclée de Brouwer, 2005.

Vandermersch, Edmond. "Catholicisme et laïcité depuis 1984." *Autres Temps. Les cahiers du christianisme social* 30 (1991) 5–7. Online. http://www.persee.fr/doc/chris_0753-2776_1991_num_30_1_1449.

Vaucelles, Louis de. "Laïcité en débat." *Archives de sciences sociales des religions* 78 (1992) 179–90. Online. http://www.persee.fr/doc/assr_0335-5985_1992_num_78_1_1528.

Viennot, Bérengère. "Pourquoi l'Amérique ne comprend pas la laïcité à la française." *Slate,* September 22, 2016. Online. http://m.slate.fr/story/123709/amerique-laicite-france.

Viguier, Jacques. "La laïcité dans les *Souvenirs d'enfance* de Marcel Pagnol." In *Laï-cité(s) et discrimination(s),* edited by Brigitte Esteve-Bellebeau et al., 77–87. Online. Paris: Éditions L'Harmattan, 2017.

Villepin, Dominique. "Une certaine idée de la République." In *1905, la séparation des Églises et de l'État: Les textes fondateurs,* edited by Yves Bruley, 7–18. Paris: Éditions Perrin, 2004.

Voltaire. "The Presbyterians." In vol. 19 of *The Works of Voltaire: A Contemporary Version*, edited by Tobias Smollett, 216–19. Translated by William F. Fleming. New York: DuMont, 1901. Online. https://oll.libertyfund.org/titles/666#Voltaire_0060-19p2_965.

Vovelle, Michel. *La Révolution française:1789–1799*. Paris: Armand Colin, 2006.

Waldeck-Rousseau, Pierre. *La défense républicaine*. Paris: Bibliothèque-Charpentier, 1902.

Walker, Williston, et al. *A History of the Christian Church*. 4th ed. New York: Scribner's Sons, 1985.

Wawro, Geoffrey. *The Franco-Prussian War: The German Conquest of France in 1870–1871*. New York: Cambridge University Press, 2003.

Weil, Patrick. *Politiques de la laïcité au XXe siècle*. Paris: Presses Universitaires de France, 2007.

Wessels, Anton. *Europe: Was It Ever Really Christian? The Interaction Between Gospel and Culture*. London: SCM, 1994.

Willaime, Jean-Paul. *Europe et religions: Les enjeux du XXIe siècle*. Paris: Éditions Fayard, 2004.

———. "European Integration: Laïcité and Religion." In *Religion, Politics, and Law in the European Union*, edited by Lucian N. Leustean et al., 17–30. Abingdon, UK: Routledge, 2010.

———. "La sécularisation: Une exception européenne? Retour sur un concept et sa discussion en sociologie des religions." *Revue française de sociologie* 47 (2006) 755–83. Online. https://www.cairn.info/article.php?ID_ARTICLE=RFS_474_0755.

———. "L'expression des religions, une chance pour la démocratie." *Revue Projet* 342 (2014) 5–14. Online. https://www.cairn.info/revue-projet-2014-5-page-5.htm.

Yacoub, Joseph. "Islam politique et laïcité: Regard sur les constitutions arabes." *Revue Politique et Parlementaire* 1038 (2006) 85–94.

Yelle, Robert A. "Moses' Veil: Secularization as Christian Myth." In *After Secular Law*, edited by Winnifred Sullivan et al., 23–42. Palo Alto, CA: Stanford University Press, 2011.

Zarka, Yves Charles. "Éditorial: Le pouvoir sur le savoir ou la légitimation postmoderne." *Cités* 45 (2011) 3–7. Online. https://www.cairn.info/revue-cites-2011-1-page-3.htm.

Zarlenga, Franck. "Le régime concordataire des Cultes non reconnus dans la France concordataire (1801–1905)." PhD diss., Université Paris-Est, 2018.

Zeghal, Malika. "La constitution du Conseil Français du Culte Musulman: Reconnaissance politique d'un Islam français?" *Archives de sciences sociales des religions* 129 (2005) 1–14.

Zola, Émile. "J'accuse . . . ! Lettre au Président de la République." Letter published January 13, 1898. Online. https://www.atramenta.net/lire/jaccuse/2575/1#oeuvre_page.

———. *Vérité*. Paris: Bibliothèque-Charpentier, 1903. Online. https://archive.org/details/veriteoozola.

Zylberberg, Jacques. "Laïcité, connais-pas: Allemagne, Canada, États-Unis, Royaume-Uni." *Pouvoirs, Revue française d'études constitutionnelles et politiques* 75 (1995) 37–52. Online. http://www.revue-pouvoirs.fr/Laicite-connais-pas-Allemagne.html.

Index

Printed in Great Britain
by Amazon